NOTED NEGRO WOMEN

M. A. Majors, M.D.

NOTED NEGRO WOMEN
THEIR TRIUMPHS AND ACTIVITIES

By

MONROE A. MAJORS

AYER COMPANY, PUBLISHERS, INC.
SALEM, NEW HAMPSHIRE 03079

Reprint Edition 1986
AYER Company, Publishing, Inc.
382 Main Street
Salem, New Hampshire 03079

INTERNATIONAL STANDARD BOOK NUMBER:
0-8369-8733-0

LIBRARY OF CONGRESS CATALOG CARD NUMBER:
73-138341

PRINTED IN THE UNITED STATES OF AMERICA

NOTED NEGRO WOMEN

THEIR TRIUMPHS AND ACTIVITIES.

BY

M. A. MAJORS, M. D.

"A race, no less than a nation, is prosperous in proportion to the intelligence of its women."

The criterion for Negro civilization is the intelligence, purity and high motives of its women.

THE HIGHEST MARK OF OUR PROSPERITY, AND THE STRONGEST PROOFS OF NEGRO CAPACITY TO MASTER THE SCIENCES AND FINE ARTS, ARE EVINCED BY THE ADVANCED POSITIONS TO WHICH NEGRO WOMEN HAVE ATTAINED.

"I will go forth 'mong men, mailed in the armor of a pure intent.
"Great duties are before me, and great deeds, and whether crowned or crownless when I fall, it matters not, so as Gods work is done."

DONOHUE & HENNEBERRY,
PRINTERS, BINDERS AND ENGRAVERS,
CHICAGO.

DONOHUE & HENNEBERRY
PRINTERS, ENGRAVERS AND BINDERS
CHICAGO

DEDICATION

The surest way to demonstrate our true devotion to our sisters is to write a volume depicting their lives, achievements and activities.

The strongest proof that we appreciate the high ground our sisters have reached, consequent of their tireless efforts for the good of humanity, is to DEDICATE this volume to their unspotted lives.

THE AUTHOR.

INTRODUCTION.

Dr. M. A. Majors, who in this work has, in my opinion, given the world a book covering rich and hitherto neglected ground, was born in Waco, Texas, October 12, 1864, of honored parents—Andrew and Jane Majors—who now reside in Austin, whither they moved, in 1869, to secure the at that time best educational advantages for their children in the State; Waco being not then as now the Athens of Negro education, where is situated Paul Quinn College, a very superior school of high and industrial education.

After attendance continuously and successively upon the public schools, West Texas College, managed by the Freedmen's Aid Society; and Tillotson Institute, under the auspices of the A. M. Association, he was appointed assistant mailing clerk in the post-office, which position he resigned, in 1882, to enter Central Tennessee College, Nashville, Tenn.

He relinquished his literary course in October, 1883, to enter the Meharry Medical College, from which he graduated in February, 1886, with honor, being salutatorian in a class of ten, thus completing his professional course at twenty-one years of age.

During his school life at Nashville he conducted the department of penmanship for the whole college, and was conspicuous as a reporter for the local daily and weekly papers on all public occasions.

Since graduation as a physician he has practiced in different parts of the State of his birth, as well as for some time in Los Angeles, California. He is the first to advocate the organization of the Lone Star Medical Association, the first Negro medical association ever organized in America.   While in California, Dr. Majors married Miss Georgia A. Green, of Texas, an accomplished lady, in 1889.

Dr. Majors was a welcome associate in the medical societies of California, where his color was no bar to his participancy in the proceedings.   He was invited to lecture on medical topics before the Los Angeles Medical College.

He was also very active in the political life of the State, and through *The Western News*, a paper which he edited, secured recognition of his race on the police force, in city public works, and in the office of assessor and collector.   Prior to this no Negro had ever been so employed in any of the departments of the city.

Returning to Texas, in 1890, he at once began the compilation of "Noted Negro Women."

This merited recognition of the virtues and force of the noted women of the race, whose work and influence have all too long been unnoticed, will receive at the hands of a discriminating public the attention its importance demands.

Epic in subject, inspiring in effect, it is no less true in fact, and only a culling from the wealth of similar material supplied in the lives of hundreds of others, who, though possibly less eminent in the public eye, are no less true, devoted, capable, and noble exemplars of our possibilities and queens in our homes.

H. T. KEALING,
President Paul Quinn College.

WACO, TEXAS.

PREFACE.

I regard a true woman as the best, the grandest of all God's human creatures; a being of light, immaculate in her chastity, a paragon in her purity and capable of ennobling the man of her liking. A woman's gentle spirit is an all-pervading virtue, whose influence softens the spell and fills our life niche with its calm soul fragrance. Her smile intensifies our joys and leads us to forget the bickerings, the sins, the hard, angular elbowing in the avaricious competition of a calloused world and opens our eyes to the brighter, the better side of earth's paradise.   FOSTER.

"Here are spaces of labor, wide as the world, lofty as heaven." A virtuous enthusiasm is always self-forgetful, virtuous and hence noble. It is the only inspiration now vouchsafed to man. Like Pickering, blend humility with learning. Like Story, ascend above the present in place and time. Like Alston, regard fame only as the eternal shadow of excellence. .Like Channing, bend in adoration before the right. Cultivate alike the wisdom of experience and the wisdom of hope. Mindful of the future do not neglect the past; awed by the majesty of antiquity, turn not with indifference from the future. True wisdom looks to the ages before us, as well as behind us. Like the Janus of the Capitol, one front thoughtfully regards the past, rich with experience, with memories, with the priceless traditions of virtue; the other is earnestly directed to the All Hail Hereafter, richer still with its transcendent hopes and unfulfilled prophecies. We stand on the threshold of a new age, which is preparing to recognize

new influences. The ancient divinities of violence and wrong
are retreating to their kindred darkness. The Son of our
moral universe is entering a new ecliptic, no longer deformed
by those images of animal rage, Cancer, Taurus, Leo, Sagit-
tarius, but beaming with mild radiance of those heavenly
signs, Faith, Hope and Charity:

> "There's a fount about to stream,
> There's a light about to beam,
> There's a warmth about to glow,
> There's a flower about to blow,
> There's a midnight blackness changing
>   Into gray ;
> Men of thought and men of action
>   Clear the way.
> Aid the dawning tongue and pen ;
> Aid it, hopes of honest men
> Aid it, paper, aid it type ;
> Aid it, for the hour is ripe,
> And our earnest must not slacken
>   Into play.
> Men of thought and men of action
>   Clear the way."

In presenting this book to the public, the author has taken
into consideration the Latin proverb, Qualitatum non Quantum.
And in a work so promiscuous, yet tedious, we find it a pleasing task to bring into reality the object of which our highest
hopes have at times wavered. Now undaunted, with energies
concentrated we spring upon the nation this little effort, hoping
that many firesides will be made brighter, many a father's and
mother's darling daughter will catch the inspiration of womanly
attainments, and bloom into beautiful and useful womanhood.
What our intelligent women will do, to glorify our race in this
hospital of tears, fears, doubts and dogmas depends largely our
success as a race. The present era is teaching humanity the
moral, intellectual and religious worth of our women. We are
living in a classified era of goodness. Whether our leading

women have cleared the culminating point and out-distanced our great men, is a subject now engaging the attention of the thinking and agitating world. And jubilant of what we see around and about us, where continual changes are coming to view, we look forward to brighter and grander days. The effulgent rays of God's glory cast their meteoric sparks upon our pathway as never before, and the goodness of the nations join our feeble efforts to rise higher and higher, day by day. A wholesomeness of looking upwards is the fruition of a Mighty Power actuating mankind, with the universal acknowledgment of mankind that no race is making more rapid progress under the circumstances than ours. To our readers allow us to emphasize, we are not attempting to say anything new. For in the mind and heart of humanity there is nothing new. We are intensely concerned, when our duty prompts us to cast our might in defense of the race. Now that we have painstakingly projected this unit to the catalogue of the literary world, let us say to the critic, do unto others as you would have them do unto you, we do not claim widespread authority, nor more than meager attainments, and since perfection is not the rule on this mundane sphere, " no writer can be free where all have power to judge." We pursued this gentle and timid toil, not because we were so well fitted for the task, but because of its extreme necessity. Being accompanied this pleasant journey through the field of literature we have participated in many a joyous argument, striving at all times to deal as mildly with our company as it became our better nature. Unspeakable pleasure and good humor have characterized all our efforts to insert, or cut down, as the case necessitated, and without overdrawing, or magnifying too much, we hope we have pleased all.

We present this little volume to our race and friends of the race, with the hope that the many and varied avenues into which our women are crowding may give inspiration to the girls of present and future generations. They can " make *their* lives sublime."

We have not by any means exhausted the subject, but feel that we have given a far-off view to the beautiful landscape. Others no doubt less conspicuous but possibly more capable than many whose biographies appear in this book, owing to disadvantages under which we have labored, have no lengthy mention, possibly do not appear upon the scene.

The world is full of books, yet few of them appeal directly and peculiarly to the Negro race. Many books written of persons and things have their beginning and their ending in fancy, without special design for the elevation of mind or the culture of literary taste and pure morals, but for entertainment and amusement and gratification of sentiment without utility to the reader in any sense whatever. We commend these pages to the reading world, trusting that they will for long stand out in bold relief, a signification of Negro progress.

THE AUTHOR.

CONTENTS.

CONTENTS.

NOTED NEGRO WOMEN,

THEIR TRIUMPHS AND ACTIVITIES.

"Good heaven ! what sorrows gloomed that parting day
That called me from native walks away! "

PHILLIS WHEATLEY,

Great Poetess, Guest of the Royal Family.   Friend and Associate to Lady Huntingdon.

PHILLIS WHEATLEY was a woman whose greatness of soul the whole world admired.   Her generosity was such that it evaded demands and saved the receivers the confusion of requests.   In referring to Webster's unabridged biographical names, we find that she was born in Africa, 1753.   Professor William T. Alexander, in his History of the Colored Race in America, in paying tribute to Phillis Wheatley and the colored race, beautifully says : "There is little doubt but when once furnished with these keys, the colored race are capable of reaching andunlocking all the doors accessible to any other people. We need not dip into the future for the law of higher inheritance to note examples of this truth, or even to depend entirely upon the present, with its increased facilities to this end, but may go back and take an instance from the dark days of slavery, and of one direct from Africa.   We refer to Phillis Wheatley, who, tho' a "child of Africa," was, for her literary talent and virtue, accorded the highest distinction and honor both in the United States and Europe.   It seems that she was brought over to this country in a slave vessel from Africa when but a little child."

The following from her biography by Benson J. Lossing,

L. L. D., will be interesting. The wife of a respectable citizen, of
Boston, named Wheatley, went to the slave market in that city
in 1761, to purchase a child-negress, that she might rear her to
be a faithful nurse in the old age of her mistress. She saw
many plump children, but one of delicate frame, modest
demeanor and clad in nothing but a piece of dirty carpet
wrapped about her, attracted her attention, and Mrs. Wheatley
took her home in her chaise, and gave her the name of Phillis.
The child seemed to be about seven years of age, and exhibited
remarkable intelligence, and apt imitative powers. Mrs.
Wheatley's daughter taught the child to read and write, and
her progress was wonderful. She appeared to have very little
recollection of her birthplace, but remembered seeing her
mother pour out water before the sun at its rising. With the
development of her intellectual faculties, her moral nature kept
pace, and she was greatly loved by all who knew her for her
amiability and perfect docility. She soon attracted the attention of men of learning ; and as Phillis read books with great
avidity, they supplied her. Piety was a ruling sentiment in
her character, and tears born of gratitude and love for her mistress often moistened her eyes. As she grew to womanhood
her thoughts found expression through her pen, sometimes in
prose, but more often in poetry, and she was an invited guest in
the families of the rich and learned, in Boston. Her mistress
treated her as a child and was extremely proud of her. At the age.
of about sixteen years Phillis became a member of the "Old
South Church," then under the charge of Dr. Sewall. It was
about this time that she wrote the poem of which a verse
below is an extract. Earlier than this she had written poetry,
poems remarkable for both vigor of thought, and pathos in
expression. Her memory in some particulars appears to have
been extremely defective. If she composed a poem in the
night and did not write it down, it would be gone from her
forever in the morning. Her kind mistress gave her a light and
writing materials at her bedside that she might lose nothing,
and in cold weather a fire was always made in her room at
night.

In the summer of 1773 her health gave way, and a sea voyage was recommended. She accompanied a son of Mr. Wheatley to England, and there she was cordially received by Lady Huntingdon, Lord Dartmouth and other people of distinction. While there her poems, which had been collected and dedicated to the Countess of Huntingdon, were published, and attracted great attention. The book was embellished with a portrait of her, from which our picture was copied. She was persuaded to remain in London until the return of the Court, so as to be presented to the king, but, hearing of the declining health of her mistress, she hastened home. That kind friend was soon laid in the grave, and Phillis grieved as deeply as any of her children. Mr. Wheatley died soon after, and then his excellent daughter was laid by the side of her parents. Phillis was left destitute, and the sun of her earthly happiness went down. A highly intelligent colored man of Boston, named John Peters, offered himself in marriage to the poor orphan, and was accepted. He proved utterly unworthy of the excellent woman he had wedded, and her lot became a bitter one indeed. Misfortune seems to have expelled her muse, for we have no production of her pen bearing a later date than those in her volume published in 1773, except a poetical epistle to General George Washington, in 1775, and a few scraps written about that time. Washington replied to her letter on the 28th of February, 1776. His letter was written at his headquarters at Cambridge:

Miss Phillis: Your favor of the 26th of October did not reach my hands till the middle of December, time enough you will say to have given an answer ere this. Granted. But a variety of important occurrences continually interposing to distract the mind and withdraw the attention, I hope will apologize for the delay, and plead my excuse for the seeming, but not real neglect. I thank you most sincerely for your polite notice of me, in the elegant lines you enclosed, and however undeserving I may be of such encomium and panegyric, the style and manner exhibit a striking proof of your poetical talents, in honor of which as a tribute justly due to you, I would have published the poem, had I not been apprehensive that, while I only meant to give the world this new instance of your genius, I might have incurred the imputation of vanity. This, and nothing else, determined me not to give it a place in the public prints. If you should ever come to Cambridge, or near headquarters I shall be happy to see a person so favored by the muses, and to whom nature has been so liberal and beneficent in her dispensations.

I am, with great respect,

Your obedient, humble servant,

GEORGE WASHINGTON.

A few years of misery shattered the golden bowl of her life, and in a wretched apartment, in an obscure part of Boston, that gifted wife and mother, whose youth had been passed in ease, and even luxury, was allowed to perish alone! She died on the 5th of December, 1794, when she was about thirty-one years of age. The following is an extract from one of her poems previously referred to:

> " Twas mercy brought me from my pagan land,
> Taught my benighted soul to understand
> That there's a God—that there's a Savior too.
> Once I redemption neither sought nor knew."

Among other noticeable features in this touching story, we find that the great George Washington—" first in war, first in peace, and first in the hearts of his countrymen"—did not hesitate to speak in the highest terms of the genius of this gifted colored woman, nor to pay her an honor which might well be coveted by the greatest intellects of our land to-day.

And Goldsmith adds:

> " Thine, Freedom, thine the blessings pictured here,
> Thine are those charms that dazzle and endear !
> Too blest indeed were such without alloy ;
> But, fostered e'en by Freedom, ills annoy ;
> That independence Britons prize too high,
> Keeps man from man, and breaks the social tie;
> The self-depending lordlings stand alone,
> All claims that bind and sweeten life unknown."

Under the caption of " Women of the Century " Mrs. Hannaford, in her illustrious work, " Daughters of America," says of Phillis Wheatley: She was one of the four illustrious women who dwelt in the United States previous to the United States century. She (Phillis) was brought from Africa to Boston in 1761. When but six years old, she wrote a volume of poems, which was published in London in 1773, while she was in that city with the son of her owner, for she was a slave. She was educated through the favor of her mistress, and was quite proficient in the Latin language. A poem, which she sent to General Washington, gave her enduring fame. Her life bore evidence that the colonial women, though some of them slaveholders, were not destitute of a lively interest in those the custom of the times placed wholly in their charge. Phillis herself is a proof that even African women, despised as they have been, have intellectual endowments, and with culture and Christian attainment may rival their fairer sisters in the expression of high thoughts in poetic phrase."

BROUGHT TO LIGHT.

Phillis Wheatley Poem, Dedicated to General Washington.

From the Boston *Courant:* Last week we attempted to offer a few remarks on the life and uncollected works of Phillis Wheatley, thinking thereby that the attention of our readers might once more be called to the contemplation of her genius and writings. If we have been successful, if we have succeeded in arousing even a transitory interest in her now waning memory, we could ask no more. But we shall take advantage of it, transient as it may be, to offer to the public Phillis' letter and poem to General Washington.

This poem was sent to General George Washington just after he took command of the continental army in 1775, and was intended to celebrate that event; by Sparks, the biographer of Washington; by Williams, our best historian; in truth, by almost all writers of this period, this poem was supposed to be lost. But such was not the case. The poem was sent to the publisher by the old general himself, though he said otherwise in his letter to Phillis.

Phillis Wheatley to General Washington.

Sir: I have taken the liberty to address your excellency in the enclosed poem, and entreat your acceptance, though I am not insensible to its inaccuracies. Your being appointed by the Grand Continental Congress to be Generalissimo of the armies of North America, together with the fame of your virtues excite sensations not easy to suppress. Your generosity, therefore, I presume, will pardon the attempt. Wishing your excellency all possible success in the great cause you are so generously engaged in, I am your excellency's most obedient, humble servant.

Phillis Wheatley.

Providence, October 26, 1775.

HIS EXCELLENCY, GENERAL WASHINGTON.

Celestial choir! enthroned in realms of light,
Columbia's scenes of glorious toils I write,
While freedom's cause her anxious breast alarms,
She flashes dreadful in refulgent arms.
See mother Earth her offspring's fate bemoan,
And nations gaze at scenes before unknown ;
See the bright beams of heaven's revolving light
Involved in sorrows and in veil of night!
The goddess comes, she moves divinely fair,
Olive and laurel bind her golden hair ;
Wherever shines this native of the skies,
Unnumbered charms and recent graces rise.
Muse! Bow propitious while my pen relates
How pour her armies through a thousand gates ;
As when Eolus heaven's fair face deforms,
Enwrapped in tempest and a night of storms ;
Astonished Ocean feels the wild uproar,
The refluent surges beat the resounding shore ;
Or thick as leaves in Autumn's golden reign,
Such, and so many moves the warrior's train.
In bright array they seek the work of war,
Where high unfurled the ensign waves in air.
Shall I to Washington their praise recite?
Enough, though knowest them in the fields of fight.
Thee first in place and honor we demand,
The grace and glory of thy mortal band,
Famed for thy valor, for thy virtue more,

Hear every tongue thy guardian aid implore ;
One century scarce performed its destined round
When Gallic powers Columbia's fury found ;
And, so may you, whoever dares disgrace
The land of freedom's heaven-defended race.
Fixed are the eyes of nations on the scale,
For in their hopes Columbia's arm prevails.
Anon, Britannia droops the pensive head,
While round increase the rising hills of dead.
Ah! cruel blindness to Columbia's state,
Lament thy thirst of boundless power too late.
Proceed, great chief, virtue on thy side ;
Thy every action let the goddess guide.
A crown, a mansion, and a throne that shine
With gold unfading, Washington, be thine.

It will be seen that Phillis refers to America as Colùmbia, the origin of which saying is erroneously ascribed by historians to Dr. Dwight. But the name Columbia must have been applied to America long before Dr. Dwight, and possibly before either writer lived.

The line beginning "When Gallic power," etc., refers to the old French and Indian war, which began in 1755.

"FERRET."

FRANCES E. W. HARPER,

Temperance Lecturer and Authoress.

FRANCES E. W. HARPER was born in Maryland in 1825 and reared there. Her early education was meagre, having left school at the age of fourteen. She is truly a self-made woman. As a lecturer she has few equals. She has also contributed largely to the most prominent Afro-American journals. Her poetical and prose writings are extensively read by white people as well as black and she has furnished inspiration to many of the young writers of the race. Of late years she has been prominently connected with the Woman's Christian Temperance Union, and has augmented the work among the women of her race.

When great minds agree upon a fact which is thus made

popular, lesser minds have nothing more nor less to do than assent. Mrs. F. E. W. Harper, such as Mrs. Phoebe A. Hannoford has already briefly described, possesses the happy faculty of equilibrium upon all the prominent issues of the day.

MRS. F. E. W. HARPER, PHILADELPHIA.

Eloquent, fluent in speech, forcible in argument, versatile with the pen, rhythmical in poetry, logical in prose, and blessed with the rareness of congeniality, she becomes at once to those who have heard or read her thoughts a lover, a friend, yea! a disciple.

Her "Story of the Nile" is one of her latest achievements, and as our power of judging is meagre we fully and freely assent to its grandness. Dr. Marshall W. Taylor says: Of the Negro race in the United States since 1620, there have appeared but *four* women whose careers stand out so far, so high and so clearly above all others of their sex, that they can with strict propriety and upon well established grounds be denominated great. These are Phillis Wheatley, Sojourner Truth, Frances Ellen Watkins Harper and Amanda Smith.

Mrs. Harper, possessing superior advantages, is superior to any one of the four great women here mentioned in mental drill and versatile literary culture ; she is an erudite scholarly woman; she too is a reformer, an agitator, but not in the rough, or with any political tendency; she is polished, and may be called the greatest of school-made moral philosophers yet developed among the women of the Negro race. If Sojourner Touth was a blind giant, Frances Harper was an enlightened one. Standing outside of the church and churchly relations, Mrs. Harper is without an equal among Negro men of her times and type of thought.

As early as 1845, Frances Ellen Watkins Harper began to figure conspicuously as a literary leader and teacher, starting out in her career as assistant instructress under the principalship of, now, Bishop John M. Brown. Whether she has kept pace with this learned prelate, we leave our readers to judge. Her activities then as now, in the cause of the Negro, battling for its education and equal rights, startle us with love and admiration, while our hearts go out in search of even the crumbs of her wonderful pioneer life. As to the world did God give Adam and Eve, not only to dwell upon the earth, but to be master over every living creature, so did he almost spontaneously give to the Negro race two people, a man and a woman, to stand ont beyond opposition intellectually, the man Rt. Rev. Bishop D. A. Payne, the woman Mrs. Frances E. Watkins Harper, the equals of any of our nineteenth century civilization.

Phœba A. Hanaford, in her "Daughters of America," under the caption of "Women Lecturers," says:

Francis E. W. Harper is one of the most eloquent women lecturers in the country. As one listens to her clear, plaintive, melodious voice, and follows the flow of her musical speech in her logical presentation of truth, he can but be charmed with her oratory and rhetoric, and forgets that she is of the race once enslaved in our land. She is one of the colored women of whom white women may be proud, and to whom the abolitionists can point and declare that a race which could show such women never ought to have been held in bondage. She lectures on temperance, equal rights, and religious themes, and has shown herself able in the use of the pen.

Prof. George W. Williams, in his "History of the Negro Race in America," says of our subject: "She was born in Baltimore, Md., in 1825. She was not permitted to enjoy the blessings of early educational training, but in after years proved herself to be a woman of most remarkable intellectual powers. She applied herself to study, most assiduously; and when she had reached woman's estate she was well educated.

She developed early a fondness for poetry, which she has since cultivated, and some of her efforts are not without merit. She excels as an essayist and lecturer. She has been heard upon many of the leading lecture platforms of the country; and her efforts to elevate her sisters have been crowned with most signal success.

A clear, strong, musical voice, capable of expressing all human feelings and passions, is among the most desirable qualities in the formation of a consummate orator.

> Her words have such a melting flow,
> And speak of truth so sweetly well,
> They drop like heaven's serenest snow,
> And all is brightness where they fall.

> "There is a charm in delivery, a magical art,
> That thrills, like a kiss, from the lips to the heart;
> 'Tis the glance, the expression, the well-chosen word,
> By whose magic the depths of the spirit are stirred—
> The smile—the mute gesture—the soul-stirring pause—
> The eye's sweet expression, that melts while it awes—
> The lip's soft persuasion—its musical tone:
> Oh! such are the charms of that eloquent one."

A hearer might well say, as he listens to the charming accents of her musical voice:

> Thy sweet words drop upon the ear so soft,
> As rose leaves on a well; and I could listen,
> As though the immortal melody of heaven
> Were wrought into one word—that word a whisper—
> That whisper all I want from all I love.

EDMONIA LEWIS,

Sculptress.

NICHOLIS FRANCIS COOKE, M. D., LL.D., in his work styled Satan in Society, in his article, What can Woman Do in the World? says, as sculptors there are already several who have achieved both fame and fortune. In a foot-note we find the following tribute from his liberal and descriptive pen: "Edmonia Lewis, a colored sculptress, not yet twenty-five years old, whose studio at Rome is sought by the cultivated and wealthy, and whose works command almost fabulous prices, furnishes a remarkable instance of perseverance, not only against disadvantages of sex, but the still greater obstacles of race and color. Her father a Negro, and her mother an Indian, both dying early, she was "raised" among the Chippewa Indians, but, through the generosity of her brother, was enabled to obtain a few years at school. Thence she made her way to Boston, where she landed penniless and friendless. Wandering abstractly through School street, she gazed in wonder and admiration upon the statue of Franklin, and, to use her own words, "was seized with the desire of making something like that man standing there." She asked a kindly looking lady "what it was made of," and being informed, sought the studio of Mr. Brockett, from whom she obtained some clay, some modeling tools and "a baby's foot." In about three weeks she returned with a tolerable reproduction of the foot, which the artist commended, and lent her "a woman's hand." Meanwhile she made herself a set of implements the exact counterpart of those she had borrowed, and, being equally successful in modeling the hand, she received from the artist a letter to a lady who gave her eight dollars. With this modest "capital" she established a studio, on the door of which a simple tin sign announced: "Edmonia Lewis, Artist." From that time forward her career has been one uninterrupted triumph. Her latest work, "Hagar," is valued at six thousand dollars, and has earned a handsome revenue by its exhibition.

Among the great women in Daughters of America, we find her classed among the women artists of their first century in art.

Phœba A. Hanaford justly says Edmonia Lewis is entitled to be mentioned with the women artists of our first century. Let "The Christian Register" tell her story:

"All who were present at Tremont Temple on the Monday evening of the presentation to Rev. Mr. McGrimes of the marble group of 'Forever Free,' executed by Miss Edmonia Lewis, must have been deeply interested. No one, not born a subject to the "Cotton King, could look upon that piece of sculpture without profound emotion. The noble figure of the man, his very muscles seeming to swell with gratitude; the expression of the right now to protect, with which he throws his arm around his kneeling wife; the 'Praise de Lord' hovering on their lips; the broken chain,—all so instinct with life, telling in the very poetry of stone the story of the last ten years. And when it is remembered who created this group, an added interest is given to it. Who threw so much expression into those figures? What well-known sculptor arranged with such artistic grace those speaking forms? Will any one believe it was the small hands of a small girl that wrought the marble and kindled the life within it?—a girl of dusky hue, mixed Indian and African, who not more than eight years ago sat down on the steps of the City Hall to eat the dry crackers with which alone her empty purse allowed her to satisfy her hunger; but as she sat there and thought of her dead brother, of her homeless state, something caught her eye, the hunger of the stomach ceased, but the hunger of the soul began. That quiet statue of the grand old Franklin had touched the electric spark, and kindled the latent genius which was enshrined within her, as her own group was in the marble till her chisel brought it out. For weeks she haunted the spot, and the State House, where she could see Washington and Webster. She asked questions and found that such things were made of clay. She got a lump of clay, shaped her some sticks, and her heart divided between art and the great struggle for freedom, which had just received the seal of Colonel Shows' blood. She wrought out, from photographs and her own ideal, an admirable bust of him. This made the name of Edmonia Lewis known in Boston. The unknown waif on the steps of the City Hall had, in a few short months, become an object of interest to a large circle of those most anxious about the great problem of the development of the colored race in their new position.

We next hear of Edmonia in Rome, where her perseverance, industry, genius and *naiveté* made her warm friends. Miss Charlotte Cushman and Miss Hosmer took great interest in her. Her studio was visited by all strangers, who looked upon the creations of this untaught maiden as marvelous. She modeled there " The Freed Woman on First Hearing of Her Liberty," of which it is said : " It tells with much eloquence a painful story." No one can deny that she has distinguished herself in sculpture ; not, perhaps, in the highest grade, but in the most pleasing form. Six months ago she returned to her own country to sit once again on the steps of the City Hall, just to recall the "then," and to contrast it with the "now." "Then," hungry, heart-weary, no plan for the future. " Now," the hunger of the soul satisfied; freedom to do, to achieve, won by her own hands, friends gained ; the world to admire.

She brought with her to this country a bust of "our" poet, said to be one of the best ever taken. It has been proposed by some of Longfellow's friends to have it put in marble for Harvard. It would be a beautiful thought that the author of Hiawatha should be embalmed in stone by a descendant from Minnehaha. And certainly nothing can be more appropriate than the presentation to Rev. Mr. Grimes, the untiring friend of his race, the indomitable worker, the earnest preacher, of this rare work, "Forever Free," uniting grace and sentiment, the offspring of an enthusiastic soul, who consecrates her genius to truth and beauty.

Professor George G. W. Williams in his History of the Negro Race in America says: "Edmonia Lewis, the Negro sculptress, is in herself a great prophecy of the possibilities of her sisters in America. Of lowly birth, left an orphan when quite young, unable to obtain a liberal education, she nevertheless determined to be something and somebody.

This ambitious Negro girl has won a position as an artist, a studio in Rome, and a place in the admiration of the lovers of art on two continents. She has produced many meritorious works of art, the most noteworthy being *Hagar in the Wilderness*; a group of the *Madonna with the Infant Christ and Two Adoring Angels; Forever Free; Hiawatha's Wooing;* a bust of *Longfellow, the Poet;* a bust of *John Brown,* and a medallion portrait of *Wendell Phillips.* The *Madonna* was purchased by the Marquis of Bute, Disraeli's Lothair.

She has been well received in Rome, and her studio has become an object of interest to travelers of all countries.

MRS. BLANCHE V. H. BROOKS,

Able Pioneer Teacher, Able Writer, President W. C. T. U.

MRS. BLANCHE V H. BROOKS, the subject of this sketch, is deserving a place in the galaxy of noted Negro women. She was born in Monroe, Michigan, where she lived until thirteen years of age.

The prejudice which forbade the girl entering the young ladies' seminary with her associates in the high school only paved the way for her entering the world-renowned Oberlin college. The prejudice before mentioned induced her parents to send her to Oberlin, where she could procure the best educational facilities; here she remained until she was grad-

uated in the class of '60, endearing herself to the faculty
teachers and to her classmates.

Though quite young at the time of the late war, and the
call for teachers for Freedmen came, she responded to Rev.
George Whipple: "Here am I; send me." Leaving home,
friends, and all comforts, she
entered upon her life work
in that demoralized region,
demoralized because of the
effects of the late war.

The hospital needed
nurses; the Freedmen,—men,
women and children—needed
teachers, not only in books,
but in every department, and
there she found earnest, hard
work; when not in the
school-room night after night
she could be found by the
cot of the sick and dying.

So firm an advocate of
temperance is she that
through her influence she
was instrumental in saving
many from drunkards'

MRS. BLANCHE V. H. BROOKS.

graves; through her influence an opening was made for
other young women to go to the South land. When her labor
was no longer needed as a pioneer she returned to the North
to re-engage in school work. To direct young minds is a task
for which Blanche V. H. Brooks is fitted by her natural
endowment of taste, judgment, firmness and decision of character, softened and modified by sweetness of temperament.

For seventeen years she has been engaged in the public
schools of Knoxville. Since her graduation, until the present
time, the productions from her pen have been a source of
entertainment and instruction. As we before mentioned, she
is a strong advocate of the temperance cause; for five years

she has held the position of president of the **W. C. T. U.**, and works earnestly, it may seem, in season and out of season, to bring the wine-drinking habit into disfavor.

MRS. DELLA IRVING HAYDEN,

Eminent Educator.

AT the close of the Civil war we find the subject of our sketch in the town of Tarboro, N. C., without a mother's care, her mother having in the early days of the war moved to the "Old Dominion."

MRS. DELLA IRVING HAYDEN.

In her incipiency she knew not the care of a mother, but had a loving grandmother to whom she was devoted with all the devotion a child could bestow. Though separated for years by landscape, there continued in the mother's breast that love and devotion that are peculiar to her sex; hence she returned in search of her lost child in 1865. Finding her in vigorous health, she, as the shepherd doth the lost sheep, took her child upon her breast, and over rocky steeps and swollen streams, wound her way back to Virginia. As the infant grew she proved to be of a brilliant mind, and even when but a child exhibited great tact in the management of little folks around her. There being no free schools in operation at that day for colored children, she was taught to spell by a white friend, who consented to teach her at the request of her mother.

From an old Webster spelling book she made her first start, and soon learned as far as "baker," a great accomplishment in those days. After getting a foretaste of an education she then, a young miss, became very anxious for an education. Free schools were not yet in existence, so she entered a school seven miles away in Nansemond county. This school was under the control of the Freedman's bureau, and was taught by a Mr. A. B. Colis, of New Jersey. The next year her parents moved from Nansemond county to Franklin, South Hampton county, Virginia, where she entered the public school.

In school she was obedient, docile, kind and punctual. Out of school she was the delight of her playmates and apparently the life of the school.

Early in life she was converted and joined the Baptist church. As a Christian she was a shining light and an ardent worker in the cause of Christianity.

Years and deeds having hastened her near the verge of womanhood, she became a faithful teacher and an ardent worker in the Sabbath-school, to which work she became very much attached.

She was secretary for Sunday-school and church clerk for several years.

In 1872 she entered the Hampton Normal and Agricultural institute with very limited means, with none to look to but a widowed mother. And just here it is fitting to say that that mother was a mother in the truest sense. For she made great sacrifice to help her daughter through school. Lapse of years having brought her to the age of womanhood, we may now call her Miss Irving. She being of an industrious turn of mind and eager to go through school, was glad to do any work assigned her to assist in paying school bills. During her school days at Hampton she stood high in the esteem of both her schoolmates and teachers. In her second term in school she made the acquaintance of Mrs. G. M. Jones, of Philadelphia, who gave her some financial aid, and has ever since been a warm and devoted friend.

In 1874 Miss Irving (as she was then), having a determined will of her own, and hearing continual appeal of her people to "come over in Macedonia and help us," could no longer resist the pitiful cry, but laid down the pursuit of her studies, and, with that burning zeal of a missionary, laid hold of her work that she had for so long desired. By so doing she did much to dispel the gloom which overshadowed her people, and financially enabled herself to resume her studies in 1875. Her first school-house was a little log-cabin in a section of her own county known as Indian Town.

Her first term was marked with great success, and she filled the first place in the hearts of the people among whom she labored.

There she organized a Sunday-school in which she acted as teacher, chorister and superintendent. So great was the love of the people for her that they said they didn't believe that the county paid her enough for the valuable services she rendered them, and as a unit came together and made up the deficiency as nearly as they could, for they thought that currency could not compensate for the great good and the blessings that she had been the means of bestowing upon them. Her second term was taught four miles from this place, where it was difficult to find a family near the school with sufficient room to board a teacher (most of the houses having only one room). She was sent to such a house to board. This was too much for the young teacher. The people looked upon her as a jewel and would do anything to please her, so she called the parents together and they willingly united and built another room, the teacher furnishing the nails.

In 1875 she returned to the Hampton Normal and Agricultural institute and resumed her studies. In 1877 she graduated with honor and was the winner of a $20 prize, offered to the best original essayist of the class. On her return home to resume the work among her people, to which she felt so closely espoused, she was elected principal of the town public school. Here she met with some competition for the position, but energy, push and competency always hold sway over all opposition when fair play is granted. She outstripped her rivals and filled the position with credit three years. She was looked upon as the spiritual, educational, and political adviser of her neighborhood, for the colored people. In the church and Sunday-school she had no peer, for both minister and Sunday-school superintendent sought her advice as to the best means of spiritualizing the church and enlivening the Sunday-school. She stands in the ranks among the best educators of her race. Through her influence and recommendation a great many young men and women have gained admission into some of the best institutions of learning in the United States. Many of them she assisted financially while in school from her scanty income, which was a sacrifice, but a pleasure. Quite a number of them have graduated and are now filling honorable positions.

As a politician she was so well informed, and could discuss so intelligently the public issues of the day, that in her town, in the campaign of 1884, she was styled the "Politician's Oracle." She, as did Paul, ceased not day nor night to warn her people of the danger that awaited them. While teaching she did not fail to practice economy, for she saved means to lift a heavy debt off her property, which she mortgaged to secure means to finish her education.

In 1880 she married Mr. Lindsey Hayden, an accomplished gentleman who was principal of the public school of Liberty (now Bedford City), Virginia. Unfortunately for her, Mr. Hayden lived only a few months after marriage. During his short illness Mr. Hayden found in her every requisite of a true wife and ever his administering angel. After the death of her devoted husband, she resigned the position as first assistant teacher in the school in which her husband had so recently been principal, and returned to Franklin to live with her widowed mother. Notwithstanding all hearts went out in sympathy for her in her bereavement, there was a sort of mingled joy at her return to her old field of labor, since it seemed a matter of impossibility to fill her place as a worker among her people. In the fall of 1881 she was again elected principal of the town school, which position she held for nine years. As a temperance lecturer and worker in general, the United States can not boast of one more ardent. She served three years as president of the W. C. T. U. and the Home Missionary Society, organized by Mrs. Marriage Allen, the wonderful messenger of England, and for four years recording secretary of the county Sunday-school union, and one year corresponding secretary of the Bethany Baptist Sunday-school convention.

She has organized a great many temperance societies and hundreds have taken the pledge. She is at present president of the Virginia Teachers' Temperance Union, and an active worker and officer of the Virginia Teachers' Association.

In 1890 she was elected lady principal of the Virginia Normal and Collegiate Institute, which position she now holds. Says General S. C. Armstrong, principal of the Hampton Normal and Agricultural Institute:

"Mrs. Della Irving Hayden was at Hampton school four years, and made her a most excellent record. We all here, teachers and friends, expected a great deal of her, and have not been disappointed. She married a noble young man, Mr. Lindsey Hayden, who soon died—a great loss. Since her bereavement Mrs. Hayden has devoted herself nobly to her people. We hope she may be spared many years. She is among the famous women of her race."

To the Author of Noted Women.

Dear Sir: I can most heartily endorse all that Mr. W. B. Holland has said of the life and work of Mrs. D. I. Hayden, of the Virginia Normal and Collegiate Institute, Petersburg, Virginia. She is indeed an earnest laborer for the elevation of her people, as hundreds of others can testify. I was once her pupil and by her taught the most useful lessons of life I know.

Mrs. Hayden is a born teacher, and her sixteen years of

faithful service in the school-room rightly places her among the Noted Women of the Colored Race.

Mrs. A G. Randolph.

Hempstead, Texas.

Says Miss Maggie I. Stevens: "Mrs. Della Irving Hayden well deserves the name woman. I was a pupil in her school thirteen years ago. It was through her I gained admission into the Hampton Normal and Agricultural Institute. It is to her (through the help of God) I owe my success in literary attainment. She has no peer as a quick thinker and an earnest worker."

James H. Johnston, A. M., president of the Virginia Normal and Collegiate Institute, in speaking of her work as connected with that institution, says: "Since Mrs. Hayden's election as lady principal of this institution, she has exhibited unusual tact and ability in the performance of her duty, thereby gaining the love and esteem of the students and commendation of the board of visitors. Aside from her special work, she has been exceedingly active in organizing temperance societies among the students and among the teachers of our annual summer session. As a result of her labors in this direction there now exists in the school a society of more than one hundred members, and among the teachers a State temperance association. In our school, where once temperance views were unpopular, the leading students are the most active temperance advocates. Doubtless the teachers of the State organization, in their several localities, have disseminated seed the fruit of which can only be estimated in eternity. She has also been instrumental in planting in our midst a branch of the "King's Daughters," which has done good work both in the school and out. In holiday seasons she has been active in good work in the Sunday-school, church and among the people generally. She does not fail to use her pen and power of speech, which she possesses in no ordinary degree, to advance the Master's kingdom by the promotion of temperance. Southampton and the State of Virginia need many more Della I. Haydens."

Dr. J. F. Bryant, county superintendent of Southampton county, in speaking of her qualifications as a teacher, said: "Mrs. Della I. Hayden taught twelve (12) years in the public schools of Southampton, to the entire satisfaction of patrons and school officers, the most of the time under my supervision. She was principal of a large graded school in this place. Her executive capacity is of a high order. And she manages a school of a hundred or more pupils with as much dexterity and ease as most teachers with twenty or twenty-five pupils. Her ambition in her chosen profession is unbounded, and she never tires.

Beginning with a third grade certificate she was enabled to attend the Hampton Normal and Agricultural Institute, teaching one year and returning to the school the other, until she graduated with distinction at that institute. She finally obtained a professional certificate, the highest grade under the public school system, as a reward for her persever- ance, energy and ability."

The foregoing statement will give our readers a faint view only of the wonderfully useful life that Mrs. D. I. Hayden has lived for and among her people.

WILLIS B. HOLLAND.

MRS. RT. REV. B. W. ARNETT,

W. C. T. U. Advocate.

"The growing good of the world is largely dependent on unhistoric acts ; and that things are not so ill with you and me as they might have been, is half owing to the numbers who lived faithfully a hidden life."

Geo. Eliot in Middlemarch.

I HAVE often felt how true this is of the wives of great men. The patient, unseen, devoted toiler with loving self-forget fulness, standing ever true at her husband's side, kindling his belief in himself by her pure belief about him, urging him on to his highest endeavor by expecting from him his best, applauding his noblest achievements and giving nerve and stimulus to his success, cheerfully sharing and smoothing over his disappointments, shielding him from the petty irritations of the domestic machinery, thus making it possible for him to throw his whole soul into the larger outer work for God and the race; soothing, comforting, cheering, inspiring—and then quietly drinking in as her reward the praise and appreciation lavished by the world on him.

Of no woman is all this more true than of Mrs. Bishop Benjamin W. Arnett, one of the strongest of our mothers in Israel, and one whose life and example should be studied by every girl that stands hesitantly " where the brook and river meet," wondering with throbbing pulses what life has in store for her.

Mary Louise Gordon was born near Geneva, Pa., August 1st, 1839. Her parents, William and Hester Ann Gordon, were substantial hardworking people who had removed from Virginia some years before Louise was born. In 1845 they left Geneva to live in Uniontown, Pa., where they lived till 1865, when they moved to Brownsville, Pa., where they still reside.

Little Louise was put in school at an early age, Miss Sarah J. Allen being her first teacher, followed by Keziah Brown Jackson and John Bellows in private schools. Public schools in those days ran four months of the year, and were generally taught by superannuated white teachers without maps or charts or any of the modern furnishings which we think so indispensable in our day. But they managed to get through the three R's and teach the little folks to " sit up straight and look on the book," and I don't know but these same little folks, now grown up, look back with just as much pleasure on those " good old days " as will our highly developed kindergartners with all their stick laying, and paper folding, and clay molding. The school house in which my young heroine's ideas were first taught to shoot was the typical log-house, 15x12, adorned with long benches made of slabs with four wooden pegs stuck in for legs. It stood on the site of the present A. M. E. Church of Uniontown and managed to attract colored children from two and three miles around. ·Private schools supplemented the short terms of the public sessions, serving to keep the children out of the streets certainly, if not for very extensive scholarly advancement.

Louise at first attended a Presbyterian Sunday-school, Miss Mary Duncan being her first teacher. When a little later she entered the A. M. E. Sabbath-school, Mr. J. H. Manaway was superintendent and Mrs. Eliza Moxley, still living in Uniontown, her first colored Sabbath-school teacher. She was converted in 1855 and received into the church by Rev. Solomon H. Thompson and into the class of Alexander Moxley, one of the leading men of Uniontown in his day—long since gone to his reward.

In the fall of 1855 she went to spend some weeks with a married aunt living in Brownsville. Now it so happened that the husband of this aunt had a nephew, a promising lad, christened Benjamin William, but popularly dubbed Bennie by his numerous friends, young and old. Naturally enough Bennie went in the course of events to pay his dutiful respects to his uncle and aunt; and there he met the interesting young maiden who was making a visit from Uniontown. The gallant lad of course did all in his power to keep the young stranger from feeling homesick, and she naturally enough felt grateful for the endeavor and both were pleased at the success of their dutiful visits to uncle and aunt. Well, the course of true love didn't run any smoother in those days than now. The young people parted with palpitating hearts and many magnetic pressures of the hand and promises of eternal remembrances, when the day came for Louise to return to her home in Uniontown, twelve miles away. They had promised a regular correspondence and Tuesday was the day for Ben to get his letters. Life rolled on deliciously for several elysian weeks. But one Tuesday no letter came; Wednesday, again disappointment; Thursday—misery; Friday—despair; Saturday—rage; and the exasperated boy, surcharged by his pent-up feelings, exploded in a bitter reproachful letter. For six months a long and dreary silence! At length Ben drove over to Uniontown for a Sunday service. He met Louise at church and asked the privilege of walking home with her. It was granted with averted eyes; and, hearts beating furiously, they walked along some distance in silence. After awhile the lad in a tremulous low tone inquired "Why didn't you write that week?" "I could not, I had a felon on my finger and there was no one to write for me," was the low reply. And the two foolish hearts, smiling through tears at all their self. inflicted torture, were one again and forever.

But the old folks had to be approached! for it was in the good days long ago when parents were *asked* for their daughters. And the redoubtable Ben, ready enough with his tongue on all ordinary occasions, had a most stammering and trembling time of it, getting to the point with the "old lady." From early morn till dewy eve he sat. He exhausted every available topic under the sun. He talked of the weather, talked of the crops, the probable price of coal and the usual cost of ice. All of which good mother Gordon submitted to most serenely. At last about supper time he desperately gulped down a great lump in his throat and took the bull by the horns, plunging blindly right into the middle of the thing. The old lady smiled on him benignly, saying after a pause : "Well, Bennie, you may have Louise if you can take care of her and will be good to her." The ice once broken, Ben's tongue was now loosed and discoursed volubly enough on his prospects and hopes for their future. When father Gordon came in he said, reassuringly : "Well, whatever mam says—whatever mam says." And so the happy young couple began to prepare for their union.

But a great shadow casting its gloom clear down a life came athwart their path. Young Arnett was working on the river when he met with an accident which cost him a limb. All that friendship, skill and money could devise were exhausted in trying to save the fatal operation. But after weeks of weary but heroically cheerful suffering the leg was amputated. Then came the test of love and the triumph of devotion. The stricken lover stoically released his fiancée, firmly saying: "I cannot ask you to accept a shattered life of

poverty and misery on my account." Louise's own friends and
relatives urged that she accept her release, saying : "Of course
he can never take care of you now." But the brave little
woman, with lips set and determined, rejoined : " *Well, if he can't
take care of me, I can take care of him.*" Accordingly on the
25th of May, 1858, they were quietly married by Rev. Geo.
Brown, President of Madison College at Uniontown.   That
heroic little woman could not at that time foresee the rounds
of the ladder then hid in cloud and gloom by which the
resolute heart to whom she had committed her happiness and
the arm on which she leaned would one day mount to the
stars and fill the gaze of his fellows by his dauntless courage,
untiring energy, unblemished integrity and lofty purpose.
But then, she could only trust and love *and inspire.* In these
days to be able to meet the rent (twelve dollars a year)
for a model three-room cottage to her was wealth ; and to
preside with wifely thrift and economy over that mansion in
union with the husband of her heart's first choice was her
ideal of earthly bliss, and richly has she been rewarded.

At first there was some uncertainty as to what employment
young Arnett would settle down to.   With ready pluck and
energy he took hold of every means in reach of turning an
honest penny.   He sold fish, sold coal, tried his hand at bar-
bering and even steeled his conscience to torturing as a dentist.
But Louise declared she didn't want any barber nor dentist
either ; she thought he could aim higher than that if he tried,
and so the ardent young husband was constrained by the
sweet insistence of love to buckle his powers down to a course
of study preparatory to a more intellectual calling.   Meantime
by her skilful needle and untiring thrift Louise successfully
kept the wolf from the door, till the needed preparation
obtained, her husband was able to earn the enormous salary
of twenty-five dollars a month as village school-master, and I
know the black eyes danced when the first month's roll of bills
was presented and the lips melted into a roguish smile as she
whispered softly " *That's right. I told you so!* "   The other
rounds were speedily gained and passed after that ; and at what-

ever station the ambitious toiler found himself—whether the struggling boat hand, the anxious student, the village teacher or an honored instructor at the nation's capital ; whether local preacher, presiding elder, or financial secretary of a great connection ; whether the eloquent speaker or the powerful worker in the legislative halls of his adopted State ; whether as bishop or as president of a theological seminary, there has ever been helpfully near his side a true and loving wife. Wherever his checkered life has called him to reside, her rare intelligence and womanly tact and, withal, her Christian worthiness and sincere benevolence, have drawn unusual esteem and appreciation to herself and won many friends to her husband. She is in the highest sense a *help-meet* for him.

They have reared a family of children of whom any parents might be proud. The eldest, Alonzo, now working at home; Benjamin W. Jr., ex-president of Edward Waters College, Jacksonville, Fla.; Henry Y., professor of mathematics at Allen University, Columbia, S. C.; Anna L., music teacher and private secretary of her father; Alphonso T. and Flossie G., attending school ; and Daniel A. Payne, "captain of the Arnett house."

One can scarce resist the temptation to moralize over such a life for the benefit of those luckless young souls who, carried away with the shimmer and tinsel of superficial young dudes, wreck their happiness on good looks and fine clothes by marrying some fellow without purposes or ambitions and with no higher conception of woman than as one to minister to his vanity and pleasures. But such a life as Mrs. Arnett's preaches its own sermon. I will not add to it.

A. J. COOPER,
Tawawa Chimney Corner.

September 19, 1892.

JOSEPHINE A. SILONE YATES,

Scientist, Educator, Writer, Known as Mrs. R. K. Potter.

MRS. JOSEPHINE YATES, youngest daughter of Alexander and Parthenia Reéve-Silone, was born in 1859, in Mattituck, Suffolk county, New York, where her parents, grandparents and great-grandparents were long and favorably known as individuals of sterling worth, morally intellectually and physically speaking. On the maternal side she is a niece of Rev. J. B. Reeve, D. D., of Philadelphia, a sketch of whose life appears in "Men of Mark."

MRS. JOSEPHINE A. SILONE YATES.

Mrs. Silone, a woman of whose noble, self-sacrificing life of piety from early youth until her latest hours volumes might be written, began the work of educating her daughter Josephine in her quiet Christian home, consecrating her to the service of the Lord in infancy and earnestly praying that, above all else, the life of her child might be a useful one. Possessed herself of a fair education, she well knew the value of intellectual development and spared no pains to surround her daughter with all possible means of improvement; the latter, now grown to womanhood, delights to relate that the earliest event of which she has any distinct remembrance is of this sainted mother taking her upon her knee and teaching her to read from the Bible by requiring her to call the words after her, as she pointed them out.

Josephine was sent to school at an early age and had already been so well advanced by her mother in reading, writing and arithmetic that she was at once able to enter one of the higher classes of the district school, and because of her eagerness and readiness to learn, soon became a favorite with her teachers, although the only colored pupil in the school. She possessed an excellent memory, good reasoning powers, and at the age of nine was studying physiology and physics, and was well advanced in mathematics. Through the kindness of a Mrs. Horton, her Sunday-school teacher, she had at this time access to a large and well selected library for young people and in all probability thus acquired an additional taste for literature which was, perhaps primarily, an inheritance from her ancestors ; however this may be, a keen ambition to write, coupled with a corresponding appreciation of first-class literature, began to assert itself at an early period. Her schoolgirl efforts at composition were very favorably commented upon by her teachers, and while yet in her ninth year she wrote a story which she sent to one of the prominent New York weeklies, and although the manuscript was returned, it was accompanied by a letter of such kind encouragement and suggestion that it served to increase rather than diminish her ambition.

At the age of eleven her uncle, the Rev. J. B. Reeve, believing that her desire for knowledge should have better opportunities for fulfillment than could be obtained in a district school, very kindly invited her to his home in Philadelphia that she might attend the institute conducted by Mrs. Fannie Jackson-Coppin. Here for the first time brought in contact with a large number of cultured persons of her own race in society, church and school she received a new and stronger inspiration for the acquisition of knowledge.

Rapid progress was made during this school year. Mrs. Coppin, who has ever since manifested much interest in her welfare, still often refers to her as a brilliant example of what a girl may do. The following year the Rev. Dr. Reeve was called to Washington to accept the chair of theology in Howard University and Miss Silone returned to her home. A year later Mrs. Francis L. Girard, of Newport, Rhode Island, her

maternal aunt, a woman well known for the moral and intellectual strength of her character, and revered by many
students for her benevolence and kindness, made her a proposition which she accepted ; and in her fourteenth year went to
Newport, and became a resident of that beautiful "City by
the Sea."

Here she at once entered the highest grade of the grammar
school and maintaining her usual scholarship, the only colored
pupil in the school at the time, she attracted the attention of
Col. T. W. Higginson, then a citizen of Newport and a prominent member of the School Board ; of the Hon. George T.
Downing, through whose untiring efforts the doors of the
public schools of Rhode Island were thrown open to all, without regard to race or color ; of Thomas Coggeshall, at that
time chairman of the school board ; of Rev. Dr. Thayer and
wife and other persons of distinction.

The year following she entered the Rogers High School, an
institution which takes first rank among the schools of the
land. Taking the four years course in three, she graduated
from this school in the class of '77, delivering the valedictory
address, and receiving the Norman medal for scholarship. She
had the honor to be the first colored graduate of the above
mentioned school and here, as in the other institutions which
she attended, gained the love and admiration of her teachers
by her demeanor and devotion to her studies.

Her instructor in science considered her his brightest pupil,
and especially commended her for her work in chemistry, a
study in which she was particularly interested (although, if
the statement were not paradoxical, it might be said that she
was particularly interested in each study), and by doing additional laboratory work at odd hours under the guidance of her
instructor, became quite an efficient and practical chemist.

On graduating from the High School she was urged to
take a university course ; all of her own purely personal desires
and inclinations led her that way, but from the beginning it
had been her purpose to fit herself for teaching and if possible
to be—not an artisan, but an artist in the profession ; therefore,

after reflecting calmly upon the subject, taking the advice of Colonel Higginson and other stanch friends, she decided to take a full course in the Rhode Island State Normal School. She was already well known in the capacity of an earnest student to the principal, Professor James C. Greenough, and found him and his able corps of teachers very willing to assist her to gain what she needed in the line of preparation for her professional career. In '79, the only colored scholar in a class of twenty or more, she graduated with honor from the Normal School.

While attending this institution she entered a teachers' examination in Newport with sixteen Anglo-saxon candidates and came out of it with a general average of $94\frac{1}{3}$ per cent.; this, while not exceptionally high, was, according to official statement, the highest average that had up to date been gained in that city in a teachers' examination.

A regulation certificate duly signed, allowing her to teach in the public schools of Rhode Island, was granted her, the first time in the history of Rhode Island that anything of the kind had occurred.

In the fall of '79 she began her life-work as a teacher and ten continuous years were thus spent in an enthusiastic and self-sacrificing manner. Eight of these years were spent at Lincoln Institute, Jefferson City, Missouri, to which institution she was called by Professor Page soon after he became its official head. He had been made acquainted with her success as a student through her former instructors. She was at once put in charge of the subject chemistry and succeeded so well with this and other scientific branches assigned her, that eventually the entire department of natural science was turned over to her. At the time of her resignation, she was professor of natural science in the above mentioned institution at a salary of one thousand dollars per school year and was at the time probably the only colored lady in the country holding such a position. During this entire period her summers were invariably spent in the East, where, seizing every opportunity afforded by teachers' associations, summer schools and individual effort, she endeavored to find out the best methods of pre-

senting the subjects which she taught. It was not long before
her work as a teacher and writer became well known to the
public, and among others, it attracted the attention of such
well known educators as President Mitchell, of Wilberforce,
Booker T. Washington, of Tuskegee, and the late Miss Briggs,
Washington, D. C.   In '86 Mr. Washington, feeling that she
was just the one needed for the work in Tuskegee, urged her
to become the lady principal of that institution, but after giving the matter careful thought, she decided to remain at Lincoln Institute.   In '89 she resigned her position in this institution to become the wife of Professor W. W. Yates, principal of
Wendel Phillips school, of Kansas City, Missouri.   Mrs. Yates
carried with her the love of the students, the best wishes of
President Page and the Board of Regents ; and all felt that in
parting with her they were losing the services of an able and
enthusiastic educator.

Mrs. Yates has many warm friends among both the colored
and white citizens of Kansas City, where she was well and favorably known in educational circles before her marriage.
Previous to this event, she had on request read a paper before
the general section of the Kansas City Teachers' Institute, a
highly educated body, consisting of a large number of white
and colored teachers of the city public schools and outlying
districts ; during the first winter of her stay in Kansas City,
she was invited by Superintendent James C. Greenwood to read
a paper before the Greenwood Philosophical Club, a circle
composed of the leading educators and literary lights of Kansas City.

Her doors and heart are always open to young people, for
whom she has an intense love and sympathy, as many students
in various States will testify.   In the midst of a round of
social household and maternal duties she finds time to pursue
a regular line of study and literary work; in the latter she has
the full sympathy of her genial husband.   He is very proud
of his wife's attainments and she feels that his searching
criticism aids her not a little in her literary work. · Since her
marriage, in addition to the work before mentioned, she has

taught for a portion of the time in Lincoln High School of Kansas City, performing the work assigned her to the entire satisfaction of all parties concerned.

Reading French and German with ease, she has made quite a study of literature of both these languages and a few years ago wrote a series of articles upon German literature which were very well received by the press. Russian life and literature also possess for her a peculiar fascination; possibly because of the large class of persons in Russia, which, in some respects like the Negro in America, is struggling for a more complete independence. Gogol, Turgenief, Tolstoi, Stepniak and other Russian authors setting forth the cause of the people, find in her an appreciative reader.

She has a great amount of race pride and fully believes in the bright future of the Negro, provided the young people for the next quarter-century are fully alive to the great responsibilities resting upon them. For years she has been a close observer of human nature and of the great problems of the age.

As a writer, her articles are characterized by a clear, vigorous, incisive style and have embraced a wide range of thought, from the purely literary to the more practical social, economic and scientific questions now confronting us. These have appeared in various periodicals and weeklies, under the name " R. K. Potter," a *nom de plume* which she selected while yet a student and has ever since retained. In some moods the poetic strain of her nature asserts itself, and several little gems have thus found their way into print; among these may be mentioned, "Isles of Peace," " Royal Today," and " The Zephyr."

During the early years of her work in teaching she made quite a name as a lecturer and many of her friends wished her to give up teaching and enter the field as a lecturer, but feeling that the class room was the place where her efforts would result in the greatest good to the greatest number she did not make the change. Her mother used to relate that before her daughter could talk plainly, when asked what she wanted

to be when grown, the answer would invariably be " I want to
be a tool teacher."

Mrs. Yates is the mother of one child, a little daughter, and
in the line of special study much of her work is done with the
hope of being better prepared to wisely direct the education of
this child.

MRS. ZELIA R. PAGE.

Dramatist, Teacher of Natural Science; Friend of the Poor.

IT was in the old aristocratic city of Alexandria, Virginia,
that Zelia R. Page, *nee* Ball, first saw the light of day.
She was not a slave. She was reared by her mother, a woman
of remarkable ingenuity and foresight, who during the dark
days of slavery helped many a poor bondman on his way to
Canada. At one time whilst living with a wealthy Southern
family in Washington City, she kept concealed for one week
in the atic six slaves waiting for the password to march.
This mother, seeing and knowing the degradation and misery
of slavery, was determined that her daughter should know
as little of it as possible. She having faith in the girl's future
was deeply interested in her education. Having many friends
in New England and knowing of the educational facilities that
colored youths had in that section of the country, she made
up her mind to take this child to New England. But the
question was how to pass through Baltimore and Harve De
Grace alone with her child. Being intimately acquainted with
the family of the celebrated Dr. Peter Parker who had
recently returned to Washington City from China, knowing
that they intended to visit the East, she consulted them about
the matter. Dr. Parker told her the only way she could travel
with his family was to go as far as New York as their slave,
she and her child. She readily consented. And thus one Saturday morning in the month of June the mother with her
child arrived in Providence, Rhode Island. She found, after
reaching Providence, that the educational facilities were not as

good for the colored youth, as those in Boston, so she sent Zelia to Boston to school.

This girl possessed great dramatic and artistic powers. During her stay in the New England school she would always be called upon to declaim in the presence of visitors. She

MRS. ZELIA R. PAGE.

declaimed before the great educators Bigelow and Green. They said to her, "Go on. You have talent; improve it." But alas, like many others, she had no one to depend upon but a poor mother for her support. Her mother sent her to Wilberforce in 1870. She was graduated in 1875. She returned to Providence. In 1878, June 27th, she married Inman E. Page, the

first colored graduate of Brown University and now president
of Lincoln Institute at Jefferson City, Missouri.

Her life has not been one of continual sunshine, and yet it
has not been at all times the opposite. Having a strict moral
principle, she could never wink at any thing that was wrong or
seemingly wrong. Perhaps if she had been so constituted as to
be able to close her eyes to wrong doing she might have pre-
vented a good many hard, false and cruel statements that have
been made about her.

She is a diligent student constantly seeking to add to her
store of knowledge some new truths from the different departments of learning. She has written several excellent papers
that have been read before the public and published by
request. Before she was twelve years old she had read the
works of Scott, Milton, Dante and other noted authors.

She has been at Lincoln Institute fourteen years, and
during the greater part of that time she had served either as
matron or as teacher of natural science. She has been the
means of doing much good in Jefferson City. She organized
a Union Training School for the poor children, September 25,
1891, which meets every Saturday afternoon. The value of
the instruction which she gives to these children will be seen
in future years. I have often heard her say " O! if I was only
rich. I do not want money for myself, but I would like to be
rich in order to do some good in this world. I would build an
institution of learning simply for the poor colored young men
and women of my race and have them to learn everything
that would enable them to vie with the Anglo-Saxon race."

She is a devoted Christian, and always seeking to do what
good she can and to help others. Mrs. Page will long be
remembered by the students of Lincoln Institute and especially
the poor students for her deeds of kindness to them.

MRS. OLIVIA DAVIDSON WASHINGTON.

Educator, Financier and Christian Martyr.

MRS. OLIVIA DAVIDSON WASHINGTON was born in the western part of Virginia, June 11, 1854. When quite young she moved with her parents to the State of Ohio, and the family made its home at Gallipolis, Ohio, and later at Athens.

MRS. OLIVIA DAVIDSON WASHINGTON.

From her earliest childhood she had an intense desire for education and by some means managed to remain in the common schools until she was fifteen years old. When about fifteen, she had made such progress that she was able to pass a n examination in Ohio for a teacher's certificate, and taught acceptably in the State for one or two terms.

But it was in the South, among the lowly of her race, that she did her life-work and built a monument in the heart of the people that will be everlasting. About the year 1874 she went into Mississippi and began teaching, and a little later she was given a position in the city schools of Memphis, Tenn., where she taught till 1878. During the summer vacations she would teach in Mississippi and Arkansas. It was the work among the ignorant but simple country people of her race that she enjoyed most. In fact, she often said that she was scarcely ever so happy as when teaching in the country on a large cotton plantation; where she came in daily contact with those whose burdens she could lighten. She lived in the hearts of the lowly.

Often have her friends heard her tell how she has sat up all night with a sick pupil after teaching all day. At one time when a neighbor was sick with the small-pox and others seemed afraid to go to her relief, she volunteered her service and remained with the patient till she was well.

In 1879 she resigned her position in the Memphis city schools with a view of more thoroughly preparing herself as a teacher.

Soon after leaving Memphis and going to her home in Lee, Athens county, Ohio, the great yellow fever epidemic broke out in Memphis. As soon as she heard of the suffering in Memphis she at once sent a telegram to the mayor of the city offering her services as a yellow fever nurse; but as she herself had not had the disease, the health authorities refused her services for the reason that her coming would merely serve to "add fuel to the fire."

Seeing that she would be of no service to the Memphis sufferers, she decided to enter the Hampton Institute, at Hampton, Va. In the fall of 1879 she entered the senior class of that institution, and remained at the institution one year, completing the course with the highest honors and winning the love and confidence of all with whom she came in contact. General Armstrong says she was the strongest and most efficient woman ever graduated from Hampton.

While at Hampton, Mrs. Mary Hemmenway, the millionaire philanthropist of Boston, visited the institution and became so interested in Miss Davidson that she told her that if she wished to extend her education she would gladly bear her expenses in one of the best schools in New England. Accepting this proposition the following fall Miss Davidson entered the State Normal School, Framingham, Mass., where she remained two years and graduated with the highest honors of her class. While at Framingham, as at Hampton, she won the love and confidence of all with whom she came in contact.

In 1881, just before Miss Davidson's graduation from Framingham, Mr. Booker T. Washington had gone to Tuskegee, Ala., to found the Tuskegee Normal and Industrial Institute. Very soon after he arrived at Tuskegee, and seeing the field for work, he invited Miss Davidson to come to Tuskegee as an assistant teacher as soon as she finished her course. This position Miss Davidson accepted and very soon after coming was made assistant principal of the Tuskegee School.

At the time this institution was started it owned no property whatever of its own and had no resources except a promise of $3,000 a year from the State of Alabama to be used in paying teachers exclusively. Mr. Washington and Miss Davidson soon began to make plans for the purchase of a permanent location for the institution and put up buildings suitable for class work and dormitories. A large farm near the school was found and within a few months after they came to Tuskegee they had made a contract for the purchase of this farm. Miss Davidson threw herself with all the energy and zeal possible into this work. She not only went among the white and colored people of Tuskegee and collected money from them, but went North, and within two or three months was able to collect in cash several thousand dollars among her numerous friends in Massachusetts.

While in the North she got acquainted with such men and women as Rev. E. Hale, Hon. Robt. C. Winthrop, Ex-Gov. John D. Long, Mrs. Mary Hemmenway and William Lloyd Garrison.

Through the combined efforts of Mr. Washington and Miss Davidson within a few months after they came to Tuskegee they had secured not only enough money to pay for the farm on which the school was located, but over $6,000 with which to erect a large building. In the meantime the number of students was increasing very fast and new buildings had to be provided. Miss Davidson went North for a few months each year, and on these trips was most successful in securing money;

and she had a peculiar talent for reaching and interesting wealthy people. At one time she received $7,000 from two persons and on one of these trips raised $10,000. Several persons who met her became not only interested in the school, but so interested in her person that they remembered her in their wills.

On August 11, 1886, Miss Davidson and Mr. Washington were married at Athens, Ohio. After their marriage, she still kept up her work as usual. She was never strong and much of the time was only able to keep on her feet by mere strength of will. Persons who saw her in Boston and other large cities soliciting money often wondered how it was possible for a woman no stronger than herself to do such work. She never seemed to think of herself in anything she undertook to do. Sometimes when she would call on persons for funds, and while sitting waiting for them to come to see her, she would fall asleep—being so exhausted from her efforts. After several months of sickness, Mrs. Washington died May 9, 1889, leaving two bright little boys.

It is said by those competent to judge, that not one colored woman in this country has done so much to further Negro education as Mrs. Olivia Davidson Washington. The school at Tuskegee is her monument ; for, without her work in its behalf, it could not be what it is. As a result of her work, the Tuskegee Normal and Industrial Institute is the largest institution in this country in the hands of colored people. It has property valued at $160,000, consisting largely of 1,400 acres of land on which are eighteen buildings. There are also eighteen industries and the school has an annual income of $70,000 a year. There are 511 students representing thirteen States under thirty-four competent teachers.

On the occasion of her death Miss Mary F. Mackie, late lady principal of Hampton Institute (Va.), speaking of her life and work says: "She gave herself without stint, and while her life has not extended over many years, she has crowded into it that which many of double her years will never do."

Gen. J. F. B. Marshall says of her: "Mrs. Washington

was in my opinion a true Christian martyr ; giving her life, as it were, a ransom for many."

Gen. S. C. Armstrong says : "She was the finest woman who ever went out from this school. Her work for Tuskegee was as perfect and beautiful an offering for the cause of the Negro as ever was made."

Soon after her death the Springfield *Republican* contained the following notice : "Mrs. Olivia Davidson Washington, wife of the principal of the Tuskegee (Ala.) Normal School, who died recently, has done much for the cause of the Negro, and was an example of the capacity of the properly trained Negro to conduct wisely and successfully large educational enterprises. She was a teacher in Memphis when the schools were broken up by the yellow fever epidemic. Afterward she entered the Hampton Institute, to learn its methods, and through the kindness of a Boston woman took a course at the Framingham State Normal School where she graduated with the honors of her class. Booker T. Washington, a Hampton graduate, had just established the Tuskegee Normal School and thither Miss Davidson went as woman principal. To the work of establishing this school she devoted all her energy, ability and strength; and her early death is doubtless owing to her overwork in its behalf. She was successful as a teacher, and remarkably so in the wearing work of making appeals in the North for aid. A few years ago she married Mr. Washington, and her early death is not only a great loss to her husband and his two motherless children, but also to the cause of Negro education."

MRS. SARAH E. C. DUDLEY PETTEY.

Christian Temperance Advocate, Musician, Treasurer of Woman's Home and Foreign Missionary Society of A. M. Zion Church in America, Africa and the Isles of the Sea; Tourist, Linguist and Experienced Teacher.

IN the ancient town of New Berne, N. C., situated at the confluence of the beautiful sinuous Trint and historic Neuse, lived E. R. and Caroline E. Dudley, the former who by dent, energy and indomitable will secured for himself a practical education, rarely found in one who had endured the hardships of slavery, and been blunted by its curses. For four years prior to the close of the war, he was foreman of a large tobacco factory at Salisbury, N. C. After the war on returning home he was elected on the police force. Shortly afterward he was elected first deputy high-sheriff; he then held positions of city marshal, magistrate and later was appointed postmaster of

MRS. SARAH E. C. DUDLEY PETTEY.

New Berne by the postmaster-general, which he declined in favor of a colored friend who served his full term. He served the legislature of his State; in fact, for many years he was a member of the house. For ten years he was first deputy collector of internal revenue for eastern N. C.

In 1883 he retired from public life, having accumulated sufficient means to insure comfort and educate his children. He invested most of his means in real estate.

Mrs. Dudley as a slave enjoyed peculiar advantages and most favorable indeed in those poverty days of servitude. She was taught to read and write in the great house, in fact her education at the close of the war became a mite in the great educational work of the Negro in the South, and indeed we may style her a pioneer heroine who, seeing the necessity of education, plunged in for duty and championed the golden rule.

Along with the spirit of education which led her on, she gathered strength and added to her domestic life the qualifications of an expert in needle work and embroidery.

To this couple was born the subject of our sketch, November 9, 1868.

At the age of six she was reading and writing, being taught at home by her mother. She then entered the graded school. After leaving the graded school she entered and completed the course in the State Normal under the instruction of the efficient and worthy professor, George H. White. (At this writing he is now solicitor for the second judicial district of North Carolina, the only Negro in the United States filling such a position.) At the age of twelve Miss Dudley entered Scotia Seminary at Concord, North Carolina; after graduating with first honors, she began teaching in her native city as second assistant in the graded school which she held for one year. Her work thus demonstrated the necessity for her promotion to assistant principal, which position she held for six years, and for two years acted as assistant professor in the County Teachers' Normal Institute, which position she held until she married the Rt. Rev. Charles Calvin Pettey, A. M., D. D., Bishop of the A. M. E. Zion Church in America. Her peculiar fitness for teaching brought her the coveted reward she justly merited. At various times very many positions in academies, high schools and State normals have been offered her, which she declined, owing to her fondness for home and pleasant surroundings. For four and a half years she gratuitously gave her services as organist for the church of her choice. Sunday-schools and missionary societies have always had in her a stanch friend and advocate. Immediately after marriage she made a tour of the United States, Mexico and Continental Europe. We insert for our readers her own sketch of incidents by the way:

" All is ready, at last comes the sailing day, the brass gong sounds and all continental passengers board the great iron-clad steamship—" City of Chicago." The sails are hoisted. The Stars and Stripes with King George's cross are unfurled to the breezes. A signal is given when a little tug steams up and pulls us from the shore. Such a waving of handkerchiefs on the pier. Many were the eyes bedimmed with tears.

"The pilot goes with us down to Sandy Hook, and returns to New York City. We pass briggs, barks, vessels and steamships in the harbor, from every known part of this inhabited globe. Each in their way salute us as we pass. Oh how sad *it was* when we reached the "bar" and our pilot was lowered into the tug and raising his cap bade us bon voyage across the deep and started back to pilot out a steamship for some other line. Our first night out we were a little too sick to enjoy the delicious supper prepared and served. The second day dawned most beautifully. The sun seemingly rose up out of the broad expanse of water. The day passed along, all on board were feeling a little seasick.

" The very heavens seemed black with ugly clouds torn and tattered by the raging tempest and dashed forward as an avalanche. We felt doomed to a watery grave, but He whose mandates the winds and waves obey was not yet ready to engulf us, and waft our spirits to the Beulah land. The storm at last spent all its fury, and Sol's bright rays peeping over the eastern hills heralded the dawn mid thrones of sapphire beautifying and making more picturesque the landscape, bidding us once more enjoy the sublime tranquility of a glorious day.

" Two days after the storm subsided, a huge whale followed us for ten miles or more and then becoming angry because no one chanced to fall overboard, he swam away toward Greenland's icy peaks, spouting water as he went, ten or twenty feet high.

"At last on the morning of the 12th day we spied land, shouts of praise and laughter rent the air. We glided along and at high noon were passing the reefs of Ireland. A cannon was fired and a cablegram sent back to America saying that we had passed the Point. About five o'clock in the afternoon we reached Queenstown, Ireland; a walled city with beautiful gardens, terraces and overhanging festoons artistically arranged by " Dame Nature." After passing through the custom-house, where we were searched for fire-arms, etc., we started out sight-seeing. We hardly planted foot on Irish soil when one of Kate Karney's daughters insisted on bishop's purchasing a piece of shamrock—the Irish emblem which, as she said, would give him *good luck*. After visiting all of the prominent places we traveled for several miles along the banks of the river Lea. Passed the tower containing the famous Shandon Bells of which Father Prout so beautifully sings. At last Cork was reached. We registered at the Imperial Hotel where we met not a colored face. All were white, and yet we were royally entertained. Bishop preached at the French Wesleyan Church the following Sunday where we met a white minister and his wife. We four formed a party to visit the continent.

"Among the sights and wonders of the Emerald Isle we have the Giant's Causeway in the north and the famous Blarney stone.

"'If ye kiss it they say, from that blissed day ye may kiss whom ye plaze wid yer blarney.'

"Next we would notice the beautiful Bantry Bay ; it has a miniature Brooklyn bridge spanning it. Then we see the charming scenes of Glengariff and the three lakes of Killarney, all famous for many legends. We passed through the Gap of Dunloe, and upon making some inquiry our guide informed us that the giant of Ireland, wishing to visit the giant of Scotland, not desiring to go fifty miles around the mountain, drew his sword, and with one mighty stroke cut the famous Gap of Dunloe, and passed onward. We traveled by hack and stage o'er the Prince of Wales route to Dublin and were followed by bonny Irish lassies, carrying goat's milk and brandy to refresh the weary traveler, for which they expected in return the tip of a penny, a sixpence or a shilling. They were very desirous of coming to America, the basin in which flows the amalgamated tide of humanity. Being weary of Home Rule, they craved the protection of the Stars and Stripes.

"In rural districts some of the houses are low, built of stone, and thatched with straw. Oft times we would find a man, his wife and eight or ten children living in one room, a pig under the table, a donkey in the corner and the chickens roosting o'er head ; yet all seemed to be healthy and enjoying life.

"Ireland is famous for its natural beauty. You can roam at will o'er hill and dale, through meadows green, and pluck the

flowers growing in rich profusion. One of the Irish legends
goes that St. Patrick prayed all insects and serpents from his
domain. Our guide took us to the upper lake of Killarney,
and where the water formed a little whirlpool; he pointed and
said : "Look and see the box containing the last serpent which
St. Patrick conquered and chained," and he verily believed it
too. Hurriedly leaving the Emerald Isle, we crossed the Irish
channel and arrived at Holly Head in Wales.

"Wales is a mountainous country, much given to mining;
the people are kind and courteous to strangers. The Welch-
men gave us a right royal welcome. On we go with all the
steam velocity of the "Flying Dutchman," until we reached
London, which has been justly styled the center of the terres-
trial ball, for indeed it is a great sea of stone flats and moving
faces.

"Here we visit Westminster Abbey, the House of Parlia-
ment, the British Museum, London Tower, the National Art
Gallery, Piccadilly Art Gallery, Hyde Park, Regent's Park,
Crystal Palace and many places which space forbids our mentioning. We took sacrament in the lamented Spurgeon's
Tabernacle, also in John Wesley's old church. We were
received by Dr. Parker, Bishop, and by his Grace, the Lord
Archbishop of Canterbury, at Lambeth Palace. Bishop
preached and lectured in most all the prominent churches
throughout the kingdom. While in France we rode across the
beautiful river Seine, went up the Eiffel tower, in Paris, visited
the tomb of Napoleon, the Chambers of Court, the Morgue,
Notre Dame Cathedral, the Hippodrome and various other
places. We had to hire an interpreter. We walked into one
restaurant and after many hard trials I made the porter understand what I wanted by flapping my arms. He brought me a
chicken. And we enjoyed it, too. While the porter was
gone, Bishop looked up and spied a large cat in one of the
windows. He said 'Kitty, kitty,' and the cat said 'Mieu,'
and came to him. He said: 'Bless my soul, the cat is the only
thing in the house that understands a word of English.' We
visited all the prominent towns and cities in France, and then

returned to Great Britian, spent some time, and then set sail for the home of the free and the land of the brave. Our voyage home was almost without incident save the passing of many icebergs when nearing Labrador and the shores of Greenland. Bishop often joked me about being seasick, but during the gale he received a wound which cost him just two gold guineas. Of course he was not *sea*sick. Arriving in New York and planting foot on American soil we started southward, spent pleasant days in the Old Dominion, which has been justly called the home of presidents. Passing on through the Carolinas we kept on and on until we reached El Paso, Texas, then we concluded to see something of real life among the Mexicans in their adobe houses. After visiting many prominent points and securing some Mexican relics we left Mexico for the Golden Gate. We traveled through southern California, visiting many orchards and vineyards ; of times our iron horse was dashing along through fields of clover daises and alfalfa when we were gazing upon the snow-capped peaks of Mount Shasta."

On arriving home (Newberne, N. C., U. S.) a grand reception was tendered the bishop and his lady, by the affable banker and broker, Isaach H. Smith. After which they were tendered many grand receptions in all parts of the United States, including California and Oregon.

Mrs. Pettey having turned her attention to the interests of the A. M. E. Zion connection, has become a great church worker and bids fair to lead the women of her church on this line. At the last general conference held in Pittsburg, Pennsylvania, May, 1892, she was elected treasurer of the Woman's Home and Foreign Missionary Society for the A. M. E. Zion connection, which position she now holds with great honor to herself and the church.

While Mrs. Pettey is doubtless a good scholar, yet the ease and facility which characterize her instructions in the schoolroom caused a great educator to say of her: "She is a born teacher." There are many young teachers whose erudition is quite sufficient, but yet there is something wanting. Her education in every way apparently reaches farther, and gives her the reputation that many who surpass her in the classics never dreamed of.

The English language has in her a champion and devotee. The cadence, rising and falling inflections of her voice, in fact every accent portrays a musical rhythm. While her teaching is limited by a few short years, many young men and women who have been under her instruction no doubt will come forth to bless the race.

CLARISSA M. THOMPSON,

Novelist, Educator, W. C. T. U. Advocate, Poetess.

COLUMBIA, the capital of the Palmetto State, has been the home of many illustrious men. It is a beautiful city, finely located on the right bank of the Congaree. Crowning a lofty hill, with broad, level streets crossing each other at right angles, and ornamented by a double and sometimes triple row of shade-trees—with well-kept flower-gardens in which plants of almost every description flourish so luxuriantly as to give it the name of "City of Flowers," Columbia seems to merit the praise bestowed on it by tourists as the loveliest city in the South—if we take *natural* beauty as the criterion. It is the seat, too, of many well-known institutions of learning ; one of these, the South Carolina University, which has been the Alma Mater of so many men who have figured in the history of our country, was established as long ago as 1801. An atmosphere of intellectuality has always characterized the town, and it is not surprising that, notwithstanding its lack of enterprise and its general conservatism, Columbia possesses a charm sufficient to attract to it a population far above the average in intelligence and moral worth.

In *ante-bellum* times, Columbia was the aristocratic center of one of the most aristocratic commonwealths of the South ; and, as those Southerners with the bluest of blue blood in their veins are almost invariably the most courteous and considerate in their dealings with our race, Columbia has always been noted for the kindly feeling existing between the two classes of its citizens.

Since the dawn of a new and brighter era, Columbia has been the home of many of our leading Afro-Americans. James Smith, who, way back in the seventies, knocked at the doors of West Point, and was the first colored youth to do so, was a native Columbian, and so were many others who have made their mark in different avocations of life. Among the adopted citizens of Columbia, for a time at least, were R. H. Cain, who once represented South Carolina in the national councils, and latterly was elected to the bishopric of the A. M. E. Church; the gifted lamented Bishop William F. Dickerson; Robert B. Elliott, than whom the race has produced no greater or more eloquent statesman; Francis L. Cardozo, at one time filling the honored position of secretary, and subsequently treasurer of his native State; Jonathan J. Wright, the first and the only colored man ever elevated to the supreme bench of any State; the brilliant, cultured, genial Richard Theodore

CLARISSA M. THOMPSON.

Greener; D. Augustus Straker, of whom the correspondent of a leading New York daily wrote: "One of the ablest speeches ever made before a criminal court was that made by D. A. Straker, a black lawyer from Bermuda;" and William Myrtenello Dart, one of the brainiest men the race can claim, whose early death ended a career rich in promise for himself and the people with whom providence had identified him.

Immediately after the smoke of the conflict which transformed three millions of slaves into *citizens* of the mightiest country on the face of the earth had cleared away, many of the former bondmen came to the front in their respective localities. Among these was Samuel B. Thompson. He was a man of much natural ability, and, for a time, his people "delighted to honor him." During the Republican *regime* he held many positions of trust and emolument. For eight years he filled the office of justice of the peace in the capital city, and for six years he represented his native county in the State legislature. A newspaper, edited by men of Caucasian lineage, said of him, several years afterward : " He is a colored *gentle-man*, in every essential." His wife, Eliza Henrietta, one of the most amiable of women, was a worthy helpmeet, and to this happy couple were born nine children, one of whom is the subject of our sketch.

Clarissa Thompson's opportunities have always been of the most excellent character. Those Northern societies who have done so much for the amelioration of the condition of the freedmen sent some of their noblest and best to labor in the Palmetto State; and Columbia, with her usual good fortune, secured some of the choicest spirits among these. Howard school, named in honor of the philanthropic General O. O. Howard, boasted of a fine *corps* of thirteen teachers. Miss Carrie H. Loomis, of Hartford, Conn., had charge of the most advanced grade. She was a born teacher, and manifested the deepest interest in her pupils. Clarissa had just completed her ninth year when she entered this lady's department, and she has always regarded Miss Loomis as the teacher to whom she is most indebted. A few years in Howard school, and then she is enrolled as a member of the South Carolina State Normal school, of which Prof. Mortimer A. Warren, of Connellsville, Conn., was principal, and Miss Loomis chief assistant. Professor Warren was one of the best educators on this continent. An enthusiastic believer in the inductive system of teaching, he founded his methods on those advocated by Pestalozzi, Froebel and Horace Mann. While here, Miss Thompson had the privilege of attending lectures given by members of the faculty of the South Carolina University. The standard of this university was high. The board of regents had spared no pains to secure the services of the best talent in the country. Its library has always been famous; its laboratory has always been considered one of the best in the United States, and its reputation, with such intellectual giants as McDuffie and Hayne, claiming it as their Alma Master, has always been enviable. It was the aim of the board to put it on a level with what it was in *ante bellum* times, and, judging from the graduates it turned out—such scholars as T. McCants Stewart and the lamented William M. Dart—their efforts did not lack much of being crowned with success. The normal school was, *de facto*, a part of the university; and during the last year of their course the class of which Miss Thompson was a member pursued some of their studies in conjunction with the junior class of this institution.

Immediately after graduation Miss Thompson began her career as first assistant in Howard school. Having been elected principal of Poplar Grove School in Abbeville, S. C., she resigned her position in Howard, and for fifteen months taught with gratifying success in Abbeville. Bishop Dickerson was at this time making herculean efforts to build up the school he loved so well—Allen University and, at his request, Miss Thompson accepted a position there. For fifteen months she was preceptress in Latin, algebra, physical geography, and ancient and modern History. The work at Allen was very congenial. But there has always been latent in her heart something of the missionary spirit, and, despite the entreaties of her friends, she resigned her position, and, in February, 1886, left her native home for Texas. For three years she labored in Jefferson, the former metropolis of the lone Star State. " The people of Jefferson were as kind to me as those of Abbeville, and that is saying a great deal," she writes concerning her stay there. From Jefferson Miss Thompson came to Fort Worth, the busy, enterprising, rapidly-growing railroad center of Texas. The school here has the reputation of being one of the best in the State, and she fills at present the position of first assistant.

Miss Thompson began at an early age to write for the press. While a school-girl, she wrote several essays, which were published in the *Christian Recorder*. Professor Warren spoke to her once : "I think you will be a good writer some day, Clarissa, but you must not make the mistake of rushing into print too early." But the "fury" was on her. There were some things in the social life of her people that filled her mind with forebodings. Knowing the salutary effect of a good novel, she determined to attempt one herself, to show up this "crying weakness." With this end in view, she wrote "Treading the Winepress," a serial of forty chapters which ran for several months in the columns of the *Boston Advocate.** A brief extract from this novel may not be out of place here.

Will De Verne, the hero, says to his aunt :

"What a poor opinion you have of your 'brethren after the flesh,' Aunt Madeline! One would never judge from your words that you form 'part and parcel' of that much-abused race."

"Thank heaven, very few drops of that blood course through my veins," and Madame De Verne gazed with much complacency on her dainty white hands and finely-moulded arms.

The playful look left Will's eyes.

"And yet, Aunt Madeline," he said, with all the earnestness he was master of, "as long as those few drops remain, it would be well to recognize a fact many of our people are in danger of forgetting, viz., that just one scintilla of Negro blood, be the possessor thereof as white as the driven snow, is sufficient to fix your status *forever*, as far as public opinion is concerned. If some of our leaders could be made to see this, perhaps instead of isolating themselves from the race so sorely in need of their assistance they would come down from their eyrie and try to lift up the masses. We cannot hue out for ourselves a separate destiny. It may seem to benefit us, but it will avail

---

*It was begun in the *Christian Recorder*, but, awaking to the fact that the plot and development of the story would scarcely become an ecclesiastical paper, it was withdrawn after three chapters had been published.

our children nothing. We must all rise together or fall together. There is no middle ground.

Later on, in the same dialogue, DeVerne says: "You should have been born on European soil, Aunt Madeline. Your sentiments are entirely too aristocratic to flourish under the American eagle. In an institution like ours, we could not tolerate, for a single moment, such exclusive ideas. There we have, and can have, no aristocracy but the aristocracy of genius. The aristocracy of blood must take a back seat, for blue blood does not always bestow brains; the aristocracy of wealth must follow suit, for, though money is a mighty factor in human progress, fortune is too notoriously blind and fickle for us to gauge a man's worth by the size of his pocket-book; and that peculiar aristocracy of which you and your friends are such ardent advocates—in both precept and practice—the aristocracy of color—should never be allowed to rear its serpent head among our people. The day it does, our race is doomed. We are fighting the self-same monster without; we can not afford to let it come within and live. Our social structure must have a different foundation. Moral character should be the corner-stone; mental culture one of the main columns. A man must be respected for his worth, not for the color of his skin or the strength of his bank account."

This novel has never been, and will never be, published in book form. Miss Thompson regards it as a girlish protest against what seemed to be serious dangers threatening our race. Her object was not to gain "name and fame," but to call the attention of thinking people to these blots in our social firmament.

Since coming to Texas, Miss Thompson has written a temperance poem entitled "A Glass of Wine," which was published in the Texas *Blade*, and was favorably received by the critics. Texas boasts of quite a number of race papers, and under the *nom de plume* of "Minnie Myrtle" Miss Thompson has contributed letters, poems, and, in one instance, a novelette called "Only a Flirtation," to several of them.

But, while her tastes are literary, her chief desire is to accomplish good in her profession. "We must work out our

destiny, in a great measure, in the school-room," she says.
"Among most races, the *mothers* mould the character of the
children ; but so many of our women have been deprived of
the opportunity to elevate themselves, and poverty compels so
many of them to spend most of the time away from their families, that a large proportion of the children cannot receive the
home training imperative for the production of grand men and
noble women, with heart and head cultivated to the utmost.
It may seem a thankless task, and even the most enthusiastic
among us ofttimes get discouraged ; but, if we will only perse-
vere, 'rich will the harvest be.' The elevation of our race
depends largely on the character of the work done in the
school-room. The teacher can, by a few well-chosen words,
touch the very chord that will inspire 'some mute, inglorious
Milton,' some embryo physician, financier or mechanic to
devote himself to the vocation for which Nature has designed
him, instead of frittering away his talents on something to
which he is entirely unsuited. A teacher's influence may make
a life, or it may mar it."

Some of the members of Miss Thompson's family have
attained a considerable degree of prominence in their respective localities. Among these are her paternal cousin, Dr.
Alonzo C. McClennan, of Charleston, S. C., and his partner,
Dr. John McPherson Thompson, her oldest brother, who has
made a fine reputation as a mathematician, as well as a physician. Miss Thompson says that what little of literary ability
she possesses she inherits from her father, while to her mother,
to whom she is devoted even beyond the ordinary, she owes a
retentive memory.

Miss Thompson's ideal of womanhood is very high, and in
her writing she has always endeavored to hold up to
her readers the model extolled by the great Justin J.
Holland, as contained in the following lines, with which we
conclude this sketch :

> " She was my peer.
> No weakling girl, who would surrender will
> And life and reason, with her loving heart,

To her possessor; no soft, clinging thing
Who would find breath alone within the arms
Of a strong master, and obediently
Wait on his will in slavish carefulness ;
No fawning, cringing spaniel to attend
His royal pleasure, and account herself
Rewarded by his pats and pretty words.
But A SOUND WOMAN, who, with insight keen,
Had wrought a scheme of life, and measured well
Her womanhood; had spread before her feet
A fine philosophy to guide her steps ;
Had won a faith to which her life was brought
In strict adjustment—brain and heart meanwhile
Working in conscious harmony and rhythm
With the great scheme of God's great universe,
ON TOWARD HER BEING'S END."

MRS. FRANKIE E. HARRIS WASSOM.

Teacher and Poetess.

FRANKIE E. HARRIS WASSOM, daughter of Beverly
and R. E. Harris, was born in Monroe, Michigan, and
while quite small her parents moved to Oberlin, Ohio, so that
their children might be educated. Having sprung from a
noble ancestry of which she may be proud, not many of her
race can boast of such noble parentage.

Her father figured very conspicuously in the underground
railroad with Dr. Wm. Wells Brown, of Boston, and others,
always trying to lend a helping hand to his race, while her
mother was smart, intelligent and independent, always laboring for the good of her race. Mr. and Mrs. Harris believed
that freedom was a gift from God to every man, and that all
children should be educated alike. They left their beautiful
home in Michigan, with their four children, and moved to
Oberlin. The oldest daughter, having gone on before, was in
school. Frankie was yet too young, but when she became of
suitable age was entered into the city school, where she spent
nine years ; after which she entered Oberlin College and spent
four years. During this time she also studied music and fine

arts. When through studying, although not in the best of health, she had a desire to go out in the world and make her mark.

We find her quite young, a mere child, going south to teach school. She had that force of purpose, and strong, determinate will to conquer whatever obstacles might come, and fight life's battle, aiming to reach the goal some day. She met with success, and was encouraged to go on. We next find her teaching in the public schools of Virginia. During her vacation in '71, she went with her sister, then Miss Blanche V. Harris, on a visit to Knoxville, Tennessee. Here they were both employed as principals of schools in Knoxville. Frankie E. Harris remained teaching in the city schools of Knoxville for nearly three years, when she received a letter requesting her to go to Mississippi to teach. Wages were better than in Knoxville, so she concluded to resign and go to Mississippi. The board, finding out her reason for leaving, offered to raise her wages if she would remain, but she told them it was too late; she had accepted the position in Mississippi, where she went in February, '74. Here she taught a successful term. At the close, the superintendent asked Miss Harris to please return and teach for them the next year; but as she had another engagement in June, she told him she could not come back. She left Mississippi June the 1st, and on June 10, 1874, was married to Col. George T. Wassom, who is one of America's bright sons, and who has won for himself a lasting

MRS. FRANKIE E. HARRIS WASSOM.

reputation. He is not only a politician, but a shrewd lawyer. Although quite a young man, he has filled places of honor. In 1878 he was appointed colonel of the Fourth battalion of eastern North Carolina. In 1882, under Arthur's administration, he was appointed postal clerk ; was also one of the delegates to the national convention held in Chicago which nominated Harrison ; and we find him again reappointed as postal clerk.

Frankie E. Harris Wassom published her first book of poems in '86. She wrote a number of years for two period- icals, and was on the staff of the Goldsboro *Star* for three years. After marrying, she stopped her school work for a short time, but feeling she must go back into this field of labor, resumed her teaching, and is still teaching. During this time she has contributed to a number of newspapers, and since '85 has done a great deal of work in the fine arts. In '86 she put on exhibition some of her crayon work at the North Carolina State Industrial Fair, and was awarded first premium. At the same fair ex-Senator Blair delivered the annual address, and Mrs. Wassom composed a song and music in honor of Senator Blair's coming. The piece was entitled " Coming to the Fair," and many were the compliments she received from friends and through the press. We quote only a few : The *Baptist Com- panion* said : " At the Educational Convention held in Raleigh, in 1886, in the Metropolitan Hall (and which was fully at- tended) the exercises were of a high order. Rev. J. C. Price, president of the Association, delivered an able address, after which ex-Senator Henry W. Blair delivered a powerful address. One of the most entertaining and inspiring features of the evening was afforded in a song entitled ' Coming to the Fair,' composed by Mrs. F. E. H. Wassom, who now resides and is teaching in Goldsboro, N. C. It was a quartette, and most beautifully rendered, being very appropriate for the oc- casion. No higher compliments need to be paid to the merits of this soul-stirring, highly musical composition than the enthusiastic applause tendered the author during and after its rendition at the fair. The whole audience was intensely delighted. Senator Blair, in honor of whose visit it was composed, evinced the keenest interest in its merits. No one, especially in North Carolina, should be without this piece of music. Senator Blair, at the close of the exercises, requested Mrs. Wassom to send him a copy."

Mrs. Wassom's book of poems is highly meritorious. The author possesses great proficiency as a poet, which is evidently the bent of her genius.

The Charlotte *News*, said: "The song composed by Mrs. Wassom, and sung by an able quartette in his honor, was loudly applauded at the conclusion of each verse."

We could write many such compliments from different periodicals, but we have taken enough of your good time. Mrs. Wassom is now teaching in the city graded schools of Knoxville, Tennessee, where she has been for the past five or six years. We copy one of her poems:

LIFE'S STRUGGLE.

If you wish to be successful
In the pathway of your life,
Press forward ever seeking
The burden of the strife.

If the struggle be a fierce one
Fight it with patience, vim,
The end will come before you think
And in it you will win.

If you struggle thus with courage
The barriers will surely fall,
And you'll find a way to conquer
Be that power great or small.

Let the maxims of your conscience
Guide and guard you in the fight,
And with duty as your watchword,
You will ever go aright.

Push onward then and upward,
Always strive to lead the van,
" For as fire doth prove the metal"
So do struggles prove the man.

ANNA BELLE RHODES PENN.

Pedagogue, Poetess and Essayist, Lynchburg, Virginia.

THE lady whose name we have chosen for our subject is a resident of Lynchburg, Virginia. She belongs to that younger class of women in our national life who are slowly, but

ANNA BELLE RHODES PENN.

surely, making themselves an enviable place in the literary future. She is one of that class that has been fitted for the arduous labor our women must encounter in the march to success by years of training at home and school, coupled with a few years of bitter mental experience.

The Afro-American must inevitably attain a place in the world of enlightenment and civilization, and in reaching such a place every human being of the race must share a responsibility.

It will mete itself out as the ability to do demands. In this respect some may do more than others. Man will doubtless do more than woman, yet she has a work to do in purifying every sphere of our life which she alone can do. Since emancipation the women of our race have not failed to begin this work and that our literary, our social and our moral life has been reaping the beneficent results of her labor goes without saying. Madame Penn is a Kentuckian by birth, the place and time being Paris, Kentucky, June 18, 1865. When very small she was taken to Virginia and located in Lynchburg, where her parents William and Sophia Rhodes are respected and well-to-do-citizens at this writing. At the proper time our subject was entered in a private school taught by Mrs. C. C. Ellis; from this school she matriculated at Shaw University, Raleigh, North Carolina, when a mere child. She was put under the care of Rev. H. M. Tupper D. D., LL. D., president of Shaw University, and his very estimable wife. She at once ingratiated herself in their favor, as did she in the favor of all others in authority. As a student she enjoys the record of having been a brilliant one, of having always pursued her studies with diligence and profit. She holds a full-fledged diploma from the scientific department of that university.

It was while a student at this school her friends saw in her eminent literary qualities and bade her put them to use in the betterment of mankind and the lifting up of her oppressed people. Her essays and poetical writings at this time gave every assurance that if continued with the same care and interest her life without the confines of Shaw would be decidedly a grand one and a fitting example of race possibilities. For two years she taught in the normal department of her Alma Mater and voluntarily resigned in order to return to Virginia and home. She afterwards taught in Chatham, Virginia, and then in the primary department of the Lynchburg,

Virginia, school where she is now. She ranks among the first-class primary teachers in Virginia and is one of the three best salaried lady teachers in a group of eighteen or twenty belonging to the corps. It is as an essayist and poetic writer Mrs. Penn has been brought into national notice. In these fields of literary pursuits she is the possessor of some considerable notice which is only the result of her labor. In other words, she justly merits all the notice she gets at the hands of her admirers. The many occasions upon which she has figured as an essayist are two numerous to mention, save one. At the closing exercises of the summer normal held at the Virginia Normal and Collegiate Institute, Petersburg, Va., in 1886,Mrs. Penn was assigned the duty of essayist upon the occasion. The title of the essay for the occasion was " ALL THAT GLITTERS IS NOT GOLD." It was well arranged and winningly delivered in Madame's own particular style. It was enthusiastically received. The president, John Mercer Langston, LL. D., commenting on the essay, its delivery, etc., said that for chasteness of language, beauty of diction and composition it was one of the best he had ever heard. He was very elaborate in his complimentary comment, showing that under its mellifluous flow he had grown rapturously dizzy.

In her poetical compositions, Mrs. Penn has won an admirable place in her people's esteem. It cannot easily be erased nor can it soon wither. She has read original poems on very many great public occasions, the last of which was the Quarto-Centennial Celebration of Alma Mater Shaw University. Upon invitation she was present December 1, 1890, and read a poem entitled " Light Out of Darkness," entirely of her own thought and composition, which would have done credit to any one claiming poetic ability. It was fifteen verses of eight-line poetry portraying the Afrio-American in ignorance and darkness and the light coming to him through the aid of Northern friends.

The poem was well delivered and received at the hands of the president, Dr. H. M. Tupper, Hon. Elijah J. Shaw and Rev. Dr. McVicar many warm and congratulatory expressions.

We indulge the opinion that to insert a few stanzas of this poem here will be pleasing to the reader and at the same time substantiate our assertions :

LIGHT OUT OF DARKNESS.

Once this land of light and beauty
  Was a blank, a perfect chaos,
With no call to life and duty
  And no mortals crying, "Save us!"
There were no radiant sunbeams
  To brighten the wanderers' way ;
No beautiful silver moonbeams
  To announce the death of day.

But God, in his Divine wisdom,
  From this chaos formed the world,
Bid sun and moon in their season
  Each its banner of light unfurl.
When this was fully completed
  And the Master about to rest,
He remembered man secreted
  In earth embrace, without a test.

   *   *   *   *   *   *

Thus the life of the world began
  Surrounded by riches from God ;
Cursed by the wickedness of man
  Which makes its progression still hard.
But none seem to have felt the blow
  More keenly than our forefathers,
Who for two hundred years and more
  Lived the life of slaves and martyrs.

In poetical ecstasy she begins to line out the help which has come to us through our friends in the following stanzas:

The Lord in his royal Kingdom,
  Turned a listening ear to their cries ;
And through the wealth of New England
  Were their children's wants soon supplied.
And among the institutions
  Reared in the beautiful Southland
By God as a restitution,
  For the conflicts of the bondman,

Was our noble Alma Mater
Who in the fall of '65
Amidst blame and cruel hatred,
Threw her college doors open wide
To Africa's sons and daughters
Who for knowledge were then athirst.
The enemy scorned and fought her,
But he found her on the alert.

Year after year she has labor'd
To rescue the youth of this age,
From Ignorance's thralling savor,
Which has darken'd History's page.
Some are in the rural districts,
Where the light has recently gone,
Where the neat and comely rustics
Are eager, anxious for the morn

Some are in the busy city
Where the constant and endless buzz
Makes the masses lose their pity
And many fathers void of love.
Some have crossed the briny ocean,
And are now in the heathen lands
With the Gospel's fragrant odor,
A heeling from the golden strand.

Some have gone to fairer regions,
Into the land of light and love ;
They have joined the heavenly legion
And the musical band above.
Some of us are still remaining,
And we have gathered here to-day,
Events of the past explaining,
Causing future dread to allay.

God bless our faithful president,
Who in the night of '65,
Regardless of the pestilence
Harken'd at once to our cries.
And now since the night is over
And the light with the years have come,
We will be no longer rovers
But a race with victory won.

Farewell to you, midnight darkness,
Farewell to you, dreams of the past,
Tis nearing the time of harvest,
Behold! the grain is ripening fast.

> Farewell to each comrade present,
>   Soon we may part to meet no more,
> Thoughts of to-day will be pleasant
>   We'll meet on the beautiful shore."

We also insert another of her excellent poems which has been published and read by several persons upon public occasions as an exemplification of Afro-American ability. It is entitled :

GRIEF UNKNOWN.

> Who can tell the bitter anguish·
>   Of a true and noble heart ?
> Who can quote in simple language
>   Words which bid its grief depart ?
> When its dearest earthly treasure,
>   When its life, its love, its all,
> He who ever sought its pleasure
>   From earth to heaven is called.
>
> Ask the starry orbs of midnight,
>   Seek an answer in the deep,
> Ask the sun which rules the daylight,
>   Ask the mighty ones who steep.
> Ask the queen who sways her millions,
>   Ask the king and ask the priest,
> Ask those with ancient wisdom,
>   Yea, the answer always seek.
>
> Alas! they send you no reply;
>   Not a word as yet they say.
> They dare not picture or surmise
>   That which in its mem'ry lay :
> They dare not use the phrase of poets
>   To describe its inmost grief ;
> They dare not censure or ignore it
>   In its longings for relief.
>
> But turn ye to a humble cot,
>   To a dwelling by the sea,
> To one where gladness dwelleth not
>   And where God seems not to be ;
> Where mists of sorrow always stay,
>   Where the mighty thunders roar,

Where rays of promise never stray
   And the angels never soar.

There, in the dusky twilight hour,
   Seek a maiden mild and fair,
Hid within a mystic bower,
   Enrobed in dark despair;
Whose downcast eye and pallied cheek
   Are moments of distress,
Whose twitching brow and nervous speech
   Are tokens of unrest.

And while her soul is thus confined
   Within sorrow's dungeon cell,
Strive to have her fully define
   The grief she cannot expel.
Why her young heart should thus repine
   O'er joys past, but once beheld:
When rays of hope deigned to shine
   O'er that cottage in the dell.

She may tell of a happy past,
   Of a voice so sweet and low,
Of a beautiful golden clasp,
   Which united soul to soul;
Of the gloom which was o'er her cast,
   When the jewel was from her borne;
And yet she has not told the half,
   For the depth is still unknown.

She may tell of a quiet mound
   In the city of the dead,
Where rest from labor is found
   And strangers lightly tread.
The secret she cannot expound,
   Of sorrows from heaven sped.
Only God, who is most profound,
   Would dare to answer in her stead.

" *No Footsteps Backward* " was the title of the class poem
which Madame Penn composed and read at the graduating
exercises of her class at Shaw. It was looked upon by many
as a very excellent effort, some of which declare it to have
been the effort of her life, though she was then in her " teens."
As can be seen the writings, poetical and prose, of our subject
are familiar for their rich and mellow sound. While a tinge

of the melancholy and sad pervades them, yet the language
employed is so chaste, her periods so well rounded, the rhythm
so true, the thought so pure as to attract and please one in the
most felicitous manner. Our subject's poems and prose writings have appeared at various times in our papers, such being
eagerly sought for. Expressions complimentary to her poetic
and pedagogic ability have followed the publication of her
efforts. Locally she is well known as an elocutionist, accomplished and able. Her aid in this field is very frequently called
for wherever she is once heard. She has done very little traveling, though very flattering requests have been made to her
so to do.

December 26, 1890, she became the wife of I. Garlan
Penn, who is an author, pedagogue and editorial writer of
national reputation. She was of very much service to her
husband in the preparation of his great work, " The Afro-
American Press and its Editors." But the best thought connected with this dissertation is the fact that the past career of
this young woman can not give an accurate forecast of her
future. She is young, ambitious and able; not content to be
anything less in the future than an equal of any of the litera-
teurs of her sex. The reading Afro-American must not be
surprised if the Madame gives a book to the world of letters
in the near future.

MRS. NAOMI ANDERSON,

*Lecturer, Poetess, Advocate of Woman Suffrage, Member of the W. C. T. U.,
President Orphans' Home.*

NOT in the nature of things can it be consistent for a race
so depraved by slavery, so outraged by cruel humanity, to boast of genealogy. Better it were not so for the
oppressed in the days of such barbarism. But fortunate,
indeed, for those it may be truly said, that were born in a free
state, a community of Christians, a land of enlightenment, a
section where

" Nature, mother alike to all,
  Still grants her bliss at labor's earnest call."

In this respect Mrs. Naomi Anderson was truly blessed. She was born at Michigan City, Indiana, March 1, 1843; her parents, Elijah and Guilly Ann Bowman, were natives of Ohio. Christian people they were and possessed of moderate means. Her mother hired a private teacher, as children of color were not allowed to attend the public schools anywhere in the State, except in localities where there were enough to have a separate school for themselves. This was not the case in Michigan City, there being but two families of color in the town. She early evinced a talent for versification, and this talent bespoke for her a place in the sympathetic hearts of people or community where she lived, and at the age of twelve she was admitted with the whites in the public schools, where she even amused her schoolmates by her poems. It was the heighth of her mother's ambition to have her daughters graduate from Oberlin col-

MRS. NAOMI ANDERSON.

lege. But when Naomi was only seventeen years old the good Lord called her mother to rest from all earthly labors, and this sad occurrence changed her whole after life, for her father, though kind and indulgent, could not perceive the necessity of giving her a finished education. She was married at the age of twenty to Mr. William Talbert, a tonsorial artist, of Valparaiso, Ind. In less than two months after marriage she was called back to Michigan City to watch by the bedside, and experience another sad bereavement, in the burial of her only sister, her only brother having died some months previous at Jacksonville, Florida, in the Union service. Thus the first five years of her married life was spent in the city of her birth (here also she buried her first-born boy). In 1868 she moved with her husband, little boy and her father to Chicago. Here she became actively engaged in the temperance work of the I. O. G. T., it being all the go at that time. In February, 1869, she spoke from the platform of the first Woman's Rights Convention ever held in the West at Libra Hall, Chicago, Mrs. Mary A. Livermore presiding. This stand injured Mrs. Naomi's popularity among her very peculiar people, and she was severely censured. But she never wavered from her principles, and at the earliest opportunity vindicated herself in an article published in the Chicago *Tribune*, March 6, 1869. This indeed brought out her powers with the pen, proving that she could not only talk, but could write.

In the autumn of '69 she made a lecturing tour through southern Illinois, Indiana and Ohio, and shortly after moved with her family to Dayton, Ohio. Here she was true to the cause of woman, and spoke before the convention held in that city in April, 1870. Her pen was active and her articles on the fifteenth amendment to the constitution were read by many and solicited by many thousands. In the same year a very popular song appeared in the Dayton *Journal* from her pen. She moved thence to Cincinnati, Ohio. Here as elsewhere she was active as a speaker, a writer, an advocate for Woman's Suffrage and a worker in Christianity and temperance.

Her husband's health having failed completely, she, restless and energetic and "true until death us do part," learned the hair-dressing trade, and moved with her afflicted family to Portsmouth, Ohio, working diligently to support her family. There she organized a Children's Home, and successfully managed it for four months, but finding the county appropriation too scant, the work too hard with family responsibilities, laid it down ; passed the board of examiners, and was employed as a teacher in the public school at the time of her husband's death, which occurred in December, 1877.

In the spring of 1879, she moved with her three children and aged father to Columbus, Ohio, applying herself to her trade, built up an excellent business; here as elsewhere her pen was busy. She worked with the Murphys, and spoke on a special occasion in front of the State capital. Here also she met her present husband, Mr. Lewis Anderson. She married this fortunate man at Urbana, Ohio, May 17, 1881, Rev. Phil. Tolwes officiating. Shortly after, however, they retired to a farm near Columbus, Ohio. There three happy years of married life were spent. In the wave of Kansas fevers, they as many thousands succumbed to its ravage and scourge, and in the spring of 1884 moved to Wichita, Kansas, where Mr. Anderson enjoyed a lucrative situation in the citizen's bank which he has held for seven years. By his christian life and sterling worth has influence worthy of any man. Is a member of the craft and enjoys the confidence of all men.

Mrs. Anderson, on leaving for Kansas, determined to find where she really desired to live, then she would drive a stob down deep and live there. Wichita, thou fortunate city! proud possessor of her citizenship. Here she is known as a lecturer, poetess, and an advocate of Woman's Rights. She is a member of the W. C. T. U. and actively engaged in every good and public work, affiliating with the white women as if she was one of them. Because, as she says, " Our leaders are wrong in fighting and clamoring for 'social equality' and at the same time holding themselves aloof and claiming to be a separate people." She says: "We are one and the same people, made so by the strongest ties of nature, bone and flesh of every nationality of white men in this country;" that " We are not negroes, but Americans, because we were born here in America. Negroes are foreigners, we are not foreigners, hence not Negroes, but Americans, and not until we walk side by side with the white people claiming no nationality save that of American citizens and knowing no people but God's people, will we ever get our rights."

The white women of Wichita organized a Children's Home and have managed the same for four years, but would not admit a colored child within its doors. So Mrs. Anderson called a council of intelligent women of color, and they determined then and there to organize a home of their own, which was done scarcely two years ago, electing her for their president. They now rent a comfortable little home, have a very efficient matron, and receive a monthly appropriation of $25 from the city, and $12 a month from the county, and all are jubilant at the success attending Mrs. Anderson's efforts. All admit that to her belongs the triumph, and the financial endowment from both city and county as the fruit of her energetic labor.

She is soon to engage in a biography of herself, in which will appear her productions in poetry and prose.

In all of her writings concerning the American people of color she characterizes them in the same category as that of the children of Israel.

The following is a poem written by her at Portsmouth, Ohio, 1876, on the event of the United States American Centennial, entitled:

CENTENNIAL POEM.

We come in this centennial year
   And ask to be received
The praises of your brother men,
   The race whom you have freed.

How different from our fathers !
   They one hundred years ago
Were chained down in slavery ;
   No talents did they know.

I need not tell you of their trials,
   You know how it has been :
Forced from old Afric's clime,
   Bold gold-designing men.

But there were Christians on this land,
   The hand of God did reign.
Though we've groaned beneath the fetters,
   We're thankful that we came.

For over in our fatherland
 The light of Christ was hid.
Our fathers were benighted there,
 Knew not what Christians did.

But now we hail that bleeding lamb,
 We send our greetings high.
We feel the power of God at heart,
 We know that Christ is nigh.

He held us as an Israel band,
 He's crossed us o'er the sea
Of Rebellion's cruel war just past,
 And now we know we're free.

Our Moses sleeps beneath the soil
 In yonder sister State ;
Abraham Lincoln, it was he
 Who first our bonds did break.

Charles Sumner next did lead the van
 Of equal rights to all ;
Here thanks we bring to all of those
 Responding to his call.

We come with gratitude to all
 Who lent a hand to save
Our starry banner, flaunting high,
 From floating o'er a slave.

We're free to do, as all are free,
 All o'er this mighty land,
And we will serve both Nation and State
 As justice doth command.

Heaven's greatest blessings here,
 Education, you will find,
Will bring our latent talents up
 On level with mankind.

We pledge ourselves, this July 4th
 If ever called in wars,
Our sable hands will ever
 Uphold our Stripes and Stars.

Then let us give to God the praise
 For all that He has done—
For giving us this land of bliss,
 The best beneath the sun.

MAY C. HEYERS nee REYNOLDS.

Actress, Singer, Musician, Writer of Operas.

MAY C. REYNOLDS (MRS. HEYERS) is the wife of the noted S. B. Heyers and first theatrical manager of the United States. This worthy young woman is now before the public classed as the leader of her race as an actress. In the year of 1882 she left her dear old home a mere girl, and

MRS. MAY C. HEYERS.

the sad parting will never be erased from her memory; how her loving, noble father, after having tenderly impressed upon her inexperienced mind the difference between the outer world and home, caressed his darling and turned to hide the tears. She left a home indeed made cheerless by the death of her mother when but an infant, but made happy by an indulgent father and careful stepmother; luxury and refinement were ever before them. We say them, as there were five little ones. Miss Reynolds has three beautiful and talented sisters, and one brother, a fine musician. They are all well educated and fitted for ornaments in society, or a noble cause in public life. While attending school it was discovered that Miss Reynolds possessed a remarkable voice for singing. Mr. Reynolds, her father, was advised to put her under training, which he accordingly did, sparing no means. Madam Rose Cogeshall was her first teacher, and after a series of terms left, after which Mr. Reynolds placed his daughter under tuition of Miss Lulu Borden, a graduate of the Boston conservatory, where she received good and careful training; when the term of school ended the music lessons ended also for that season. Miss Reynolds having the honor of being called a *singer* by every one at her little country home, Tioga, Pa., she did not seem to care or know the worth of the praises showered upon her by old artists, but went along with her favorite playmates, jumping rope, playing ball, running races and tagging after her big sisters. Her last vacation was in June, 1882, having at that time entered into all the highest branches, French being her last and favorite study. She was a finished bookkeeper and elocutionist as well as a singer. During vacation, with the permission of pa, she went to Hornellsville to visit her grandma and aunt, while there the famous "Hyers Sisters" company were billed to give an entertainment. Her heart was heavily burdened, as she had just received a letter from her sister Almira to return home as school commenced the following Monday. Everywhere she turned she could see the flaming letters: "*Hyers Sisters.*" It seemed to put a charm over her. She, however, wrote to her papa pleading with him to let her remain to see the first stage show of her life. Her father in his loving way answered in the affirmative. She staid and met her fate. She went and heard them warble, and saw them dance and beheld their magnificent costumes. She saw the awful funny man "Sam Lucas," who could make himself tall or short, and every one and everything was so new and wonderful that it set her brain in a whirl. "Oh, if I could only leave the hateful old school-room and go on the stage," was her first thought. Mr. Hyers called on her aunt the following morning. May was in the parlor playing on the piano and singing, "I Am Content." The manager was startled with delight and asked who was singing. He was shown into the parlor and introduced. He declared she had the most wonderful contralto voice he had ever heard. Asking her if she would like to travel with his company she said, "Yes sir, but pa would not let me." The company left and May went home with a new idea. Mr. Hyers corresponded with her father, gaining his consent. Miss Reynolds joined the company in Cleveland, She gained upon the stars rapidly and is now one of the most brilliant in the profession. She was married to Mr. Hyers the following season at her father's home. She composed a poem on the late " Johnstown Horror," which is quite dramatic, and she recites it with great success ; she also wrote a play for her company entitled, " Tip the Wharf Rat," and is now engaged in writing another play entitled the " Dreaded Witch of Africa." She thinks her profession a grand work, and when she secures the warm applause of every tongue she gives a deep-souled gratitude-filled look, and thanks her father for his tender training and her Creator for the talent he endowed her with

MRS. REV. M. J. DYER, nee EMMA FISHER.

Singer.—"Star of Evening."

WE have seen those virtues which have, while living, retired from the public eye, generally transmitted to posterity as the truest objects of admiration and praise. Such is the subject of our sketch, who was born in Catskill, N. Y., July 4, 1857. She was reared in the American metropolis, educated and trained in music by Madam Messimore, a lady of rare musical accomplishments, who originally lived in England ; also by Professor Reason. Her father having died when she was only three years old, true to the instincts of nature, where a will forced by a necessity for action existed, Providence provided a way. She suffering some physical deformity — that of a healthy body of excellent and elegant physique is minus one arm—in the place of this inconvenience God provided a rich and unparalleled voice, so at nine years of age she could sing from low soprano to E above the staff. From the general concessions and praises heralded abroad by people who were intoxicated with melody such as they had never heard from one so young, people came for miles around to catch a marvelous and deep-reaching but dying note, the quintessence of melody itself. This created rare excitement—we say rare, because such as existed at that time had never in the world's history produced such profound assertions — "a thrill of joy prophetic" of the possibilities of the colored race. The press paid glowing tributes to her, and styled her the "Star of Evening."

At the age of fifteen she suffered the misfortune of caring for her mother, who had become an invalid, and, true to her trust, as her voice never failed her, she bore her task bravely, and sang to eager and anxious audiences which crowded her concerts. Her first concert was given October 12, 1875, at Line church, on which occasion the door receipts alone were $550. With the assured appreciation of this demonstration she was forced on and on by the current which had already taken control of her soul and body, "on toward her being's end." She traveled and sang to appreciable audiences in all the large cities of New York, through the East, South, North and West, meeting with unbounded success everywhere. She grew in public favor so rapidly that her name spread all over the States and her talents were boasted by the millionaire as well as the miner, in fact such an impetus was given to her progress that nowhere was there a church barred against her.

Suffering physical deprivation in the absence of an arm, she nevertheless plied the one God-given hand to the organ and piano, with the nimbleness of the applauded disciples of Excelsior.

She sang several years with the New Orleans Jubilee Troupe, under the direction of Rev. Dr. W. D. Goodman, which traveled through the Eastern and Middle States.

In the year of 1884 the death of her invalid mother became the sad reality which tried her melancholy spirit and dejected heart, but in the midst of her despair hope pointed to her a star. The next year she married Rev. M. J. Dyer, a very estimable man, a minister of power and concentrated ability, and a distinguished member of the Louisiana Annual Conference M. E. Church.

FLORA BATSON,
Queen of Song.

FLORA BATSON was born at Washington, D. C., in 1864. Her father died from wounds received in the war. At three years of age her mother removed with her to Providence, R. I. At nine years of age, as a member of the then famous Bethel Church choir of that city, she attracted hundreds to hear the child singer.

MLLE. FLORA BATSON.

Her professional career commenced at thirteen years of age, singing two years in the interest of Stoore's College, Harper's Ferry, three years in J. W. Hamilton's Lecture Bureau for the People's Church of Boston, one year in Redpath's Lecture and Lyceum Bureau, one year in temperance work; and in 1885 Manager J. G. Bergen secured her services, and under his management Steinway Hall, New York, the Academy of Music, Philadelphia, and the largest music halls of the Eastern cities were packed to hear the new star, styled by the New York *World* the colored Jenny Lind. On December 13, 1887, Miss Flora Batson and Manager J. G. Bergen were married at the Sumner House, New York City, and since their marriage Mrs. Batson-Bergen has sung with great success in nearly every leading city in the country, and probably no American singer has been more strongly endorsed by the press of the country. The following are a few of her testimonials, which are only samples of hundreds that might be given:

The Patti of her race.—*Chicago Inter-Ocean.*

The colored Jenny Lind.—*New York World.*

The peerless mezzo-soprano.—*New York Sun.*

The unrivaled favorite of the masses.—*New York Age.*

A mezzo-soprano of wonderful range.—*San Francisco Examiner.*

She carried the house by storm, and five times was recalled to the foot-lights.—*New York Herald.*

A sparkling diamond in the golden realm of song.—*San Jose Californian.*

Her progress through the country has been one continuous triumph.—*Denver Rocky Mountain News.*

All her numbers were sung without effort—as the birds sing.—*Mobile (Ala.) Register.*

A voice of great range, and of remarkable depth and purity.—*Louisville (Ky.) Courier-Journal.*

She will never lack for an audience in the ''City of Seven Hills."—*Richmond (Va.) Planet.*

The sweetest voice that ever charmed a Virginia audience.—*Lynchburg (Va.) Advance.*

Her articulation is so perfect, her renditions seem like recitations set to music.—*Kansas City Dispatch.*

A highly cultivated mezzo-soprano, of great sweetness, power and compass, and of dramatic quality.—*Charleston (S. C.) News and Courier.*

The indescribable pathos of her voice in dramatic and pathetic selections wrought a wondrous effect.—*The Colonist, Victoria, British Columbia.*

Though of pleasing presence, she is unaffected, almost child-like in her bearing; this, with her wonderful singing, captivates the heart of the listener, regardless of the ''color line."—*Californian.*

Her voice showed a compass of three octaves, from the purest, clearest soprano, sweet and full, to the rich round notes of the baritone register.—*Pittsburgh Commercial Gazette.*

Flora Batson, with her wonderful voice, has a divine mission to aid in breaking down the stubborn walls of prejudice, which must sooner or later give way in our Nation's progress toward a higher civilization.—*Boston Transcript.*

She scored a complete success as a vocalist of high ability, and fully justified the favorable criticisms of the Eastern press.—*San Francisco Examiner.*

The flexibility, metal and purity of her vocal organ justly entitle Flora Batson to the distinction of being called the colored Jenny Lind.—*Pittsburgh Dispatch.*

In response to an encore she gave a selection from ''Il Trovatore" in baritone, showing the extraordinary range of her voice, and producing a melody like the low tones of a pipe organ under a master's touch.—*San Diego (Cal.) Sun.*

The press of the country, from the Atlantic to the Pacific, unite in crowning her the greatest singer of her race, and worthy to rank among the great singers of the world.—*Portland Oregonian.*

She wore a crown, heavily jeweled, and diamonds flashed upon her hands and from her ears. Her singing at once established her claim of being in the front rank of star artists, and there is a greater fortune than that already accumulated in store for her.—*Providence (R. I.) Dispatch.*

She sings without affectation, and has an absolute command of her voice, from the highest to the lowest register. She was a surprise to every one present, and established a reputation that will guarantee her full houses at her future engagements on the Pacific Coast.—*San Francisco Call.*

Her voice is rich in the qualities most valuable to a singer. The range is wonderful. It is clear and resonant, exceedingly flexible and pure. Her articulation is perfect, and she sings with a freedom from effort seen rarely, except in the most famous singers. The tones of her voice are powerful and thrilling. It is rather dramatic than emotional. Her renditions last night covered an extraordinary versatility and range.—*Nashville American.*

MRS. ABBIE WRIGHT LYON.

Gifted Pianist and Singer.

THE subject of this sketch, ABBIE WRIGHT LYON, was born in Stony Brook, Long Island, in the year 1862. When seven years old she was removed to Harlam, New York, where she attended school, and subsequently to New York City, where she finished a common school education. At twelve years of age she was employed as organist at the Melrose, St. Paul A. M. E. Church. Having evinced special talent for music and adaptability for instrumental playing she was, by special arrangement of her parents, placed in a condition where she could receive the very best training from well known instructors. She was organist for the Bethel A. M. E. Church, one of the largest and leading colored churches in New York City, for three and a half years. She has been a successful teacher of music.

She met and married the Rev. Ernest Lyon, a graduate of the New Orleans University, and now a prominent minister of the Louisiana Conference Methodist Episcopal Church, while he was serving his first year as pastor of the M. E. Church, at Baldwin, the seat of Gilbert seminary, in the year 1883. Since then she has been with him, sharing in the toils and hardships which come to a minister's wife. Three lovely children have been the issue of this marriage. She has followed her husband to every appointment (he having held some of the most prominent in the city of New Orleans) and by her kind and affectionate disposition has made hosts of friends.

Mrs. Lyon is a professional songstress, having been endowed by nature with a strong and lovely voice. Many souls have been converted and led into the new life, under the influence of her christian songs.

Mrs. Lyon was the accomplished organist of the New Orleans University singers for some years. Through that connection she became acquainted with the gentleman who became her husband.

The Rev. ERNEST LYON is now the popular pastor of St. Mark's M. E. Church, New York City, and Mrs. Lyon is among her old friends, who rejoice in her prosperity.

W. D. GOODMAN, A. M., D. D.

MADAME FRANCES E. PRESTON.

Elocutionist.

MADAME FRANCES E. PRESTON, *elocutionist,* born in Richmond Va., came to Detroit, Michigan, July, 2, 1855. The school advantages were then limited in this city. She being the only daughter, her parents were not willing to have her leave home to go where a better education might be obtained. The Detroit Training School in Elocution and English Literature offered an opportunity that she had long desired and although a widow with one child and a large business, that of hair-dresser, to demand her time and attention, she entered this school January, 1880, at the age of thirty-three years, taking a two years and a half course, graduating May

19, 1882, standing second among a large number of graduates, the majority being young women with much better schooling to start with. A position was secured her by the teacher Mrs. Edna Chaffee Noble, to travel with the Donivan Famous Tennesseeans. The secretary of the school accompanied her to Delaware to complete the arrangement, so interested was the

MADAME FRANCES E. PRESTON.

teacher in her pupil that in this new life she might be successful. After traveling one year with them she returned home and was appointed a teacher in the school from which she graduated, which position she still fills when at home.

In '84 she traveled through eastern Virginia, giving programs alone. In October, '88, she went to Augusta, Ga., accompanied by her daughter, L, F. Preston, to open a Baptist school for girls. The school opened in January with one teacher. Madame Preston with her daughter, traveling and giving programs, to raise means to support the school, was called from this field of labor by the illness of her mother.

In July, 1890, Dr. Derrick of New York appointed her as agent to assist in raising funds for the foreign missionary board, and in April, 1891, a position on the W. C. T. U. lecture bureau was secured her, this being the first literature ever placed upon their bureau.

Mrs. Frances Preston is prepared to make engagements with lecture associations, lyceums, clubs, churches, or other societies, for evenings of dramatic and humorous recitations.

Additional interest arises from the fact that she is a colored lady, who was formerly a slave. She has educated herself, and has been fitted for her present work by a thorough course of study in the Detroit Training School of Elocution and English Literature, under the personal instruction of the well-known reader and teacher, Mrs. Edna Chaffee Noble.

FLATTERING TESTIMONIALS.

The debut of Mrs. Frances Preston, at Abstract Hall, possessed peculiar interest, from the fact that she is the first colored lady in this city to essay public readings. She is to be congratulated on winning a very emphatic success. She has a melodious voice of excellent range and flexibility, enunciates with agreeable clearness, and manifests feeling and appreciation in selections, grave and gay. A novel feature of the programme was the introductory Bible reading; it was excellent. The miscellaneous selections were appropriate, and admirably rendered.—*Detroit Free Press.*

Insufficient space made it impossible, yesterday morning, to speak of Mrs. Preston's debut, except in a general way. There is to be said specially: "The Black Regiment" and "Howard at Atlanta" were capitally rendered. Perhaps the best read selection (certainly the one which awakened the heart. iest response of an interested and appreciative audience) was Champney's quaint, half humorous, half pathetic dialect poem, descriptive of how the trusty little negro boy, "Persimmons," rescued his baby protege from the perils of the flood. It is a favorite selection with Detroit readers, but we have heard none who could read it so well as Mrs. Preston. The hall was crowded and the lady's reading desk was heaped high with choice floral tributes.— *Post and Tribune.*

A large and select audience greeted Mrs. Preston, at Abstract Hall, on Monday evening. Mrs. Preston is a pupil of Mrs. Edna Chaffee Noble, and possesses elocutionary talent of no small order. The principal charm of her readings is her naturalness and grace of manner. All the selections were listened to with much interest, but her renditions of "Aunt Phillis' Guest," "Persimmons takes cah ob de Baby," and " How he saved St. Michael's," were undoubtedly her most successful efforts. In connection with this article it may be appropriate to state that Mrs. Preston was a slave in the Southern States during the days of bondage. She is about thirty-five years of age, and is a widow.—*Every Saturday.*

Mrs. Preston is certainly a very fine reader. Her reading, entirely devoid of rant, is simple and impressive.—*Sandusky, Ohio, Daily Register.*

There was a large audience present at the First Baptist church, on Wednesday evening, to hear Mrs. Frances Preston, the noted colored elocutionist, who gave one of her celebrated entertainments for the benefit of that church. When her recitations were over no one seemed inclined to go, but applauded and asked for more. Mrs. Preston has a rich contralto voice, over which she has perfect control. She has a fine stage presence, and whatever the character of her selection—pathetic, sentimental or humorous—she portrays each with equal skill, and is one of the most finished readers before the public.—*The Caret, Newport News, Va.*

The citizens of Lansing were highly entertained by the reading of Mrs. Preston, the well-known elocutionist of Detroit. The selections were well received and elicited much applause. Her rendition of humorous selections was admirable. " How he saved St. Michael's " was read in such a manner that the vast audience was held spell-bound until its conclusion. But the crowning event of the evening was the reading of " The Black Regiment," when the marvelous voice of the elocutionist was shown to its best advantage. She has won the hearts of the people at Lansing.—*Lansing Republican.*

Rev. F. B. Cressey, editor of the *Center*, the organ of the prohibition party of Michigan, writes as follows : Mrs. Frances Preston, Detroit. Respected Madam : Permit me, all unsolicited by yourself, to express my high appreciation of the readings and recitations which I recently heard you give. I must say that for distinctness of enunciation and naturalness and beauty of expression you have powers which will surely obtain for you a wide patronage. You have my best wishes and cordial commendation. With kind regards,　　　　　　　　　　　　　　　FRANK B. CRESSEY.

Mrs Preston read before the inmates of St. Vincent's Orphan Asylum, in Detroit, on Decoration Day. The *Michigan Catholic*, in a column article, says of the Scripture reading : " Mrs. Preston opened by reading from the Bible St. Paul's defense before King Agrippa, and listening to the eloquence thus depicted, one wondered he had not read that particular passage of the Holy Scripture with more frequency and enthusiasm." Of her rendition of "Persimmons Takes Care of the Baby," the same paper says : "In this piece Mrs. Preston had an opportunity for display of her marked and varied elocutionary power, and held her audience in a state between tears and laughter." Mrs. Preston's daughter, Miss Lillie, assisted her mother on this occasion, and speaking of her singing the *Michigan Catholic* says: "Miss Lillie has a remarkably sweet voice, showing good progress in cultivation."

Powhatan Beatty, for many years connected with the theatres of Cincinnati, says: "Mrs. Preston is a pleasant reader, and thoroughly understands the principles of elocution. Her gestures are graceful and full of expression. At times one is forcibly reminded of that eminent actress, Clara Morris. Her modulation is excellent, and in the lower and middle register of her voice she has not an equal. * * * I have heard all of the great readers, and so far as my judgment goes I would place her in the front ranks. She has a voice full of pathos, and at times her audience are melted to tears, and at other times are convulsed with laughter.

H. W. Thompson, representative in the Michigan Legislature from the Delta district, says: "I have listened with pleasure and profit to the readings of Mrs. Frances Preston, and do hereby recommend her to any who may desire her service in that direction."

D. Augustus Straker, the eminent lawyer, formerly of Columbus, S. C., at present one of the most successful lawyers of Detroit, writes: "Mrs. F. Preston. Dear Madam: It gives me pleasure to testify to your merit as an elocutionist. I have listened to your renditions in public and in private, and regard them of the most exalted style and of profound conception. It is only by such speaking as you give to the ideas of others that the hearer can fully understand and enjoy the depths of soul of our poets and other writers.

Respectfully yours,   D. A. STRAKER."

W. Irving Babcock, State senator from the Ninth district of Michigan, says: "It gives me great pleasure to say that Mrs. Frances Preston is an elocutionist of commendable ability and training. Her recitations are particularly pleasing."

The *Spring Valley Journal* says of Mrs. Preston: "She is the greatest elocutionist of her race."

The New York *Globe*, speaking of an entertainment given by Mrs. Preston, closes in these words: "One evening with Mrs. Preston will add more intellectuality to our children than many books, and we advise our readers to let no opportunity pass that will do so much for the little folks."

Mrs. Preston attracts the greatest interest wherever she goes, not only by her wonderful talent, but from the fact that she has been a slave and has had innumerable difficulties to overcome in the vocation she has chosen and for which she is so admirably fitted.—*Newport News Commercial.*

CINCINNATI, O., January 11, 1887.

Mrs. Frances Preston, elocutionist and teacher in Mrs. Noble's training school in Detroit, is well known to me, I having been her pastor two years in Detroit, Mich. During that time I have heard recitations both in the church of which she is a member and among the white people of the city. She also gave two programmes in this city at the Union Baptist church, at which she received a perfect ovation. The universal verdict here, entertained by critics and non-critics, is that she is "equaled by few and excelled by none," as she is at home equally in any part which she essays, pathetic, humorous or dra. matic. I cheerfully give this expression because I feel the lady is worthy of it.

WM. A. BURCH, Pastor Union Baptist Church.

The Springfield, O., *Republican*, in noticing an entertainment given in that city by Mrs. Preston and her daughter, after paying highest compliments to Mrs. Preston, says: "One of the most attractive features of the evening's entertainment was the 'Æsthetic Gestures,' and ' Lyre Movement,' by Miss Lillie Preston, daughter of the elocutionist. Her gestures expressing profound grief, anguish, supplication and remorse, by turn, were so natural as almost to cause a person to feel as if he were witnessing a dire disaster or calamity. Miss Preston has remarkable control over her audience as her performance was something entirely new to many."

Mrs. Frances Preston's reputation is not confined to her home—Detroit—but is becoming national.—*Springfield (Ohio) Republican.*

MISS LYLBROUNETTA F. PRESTON.

Vocalist and Pantomimist.

SHE is the only and first pantomimist of her race on the stage. Born in Detroit, Mich. Attended the public school, studied music at the Detroit Conservatory of Music, at the same time taking the junior course in the school of elocution, and finishing a thorough course of calisthenics, which thoroughly prepared her for the work of pantomimist. Has traveled for four years with her mother. Her early death disrobes the Negro race of one of its brightest meteors, and the world of an actress.

MISS LYLBROUNETTA F. PRESTON.

Truly has the poet said "Death loves a shining mark."

MRS. S. J. W. EARLY.

Teacher, Lecturer, W. C. T. U. Advocate.

SARAH JANE, the youngest daughter of Thomas and Jemima Woodson, was born Nov. 15, 1825, near the city of Chillicothe, Ohio, where she passed the happy days of early childhood. In the year of 1829 the family removed to Jackson county, Ohio. Being deprived of the privilege of attending school with the white chil-

MRS. S. J. W. EARLY.

dren, a select school, furnished with the best teachers, was provided for colored children by their parents. The subject of this sketch attended this school with other members of the family from the fourth year of her age until her fifteenth year, and in that period derived all her early advantages. Her parents were zealous and consistent Christians and she was continually brought under the best religious influences. At the age of fourteen she professed religion and joined the A. M. E. Church in the year 1840, at Berlin, Ohio.

Very early in life she showed a disposition to learn whatever came within her reach. At the age of three she could sing all the hymns used at family worship. At five she could commit large portions of the Bible to memory. As the years rolled by she longed for better educational privileges and after attending an academy in Athens county, Ohio, she attended Oberlin College, and graduated therefrom in the year 1856, and immediately entered upon the duties of a

teacher.   She was first principal teacher of the public
school of Ganesville, Ohio.   In the year 1859 she was called
to Wilberforce University, being the first colored graduate
ever employed by its trustees to teach in company with white
teachers.

She was afterward principal of the colored public school
of Xenia, Ohio, until the war subsided.   Then she went south
and held a very important position as principal of one of the
largest colored schools in North Carolina.   Thus for more than
thirty-six years she has been an efficient instructor of the
young, a leader in the church and Sabbath-school and the
reforms of the day.   In 1887 she entered the field as a public
lecturer and is now in the service of the two national societies
in the temperance work.

She was married to Rev. J. W. Early in the year 1868,
Sept. 24.

MISS HENRIETTA VINTON DAVIS.

Elocutionist, Dramatic Reader and Tragedienne.

THE subject of this sketch, Miss Henrietta Vinton Davis,
was born in the city of Baltimore, Md.   Her father,
Mansfield Vinton Davis, was a distinguished musician, and
from him she inherited a natural taste for music.   He died
within a few days after her birth, leaving a young and beautiful widow and the subject of this sketch.   In the course of a
few years her mother contracted a second marriage with
Captain George A. Hackett, who, through the period of a long
and eventful life, was the recognized leader of the colored
people of Baltimore.   He was a man of ample means and
generous heart, and gave to his stepdaughter all the advantages
which such conditions allow.   He, like her own father, died
while she was young.   Her mother, a year after the death
of Mr. Hackett, removed to and became a permanent resident
of the city of Washington, D. C.   Miss Davis here had the
advantages of admirable schools, and, having a natural fondness for books, soon made rapid progress in her studies, and,

by her studious habits and genial manners, became at once a favorite with the teacher, Miss Mary Bozeman, who was the first person to suggest that her little pupil give her attention to the study of elocution. At the early age of fifteen she passed the necessary examination and was awarded the position as teacher in one of the public schools of her native State. While holding this position she attracted the attention of the Board of Education of the State of Louisiana, who tendered her a higher position to teach, which she accepted. She remained there some time, until called home by the illness of her mother. Miss Davis left Louisiana amidst the regrets of many friends. She also bore the certificate of the Board of Education testifying to the efficiency and ability with which she had discharged her arduous duties.

Miss Davis, in 1878, entered the office of recorder of deeds at Washington as copyist, where she remained until 1884, when she resigned to follow her chosen profession. It was while holding this position that she decided to carry

HENRIETTA VINTON DAVIS.

out a long-cherished desire to study for the dramatic stage. She had in the meantime, by a wide and thorough study of the best masters in classic and dramatic literature, laid the foundation for a promising career. Miss Davis became the pupil of Miss Marguerite E. Saxton, a lady of undisputed ability and a most conscientious teacher—a lady who knows no one by his color. Under the tuition and guidance of this lady she made her debut on April 25, 1883, at Washington, before a large and critical audience. She was introduced by the Hon. Frederick Douglass, who takes a deep interest in her success. On this, her first appearance, her success was instantaneous, and she received a veritable ovation. A few weeks after her first appearance she made a tour of the principal cities of New England, under the management of Messrs. James M. Trotter and Wm. H. Dupree, of Boston, Mass.

At Boston, Hartford, New Haven, Providence and the many other places they visited, she was received with every mark of approval by both press and public.

In April, 1884, Mr. Thomas T. Symmons became her manager. Mr. Symmons is one of the few gentlemen of our race who possesses the ability and spirit of enterprise calculated to secure success. He formed a dramatic and concert company to support his star, and by novel and liberal advertising brought her to the notice of new audiences. At Buffalo, N. Y., she received most flattering newspaper notices, and was the recipient of much social attention. Again, at Pittsburg, Pa., and in fact wherever she has been, her genial manners and modest demeanor have attracted to her many friends and admirers, who have vied with each other in doing honor to a lady of whom the race may well feel proud. Miss Davis recently made a tour of the State of Florida, under the able management of that public-spirited and dignified lover of his race, Hon. M. M. Lewey, editor of the Florida *Sentinel.* Miss Davis was greeted everywhere by large and enthusiastic audiences.

Miss Davis is the pioneer of her race in the legitimate drama, and by her success has been the means of stimulating and encouraging others to emulate her example. Miss Davis has received many testimonials of appreciation. Presents of all descriptions have been showered upon her. While she has many imitators, she has no superiors.

THOUGHTS OF PROMINENT MEN REGARDING MISS DAVIS.

WASHINGTON, D. C., November 18, 1883.

Gentlemen: I have many times been called upon to bear testimony to the remarkable talents of Miss Henrietta Vinton Davis, and I always do so with pleasure. In my judgment she is one of the best dramatic readers in the country—and the best colored reader that ever came before the American people. Her personal appearance is strongly in her favor. She instantly commands attention and sympathy; and when her deep, fine voice is heard, her audience at once give themselves up to the pleasure of hearing her. I am quite sure you will make no mistake in having her read for you.

Respectfully yours, FREDERICK DOUGLASS.

**

FIRST EPISCOPAL DISTRICT, A. M. E. CHURCH,
Bishop H. M. Turner, D. D., Presiding.

ATLANTA, GA., January 21, 1891.

This is to certify that Miss Henrietta Vinton Davis has been known to me since childhood. She is in all respects a lady of the first grade, spotless in character, polished in manners, educated and finished in her profession. As a dramatic reader she has no superiors and should be encouraged by all who favor the elevation of our race. I commend her services to all ministers of the Gospel, to the public in general. H. M. TURNER.

**

ANNAPOLIS, MD., January 21, 1891.

Miss Henrietta Vinton Davis, the celebrated tragedienne and dramatic reader, entertained the people of the A. M. E. Church January 19 and 20, 1891. The audience was large the first night, and the house was crowded the second night. Her magnetic style, forcible, dramatic and eloquent voice charmed every one present. She magnetized and electrified the audience with delight, who loudly applauded each recital. Miss Davis is a first-class entertainer, a lady of character, ability and great talent; an artist who presents living pictures. She is a great help to the ministers in raising money for churches. Her terms are easy, her work laborious. May God bless her.

Yours respectfully, I. F. ALDRIDGE.

**

Miss Henrietta Vinton Davis, the tragedienne, is personally known to me, and in my opinion is the finest representative of that class of colored professionals in America. Her presence is graceful, her voice rich and flexible, and she impresses her audience at once with the fact that she is a born actress. She delights the most critical and convinces the most obdurate sceptic. The brethren and churches will do well to give her the warmest reception, as she is a lover of God's Zion, and is always willing to help it first, and herself last.

W. BISHOP JOHNSON,

Prof. Mathematics, Wayland Seminary, and Pastor Second Baptist Church. Washington, D. C., February 22, 1891.

A PLEASING ENTERTAINMENT.—A delightful entertainment was given in Touro Chapel last evening by Miss Henrietta V. Davis, in dramatic recitals. Miss Davis is the first of her race to attempt Shakespearean delineations. But her efforts last evening prove her power and skill in elocutionary art. Miss Davis excels in dramatic recitals, and especially in tragic parts. If it is possible to discriminate in the selections of last evening, perhaps the potion scene from "Romeo and Juliet" was most ably rendered. She is certainly worthy of the many encomiums of praise she has received.—*Newport Daily News.*

Miss Davis has received thorough instruction, as her recitations showed marked talent. As a public reader she is a success.—*Albany (N. Y.) Daily Press and Knickerbocker.*

The entertainment given at Waite's Hall last evening was one of high merit. The audience was appreciative and liberal in its applause. Miss Davis, who is a quadroon, has a graceful presence and a powerful and well-trained voice, and her renditions showed not only careful study, but an excellent appreciation of the various authors. Several selections were given from Shakespeare, including Portia's speech and the poison scene from "Romeo and Juliet;" in the latter selection especially marked dramatic power being displayed. The vivacious rendering of "Awfully Lovely Philosophy," "The Jiners," and "Dancing at Flat Creek Quarters" proved that Miss Davis could also read comic selections with success, and two encores testified to the enjoyment of her auditors.—*New Bedford Evening Standard.*

Her recital last evening of selections from Shakespeare's plays, especially "Cleopatra's Dying Speech," parts of "Romeo and Juliet," and the epilogue in "As You Like It" were received with warm expressions of pleasure. Her clear enunciation and full, low-pitched voice helped to her success.—*New York Sun.*

As a dramatic reader Miss Davis has considerable talent, and the selections were finely interpreted. The death scene of "Romeo and Juliet" in costume brought out powers as an actress of no mean order; that and Schiller's "Battle" were well rendered.—*New London Telegram.*

A really remarkable entertainment was that given in Association Hall on Friday night by Frederick Douglass' protege, Miss Henrietta Vinton Davis. Miss Davis is a singularly beautiful woman, little more than a brunette, certainly no darker than a Spanish or Italian lady in hue, with big, lustrously expressive eyes and a mouth molded upon Adelaide Neilson's. She has a rich, flexible and effective voice which she well knows how to manage, and her use of the English language is not only excellent, but exemplary. She is not only an elocutionist, but an actress of very decided force, as she demonstra'ed in selections from "Romeo and Juliet," particularly the potion scene, a piece of work we have rarely seen excelled. We could not help thinking what a magnificent Cleopatra she would make to a competent Anthony. Her reading of "Mary, Queen of Scots" was also very fine and elicited much applause.—*Sunday Truth, Buffalo, N. Y.*

The late entertainment under the auspices of Zion Church, and managed by Lieutenant Trotter, with the eminent tragedienne, Miss Henrietta Vinton Davis, was a grand dramatic success. It is said that Adelaide Neilson was the only true Juliet, but the rendition of the balcony and potion scene by Miss Davis caused the audience to think that Neilson had risen, "phœnix-like, from her ashes." She held the audience in amazement with her animated acting, graceful movements and correct pronunciation, forcing the acknowledgment of her great ability. She is very graceful in movement and will beyond a doubt find her proper rank of fame in the histrionic world. She made a lasting impression in "Brier Rose," by Boyensen, and surpassed even herself in the comical rendition of the "Jiners." Truly may it be said that the colored Americans have at last a true representative on the stage, whose fame in time will become universal.—*The Commercial Gazette, Cincinnati.*

The select readings by Miss Henrietta Vinton Davis, at Unity Hall, were finely rendered, showing her to be an elocutionist of genuine merit. Her modesty and gracefulness were especially noticeable, and her ways on the platform exceptionally pleasing. Her selections included "How He Saved St. Michael," by Mary A. P. Stansbury; "The Battle," by Schiller, and Mark Twain's "How Tom Sawyer Got his Fence Whitewashed." Selections from "Lady Macbeth" and "Romeo and Juliet" were also given, the renditions being in several respects equal to Mrs. Scott-Siddons' interpretations of the characters involved. In fact Miss Davis' reading reminds me very often of Mrs. Scott-Siddons.—*Hartford Evening Post.*

The testimonials show that the pulpit and press unite in endorsing Miss Davis as the most talented lady before the public.

In recounting the triumphs of Miss Davis as are presentative of the school of tragedy we find it a pleasing task to give utterance to words commensurate to our feelings. Having heard the so-called best of the dominant race (Mrs. Prescott), and having also listened to Miss Davis, we fail to see which is superior, or wherein. Her voice is the ideal, her statue is matchless, her eyes are charming and can almost read the thoughts of other people.

Her representations, dialects, gestures, poses are indeed perfection. She instructs not only her audience, but the authors of all her selections. Her own peculiar ideas have made her a teacher in gesticulation, and the wonderful management of her voice, eyes, yea, mute gestures, make her the compeer of Miss Couthoui, of Boston, Any one who has met her, conversed with her or listened to her in the role of drama could not but agree with us in our assertions. Hard study and close application to the art has made many grand artists, some great, really *good.* Nature makes Miss Davis what other things have made others. She is natural, easy and graceful. You laugh or feel sad at her will, as she takes her audience up with her. She is destined to be the brightest star in the zenith of our tragical firmament.

ANNA, MADA AND EMMA LOUISE HYERS.

Vocalists, Pianists and Actresses.

IN every human being God, the creator of all, hides a precious gem, as the costliest diamond is extracted from under the rough-edged stone, the most delicate mosses are taught to grow at the bottom of the deepest cannon. While in the former the diamond for long remains worthless in the hands of the cobbler, yet when the master of fine arts manipulates this apparently rude stone its value increases a hundredfold ratio toward completion.   In the latter the most delicate mosses, admired only by the disciplined eye or the tireless searcher after the hidden treasures, blooms out into a philosopher and argues with us to the extent of agreeing.

But the radiance and intellectual charm which in these two human beings God had hidden was not to remain so very long. For at very early ages the necessity arose of placing them in the full and promising attitude where they might be polished to shine in the realm of music and song. When once in training the advancement was so rapid and so inspiring that the celebrated Professor Hugo Sank, whose name betrays his nationality, took them on and on from the degree of good to superlative best. Unfortunately a change had to be made for their instruction, but with the ability Madame Josephine D'Ormy possessed, and most especially as a celebrity in operas, they were instructed in Italian and German, which, in fact, was necessary to be conversant and to know in order to meet the public expectations everywhere ; they pursued nobly and became quite proficient in each, and in fact they give Madam D'Ormy the praise for faith in them to learn, for the patience which was nursed by the faith. It was not long to wait for the reality.

Mr. Trotter in his literary feast entitled music and some highly musical people says : "To Madam D'Ormy the Misses Hyers owe most of their success to-day. For she it was who taught them that beautiful enunciation, and sweetness of intonation, that now are so noticeable in their singing of Italian and other music."

After finishing their training under Mrs. D'Ormy they retired seemingly from the public gaze ; being quite young, and there being no reason for a rush.

Finally at the Metropolitan Theatre in Sacramento, Cal., April 22, 1867, they made their *debut* before an audience of eight hundred people. Success, which met them and crowned them there, has followed them and has ever been a characteristic symbol of their genius, their repeated triumphs the lesson of nature to the world.

Since 1880, when the papers teemed with notices, agents of books were excited in their enthusiasm concerning " Music and Some Highly Musical People," an illustrated book by one of our first autobiographers, Mr. James M. Trotter, which leaped up into the thousands, and people were anxious about its sale, from the mere fact of it demonstrating to the world what education was doing for the colored people in that distinct sphere. Hyers Sisters, who form a part and add to its reading matter rich deeds of musical accomplishments, have traveled around the world, sang before the crowned heads of Europe and become a house word in the musical circles of the United States, are again presented to our readers, notably fulfilling their mission, having demolished the doctrine of incapacity and delighted the world with their musical chants. For them let it be said : "All places a temple, and all seasons summer." No time in their musical history have they failed to sing to crowded, eager and anxious lovers of their art, reaching their numbers in the high and low register with the facility and ease of skilled musicians. Their harmony and cadence are true to nature, but having become lost in the depth and sweetness of their rival voices trained to the finish, one would conclude that Nature had overstepped her bounds and borrowed the symphony

of heaven.   Let what has been said by masters do our bidding.
That great and grand play entitled " Uncle Tom's Cabin has
more nearly mimicked nature and actual long ago picture of slavery days, when Topsy and her twin are treated with their true,
comical, yet sublime powers. For more than one season they held
the boards of all the Northern, Eastern and Western cities, playing to crowded houses. They have demonstrated beyond the
shadow of a doubt what culture, refinement, backed by instruction of the best type, can be do for the Negro race under
similar influences.   Born in California, reared, educated in her
schools, and clothed and protected by her inalienable rights
and stringent yet equal laws, they show no trait of a low,
despised race, save the color of their skin and the texture of
their hair. " God save the mark."

DALLAS, TEX., August 20, 1892.

To a top-heavy house the McCabe & Young's genuine
darkey minstrels gave a first-class performance last night.
There is no counterfeit about these ebony-hued artists.   They
are simon-pure.   There is not a man in the company who is
not a good singer, and as for dancing, " go way, dar chilun'."
The specialty work was excellent, and provoked continuous
peals of laughter.   The Hyers sisters, whose names are almost
world-wide, made their first appearance before a Dallas audience and sustained the reputations which they have won as
possessors of peerless voices.

The matinee to-day is largely attended and to-night the
minstrels will hold down the boards of the Dallas Opera
House for the last time this season.—*Dallas News.*

DALLAS, TEX—DALLAS OPERA-HOUSE.

It cannot be said that good minstrelsy is not appreciated in
Dallas.   The opinion seemed fully warranted by the large and
enthusiastic audience that gathered at the opera-house last night
to see McCabe and Young and their support of ebony artists.
Special mention is due Harry Singleton for his rendition of a
Soldier and a Man, and Will Roberts for his pleasing rendition
of Pauline. The witticisms of Billy Young, Johnny Young and

Ed Cay were received with deserving plaudits. The event of the evening was the appearance for the first time in Dallas of the celebrated Hyers sisters. They are vocalists of exceptional ability. They have highly cultured voices of bell-like tone and faultless intonations. The show was first-class and will be repeated at matinee and to-night.—*Dallas News.*

CELIA E. DIAL SAXON.

Teacher and Sunday-School Worker.

AMONG the educators the race has produced, the subject of this sketch deserves a high place. Few teachers have met with greater success. The faculty of imparting knowledge seems innate with her. Graduating from the South Carolina State Normal School, in May, 1877, she began, in November of the same year, to teach in Howard school, long a leading institution of Columbia, S. C. Her abilities soon placed her among the foremost instructors of that seminary of learning. She proved herself a born teacher—excellent in instructing and excellent in governing. Some Northern visitors, greatly interested in the advancement of the colored people, once remarked after a visit to her class-room: "What a fine disciplinarian Miss Dial is!" On the eve of her marriage to Professor T. A. Saxon, of Allen University, in December, 1890, she tendered her resignation, but at the urgent request of the board she was induced to reconsider this action and continue to fill the position she had filled for so long and with such uninterrupted success until the close of the term, in June, 1891.

Mrs. Saxon is also a scholar of no mean rank. She completed the Chautauqua course in 1883, and has since won several of the seals offered to the graduates of this course who pursue and master some special branch of study after graduation. She is a great Sunday-school worker, and has been from girlhood a most acceptable teacher in the well-known Bethel A. M. E. Sunday-school. She is a great lover of her race—

with a high conception of its capabilities and resplendent hopes for its future. Like the lamented Bishop William F. Dickerson, she believes that "twenty-five years ago the colored people were babes; to-day they are children; twenty-five years from now, despite the pitfalls about them and the prejudices they have to contend with, they will be approaching the full stature of manhood." Long may she live to do good to humanity, and to help lift her race to that high plane which she believes God intends them to occupy.

MISS MARY A. SHADD.

Lecturer and Editor.

BISHOP PAYNE, in his recollections of seventy years, in referring to his travels in the West, says, among other things: "I also had the pleasure of hearing that extraordinary young woman, Miss Mary A. Shadd, editor of the *Provincial Freeman*, of Western Canada, in two lectures on the condition and prospects of the colored people in Canada. Her power did not consist in eloquence, but in her familiarity with facts, her knowledge of men, and her fine power of discrimination. Her energy and perseverance, as well as her ability to suffer in the cause she espoused, entitled her to rank among the reformers of the time. She went alone into Canada West in the fall of 1851, and traveled it from Toronto to Sandwich, sometimes on foot, maintaining herself by teaching school. The following spring she published a pamphlet entitled " Notes on Canada West," and in about one year from the day she landed in Canada she had nearly established the weekly sheet before mentioned of which for more than one year she was the sole editor, at the same time acting as traveling agent and financier. Her editorials compared well with those of the sterner sex, some of whom she often excelled. Indeed I could mention at least two colored editors whose editorials were far beneath hers. This leads me to note that at the close of 1859 it fell under my observation that there were but three newspapers among the colored people of the United States : The *Ram's Horn*, published in Philadelphia, and edited and owned by Thomas Van Rensselaer ; the *Christian Herald*, of the A. M. E. Church, published in Pittsburg, Pa., and edited by Rev. A. R. Green; the *North Star*, published in Rochester, New York, and edited by Frederick Douglass, a fugitive slave, but born to distinguish himself as one of the master minds of the nineteenth century. Thirty-six years have produced immense changes and progress in colored journals and journalism."

LOUISE DE MORTIE.

Christian Martyr, Elocutionist, Missionary and Financier.

VIRGINIA has the boast of being the birthplace of presidents, heroes and heroines innumerable. Let this suffice; our subject was born in Norfolk, 1833, and suffering educational inconveniences, nevertheless born of free parents, found no race restrictions in Massachusetts, hence made Boston her home in 1853. Possessing sufficient courage to master the higher sciences, she at once attracted the attention of all who came in her way. "None knew her but to love her," and in the possession of that intellectual radiance which brightened with effulgency all her companions, she, governed by such an angelic soul, portrayed a marvelously kind and genial spirit, which endeared and held all friends.

Nature, kind alike to all who will do, dare, or die, contributed to her makeup a sound, well-formed body, voluminous voice, and elocutionary powers wonderful and puzzling to describe. She has contributed dignity to her art and planted both body and name among the loving friends of New Orleans, Louisiana. 1862, Williams History of the Negro Race in America, says . "She began a most remarkable career as a public speaker and reader ; an elocutionist by nature, she added the refinement to the art, and with her handsome presence, engaging manners and richly toned voice she took high rank in her profession. Just as she was attracting public attention to her genius, she learned of the destitution that was wasting the colored orphans of New Orleans. Thither she hastened in the spirit of Christian love, and there she labored with an intelligence and zeal which made her a heroine among her people. In 1867, she raised sufficient funds to build an asylum for the colored orphans of New Orleans. But just then the yellow fever overtook her in her work of mercy, and she fell a victim to the deadly foe, 1867, October 10, saying so touchingly, 'I belong to God, our Father,' as she expired. Although cut off in the morning of her useful life she is of blessed memory among those for whose improvement and elevation she gave the strength of a brilliant mind and the warmth of a genuine Christian heart."

MRS. LAURA A. (MOORE) WESTBROOK.

W. C. T. U. Advocate, Teacher and Lecturer.

AS Tennessee has long been noted for its beautiful hills and mountain sceneries, I imagine that somewhere among the forests of Tipton county, in the year of 1859, was born the person of whom I shall attempt to write a few things. Mrs. Westbrook's parents, Richard and Amelia Moore, were both slaves, but her mother was free born and when a child was kidnapped by the slave traders, carried away from her parents, and ever afterward remained a slave until the emancipation of slaves. Her father is a mulatto, and is also closely related to the old Georgia Cherokee Indians. Mrs. Westbrook's father, being a great lover of knowledge, could not be satisfied after the emancipation until he had succeeded, through the aid of his brother Edward Harris, in obtaining one of Oberlin's best scholars as a tutor for his two children, Laura and Vara Lee, the baby. Under the tutorship of Miss Rachel Alexander—for this was the name of the lady who consented to leave home and friends and even dared to come South when brave men would tremble to think of such a thing at that time—Mrs. Westbrook, after five years of hard study, made herself a good scholar in the primary branches. There being a great demand for teachers in the South at this time, Mrs. Westbrook, who was greatly in advance of many of 'her race, though only eleven years old, was called upon to go and impart to her suffering sisters and brethren the light which she had already received. She had already received that great wisdom which cometh down from above, which makes us wise unto salvation, and being filled with a great missionary spirit, she readily accepted the call. She, after laboring with her people two years, felt her inability to execute the work as it should be, and to meet the demand of the future she made application and entered the Central Tennessee College in 1872. Under the fatherly care of Dr. J. Braden and his noble corps of teachers, after four years of hard toil and undaunted courage, she completed the normal course of that institution in the year of 1876, during which time she had proven herself an enthusiastic and studious young lady, full of moral courage and

MRS L. A. WESTBROOK.

Christian piety, which won for her the esteem of her teachers and schoolmates. Her teachers, seeing she was capable of doing much good for her people, urged her not to stop with the normal course, but to continue her studies until she would have finished the regular classical course, which victory she did achieve in the year of 1880, graduating with a class of four, she being the only female. Mrs. Westbrook was honored by her Alma Mater in the year of 1885 with the degree of A. M., which degree she heartily deserved. Mrs. Westbrook continued

to teach during vacation until she had completed her course
of study, and by this means, with the assistance of her parents,
she was enabled to continue in school. Her education being
finished, she entered fully into the work of teaching. On the
Fourth of July in the year of 1880, she was married to a class-
mate of hers, Rev. C. P. Westbrook, of Aberdeen, Miss. After
teaching in Tennessee a short time, they were urged by the
president of the college, Dr. J. Braden, to take charge of two
schools in Texas. Mrs. Westbrook, being full of the missionary
zeal, quickly answered to the call, and in December of 1880
they arrived at Victoria, Texas, where Mrs. Westbrook took
charge of the Victoria city school, as principal, while her husband assumed the principalship of the Goliad city school,
which was afterward known as the Jones' Male and Female
Institute.

Mr. Westbrook's school having increased so rapidly at
Goliad, Mrs. Westbrook was compelled to give up being principal at Victoria to assist her husband. After teaching in the
Jones' Institute for four years, Mrs. Westbrook came with her
husband to Waco, where she entered actively in the W. H.
Mission work for two years teaching a mission school in which
much good was done, during which time she was appointed
corresponding secretary of W. H. Mission Society of the West
Texas conference, which position she still holds, and has traveled quite extensively throughout the bounds of the West
Texas conference of the M. E. church and lectured in the
interest of the W.H. Mission cause. In 1888, Mrs. Westbrook
went as a delegate to the W. H. Mission convention which
convened in Boston, Mass. Mrs. Westbrook has labored in the
public school work as teacher for twenty years. She has taught
twelve years in the Texas public schools and is now engaged
in the public school of the city of Waco, where she has taught
for four years. She has been instrumental in doing a great
amount of good among her people and she hopes in the future
to be able to do a much greater work for them.

She is known as a tireless and aggressive woman in maintaining the rights of her race. She has many times been

honored in conspicuous instances and under very flattering circumstances owing to her undaunted courage.

She has served at various times upon the examining board of the twenty-second senatorial district for Texas, examining colored young men and lady applicants for State scholarships at Prairie View State Normal Institute. She has distinguished herself as a member of the Woman's Christian Temperance Union, traveling through various Southern States lecturing, electrifying and inspiring our youths, and teaching temperance and Christianity. Her motive to do good far surpasses her vanity, except when her race is attacked, then, manlike, she with the pen strikes back, and even goes beyond her loyalty to serve, but makes lasting impressions upon those who are so unfortunate to get within her range. She is a firm believer in the true, the pure, and the beautiful.

Her daily life is characteristic of her essays and lectures. The hardships and obstacles which we daily encounter are no strangers to Mrs. Westbrook. She is yet in the blooming morn of life, with many of us, who will exert our energies to keep along by her side.

GORGIA E. LEE PATTON, M. D.

Physician and Surgeon, A Meharry Graduate, African Missionary.

JUST as the cruel canon had ceased its roaring and the smoke of the powder had begun to subside, there was born in Grundy county, Tennessee, two little girls, April 15, 1864. One, too pure for this world, was immediately transplanted in the Eden above; the other, less ethereal, was left to battle with the storms of life, and was given the name of Georgia E. Lee Patton.

Shortly after this the mother heard of the glad tidings of freedom and moved to Coffee, the adjoining county, which Georgia still calls home.

Like most Negroes the mother was sent away from her taskmaster who had grown rich from others' toil, with nothing, and being a widow with a very large family depending

upon her, she had to struggle hard against the merciless hand
of poverty. But by diligence, working early in the morning
and late at night, she managed to provide for them and send
them to the few months school that was occasionally taught.
You may know that educational advantages were meager
when you are told that Georgia attended every school, yet at
the age of seventeen had gone only twenty-six months.

The child's clothing consisted of scanty underwear and a
cotton dress, the thread of
which was spun at night
by a good mother after a
hard day's work, walking
two or three miles to and
from the place of labor.

These garments were
made clean by the same
dear hands on Saturday
night, while the child,
with perfect peace of mind,
too young to think of hardships, slept the sleep of the
innocent.

Too poor to afford a tin
bucket, a tin can which had
been used for fruit was made
to serve this purpose by holes
being made and a string put
through them for a handle.

GEORGIE E. LEE PATTON, M. D.

If Georgia had even bread
and meat to put in this she tugged off to school as happy
as a brown thrush with her undisturbed nestlings ; not a
care, not a sorrow, only one ambition—to be at the head of
the class at close of school; that meant a perfect lesson, for the
children valued the few days for improvement.

Being the youngest of the family she was the favorite
with them all, and the mother would not allow her to engage
in washing and spinning, as the older sisters did. Being a

child of nature, loving the sweet songs of the birds, the fresh air, the fragrant clover blooms and the blue vault above, she turned to the field where she learned to plow before the shoulders were above the plow's handles.

The child was so delighted with the new work she easily persuaded her mother to allow her to continue. Even to-day she will not hesitate to go from the school-room or the bed-side of the sick to the plow's handle.

At the age of sixteen, death claimed her strongest earthly tie (her mother), leaving her alone in this cold, dark world. Life was indeed gloomy, only one hope found in this world : " I will never leave nor forsake thee." At last she took up life alone, and you who have had kind mothers to love know her feelings.

Georgia now moved to the home of her oldest sister. She had longed for an education, now that she must fight the war of life alone she felt the need of it the more. In the mind plans were being devised by which this might be attained.

The following year she thought she had at last come to the right plan, that of going out to live with a family. The work was easy because through it she thought she could see the way to college. Another sister objecting to this plan it was soon abandoned. She again entered public school, but with that craving still, to go off to college. The knowledge gained at the public school only sharpened this already indwelling aspiration for something higher than public school.

The way seemed entirely hedged up. It was a sore temptation to the ambitious girl to see her only hopes thus swallowed, and she began sighing.

How often we close our eyes to blessings that are for us and stand weeping for what we have, if we will but look up and claim it for our own.

Her sister secured some money and gave her five dollars; the same day her earthly possessions were collected, placed in a small wooden trunk and in a few days she was off for Nash-ville. After purchasing the ticket and a hack secured only two dollars and fifty cents was left. A strange city, strange people, books to buy and board to pay, yet she was happy. How could she be otherwise? Since God had done so much for her could she believe He had brought her here to suffer?

We should always feel thankful for to-day's blessing, not sighing for the one we fear we may not get to-morrow, thus losing the bliss of the present.

She believed the good president would give her work after he knew her, as she had written him about it. That was not God's way. See how providential! At the depot she met a long-lost brother who was married and living in Nashville, and went to his house. The board was thus settled for the year. The other two sisters sent her seven dollars and since there was only four months she made this buy the necessary books and pay the tuition, except the last month, which she paid during vacation.

Though the brother lived more than two miles from the college, in spite of the condition of the weather she was in her place in the chapel at the tap of the first bell.

February 6, 1882, will ever be a memorable day to her. When in the classes, the students laughed at her mistakes and perhaps awkward manners.

The city had no claims now for the country girl, because her heart had been wounded the first thing after entering a class, by the students laughing at her mistakes.

At the close of school the first day she left with a heavy heart, wishing she had never come, but feeling that since she had, it must be endured and make the best of it, and she resolved that they should never have occasion to laugh again. Possibly they realized her resolution, when in a few weeks she was promoted to a more advanced class.

She had that in her make-up which every one must have if he succeeds—a determination not to give up because the igno-rant acts provoke a smile on others' faces and some more cruel may even poke fun. This only made her more diligent.

In May, when the term closed, she went to Kentucky and secured a small school. This enabled her to attend school a

few months the next session. Since then she has paid her
way mostly by teaching.

She has completed the senior normal course. As a teacher
she has filled her place well; being a natural lover of the work
she has always gone into it with the whole hand and heart,
making hard places easy. She was a good, obedient student,
and such generally are successful as teachers. They who
control themselves can control others.

Several times has she been called to places where women
were not wanted because the patrons had gotten the idea that
the children could not be controlled by her or she was unfit
for teaching.

Her work made false these statements and redeemed the
credit of woman as teacher, governess. In each case she was
asked to return, and offered increased salary.

Not satisfied with her ability for usefulness, after finishing
the literary course, she has turned her attention to a profession and has now graduated from the medical course of
Meharry medical department of the same school.

"Freely you have received, freely give." Since God has
so freely given her this opportunity for mental and spiritual
development she should freely give it to others and to those
who need it most. It is not hard to decide who these are
who most need this gift. A little knowledge of the condition
of the world will at once show it to be the inhabitants of
Africa.

So she intends to take this as an offering to the poor
heathens in Africa that she may help hasten the day when
"Ethiopia shall soon stretch out her hand unto God."

Preparations are now being made for life's work on that
dark continent.

MATTIE ALLISON HENDERSON.

Teacher, Stenographer and Editor.

MATTIE ALLISON HENDERSON, a typical little
Southern woman, was born in the little mountain
town of Frankfort, Ala., Dec. 24, 1868. She was an orphan at

five years of age, and of a family of four brothers and a sister is the only living member. Falling into the hands of a foster mother who "ruled with a rod of iron," the subject of this sketch experienced many of the bitters that really seem to belong to the lives of most orphans. Her struggle for an education is somewhat wonderful. At the tender age of thirteen she was compelled to do. as an old Southerner would put it, " a woman's work."

MATTIE A. HENDERSON.

" Many a time," says she, "have I been on my feet from five o'clock in the morning till midnight. It was, 'Mattie, do this,' 'go there,' 'get that,' until I often prayed that rest, in the shape of death, would relieve my tired little body."

Time for study at home was limited, and thus it happened that she was known to give strict attention during class time. In June, 1885, she graduated from Le Moyne Normal Institute, Memphis, Tenn., with the first class honor, and composed, also, the class poem. After teaching the following year in her Alma Mater, she resolved to begin a classical course at Fisk University, Nashville, Tenn, having spent one year there. For lack of means she was caused to abandon the idea, and again she began life in the school rooms of Arkansas and Tennessee district schools, finally drifting back to the institution where her first work as pupil and teacher begun. Tiring of teaching, and heartbroken over the loss, by death, of two friends, Miss Henderson resigned her position in the Le Moyne Institute and went to Cincinnati, Ohio, for a change and to learn sten-

ography, in which she completed her course in the spring
of 1892.

At an early age she gave signs of literary talent, and her
contributions to the little weekly school-paper were much
commented upon by her fellow-students. The first newspaper
article from her pen was published in the Marion, (Ark.)
Headlight. This article was published in full and most favorably commented upon in the editorial columns of the
Avalanche, then a leading democratic paper of Memphis
and the South. This would have been a world of encouragement to most young scribblers; but Miss Henderson, at that
time, saw little in Negro journalism to encourage her, and
although from time to time acting as correspondent and occasionally contributing au article to different papers, under
assumed names, dropped out of the literary world until she
suddenly appears in Kansas City as one of the two editors of
The Future State, a weekly paper, devoted to the interests of
the Negroes of the State of Missouri, where she manages every
department of that paper with the ability of a man. Her contributions under the *nons de plume* of " Aunt Alice,', " Jack
Hastings," " Mary Allison" and "Aunt Sarah" have made
lasting impressions in the hearts of her readers. Her writings
are fast winning for her a place among the writers of her race,
and her exceptional powers of conversation make her many
friends.

MRS. DR. G. F. GRANT (nee GEORGINA SMITH).

Pianist, Vocalist.

AMONG the gifted singers and pianists of the race, Mr.
Trotter delights to honor Mrs. Grant in his book
entitled, Music and Some Highly Musical People. He says:
" She was formerly the efficient organist of the North Russell
Street Church, and has been regarded as a most pleasing
vocalist, possessing a very pure, sweet soprano voice. She
was for some time a pupil of the New England Conservatory of Music, and on more than one occasion was

chosen to represent at its quarterly concerts before large and cultivated audiences in Music Hall the system taught and fine progress made by the attendants of that institution." On such occasions her *naivete*, her graceful, handsome stage appearance, and expressive rendering, with voice of bird-like purity, of some of the best *cavatina* music, always elicited the most enthusiastic plaudits and recalls. The writer was present on one of these occasions, fortunately, and remembers with much satisfaction the delight he felt, not only in hearing this lady's melodious voice himself, but in witnessing its charming effect on the audience of nearly four thousand people, representing generally "Boston's best culture."

Her reception really amounted to an ovation. The event was a most remarkable one, and exhibiting as it so fully did the power of art to scatter all the prejudices of race or caste, was most instructive and reassuring.

Of her appearance at one of the concerts just mentioned, the Boston *Globe* thus spoke:

* * * Miss Smith, a fine-looking young lady, achieved a like success in all her numbers and in fine presence on the stage, and in her simple, unobtrusive manner, winning the sympathies of the audience.

And the Boston *Journal* said:

An immense audience, in spite of the storm and the wretched condition of the streets, assembled in Music Hall yesterday evening to listen to the quarterly concert of the New England Conservatory of Music. The spacious hall was packed in every part. The most marked success during the evening was that won by Miss Georgina Smith, who has a fine soprano voice, and who sang in a manner which could but receive the warmest plaudits.

Miss Smith was a member of the chorus composed of selected singers that sang at the memorable "International Peace Jubilee Concert," and although still quite young, has had an experience as a vocalist of which she may well be proud.

MAMIE ELOISE FOX.

Poetess.

THE accompanying cut is a most perfect likeness of Mamie Eloise Fox, who was born in Chillicothe, Ross county, Ohio, April 10, 1871. Both of her parents are Virginians and ex-slaves.

Miss Fox is of short stature, somewhat stout, and very muscular; she has large, brown eyes that look straight and squarely into those of the person with whom she is conversing; her high forehead betokens the intelligence that she certainly possesses. Her features in general are well-defined and intelligent.

In disposition, the young lady is lovable, kind and affectionate, having a great fondness for children and animals; she is noble, upright and *true*, in the highest sense of the word; having never been known to betray any confidence placed in her, she has a multitude of confiding friends. Being highly conscientious, Miss Fox will support the right, never for once condescending to anything that tends to degrade; it is this conscientiousness that makes her so dutiful in home circles, so faithful a church member, so radical a total abstainer, and so true a friend; she truly says of herself that "she is as uncompromising as General Grant was when he demanded General Lee's unconditional surrender." Although firm and immutable in her convictions of the right, Miss Fox is by no means bigoted, always endeavoring to make a practical application of the fact that "discretion is the better part of valor."

In June, 1891, Miss Fox graduated from the Chillicothe high school, having taken the Latin course. While in the high school she gave especial attention to literature, in consequence of which her natural literary inclinations were rapidly and profitably developed. She is an excellent writer both of prose and verse, being aided in the latter by her vivid imagination. At the age of nine she began to write verses, and has been doing so ever since; indeed, for one so young, she has written some commendable poems. The lines which Alexander Pope applied to himself are equally applicable to Miss Fox:

> As yet a child, and all unknown to fame,
> I lisped in numbers, for the numbers came.

Once a gentleman asked Miss Fox, "What is love?" To which she replied, "Wait a few days and I shall answer your question" One day, about a week thereafter, while in school the young poet wrote on the fly-leaf of her astronomy:

> What is love? A higher passion
> Emanating from the heart;
> 'Tis a spark of sacred impulse
> Which a word or look can start
> To a flame of heightened pleasure.
> Only those who love can know
> How the pulse and heart are quickened
> When the fires of true love glow.

After submitting the answer to the gentleman he told her she could not have written so concise and definite an answer had she not been inspired with love, whereupon she amended it by adding these lines:

> Not experience has led me
> To the thoughts expressed above,
> For I never waste a moment
> On that airy subject, love.

Miss Fox contributes poems to *Ringwood's Journal*, for which she has written some very beautiful ones, among them being "Sunset in Ohio," "Ignis Amoris," "Time's Pages," "Autumn" and some others.

Aside from her literary qualifications Miss Fox is an ardent lover of music, reading it at sight. Her chief ambition, however, is to study medicine in order to become a physician and surgeon. Although she is not yet able to enter upon her medical studies, yet she possesses the energy and perseverance that will win for her success.

As an ardent advocate of the temperance cause Miss Fox is unexcelled; she drinks neither malt, vinous nor spirituous liquors. At a recent reception she attended Miss Fox was the *only* one present who did not partake of wine. Her friends often try to persuade her to drink cider, but she absolutely refuses. When asked her reasons for being so extreme in her temperance views, she says: "Read Romans xiv. 13-23; 1st Corinthians viii., 1-13." When a girl of seventeen she wrote the following poem on

INTEMPERANCE.

There is a great and awful foe,
　That blights the human race,
It plunges men in deep despair,
　In sorrow and disgrace.

That evil is intemperance—
　The Moloch of to-day.
Upon its altars of distress,
　Millions of victims lay.

Their hopes are gone, their consciences
　Are dulled by sin and vice;
Satan has promised "more beyond,"
　And virtue is the price.

Cannot intemperance be o'erthrown?
　Must it forver stand!
Why does this blasting, withering curse
　Extend throughout the land?

Let us do all within our power
　To break the wine-cup's spell,
And try to keep our men and boys
　From going down to hell.

WHAT IS A RAINBOW?

What is a rainbow? 'Tis a blending
    Of chromatic rays of light,
Sent by tiny, sparkling raindrops,
    When the sun is shining bright.

' Tis the seven tones of music
    Metamorphosed for the eye,
Sound converted into color
    By the God of earth and sky.

'Tis the emblem of his promise,
    ' Tis the arch of Heaven's gate,
Where the angels stand and beckon,
    Where our loved ones watch and wait.

ECLIPSE OF THE SUN.

When eighty-eight its speedy flight had taken,
    And eighty-nine had dawned upon the earth,
With sunshine and with shadows which awaken
    Alternate feelings both of sighs and mirth,
Phœbus, whose smiles shone at the dawn of morning,
    As eve drew on, concealed them with a veil
Of darkness, as if he would give us warning
    Of shadows, which the night is wont to trail.
But why should Phœbus hide his face from mortals?
    Do not his rays both warm and cheer the hearts
Of men, when, as it were, the heavenly portals
    Are closed? What happiness the sun imparts!
But such is life :—with all its rain and sadness,
    Sunshine and smiles incessantly are sent ;
The Being Omnipresent looks in gladness,
    When grief makes adamantine hearts relent.
JANUARY 1, 1889.

Miss Fox has written a number of fine essays, some of which
will ere long be given to the public; she also thinks of having her
verses published in book form.   Being a great church and Sunday-school worker, and secretary of the latter, she is kept very
busy.   She has a brother to whom she is very devoted.

MRS. N. F. MOSSELL.

Eminent Writer.

A NUMBER of years ago at the closing exercises of a grammar school in the city of Philadelphia, a young girl read an essay on *Influence.* This paper was so unusually interesting and gave such promise for future power that Bishop Tanner, who was in the audience, procured it for the *Christian Recorder*, and invited the young writer to furnish more material for the columns of that journal. Thus modestly stepped into the literary world one who was destined to take high place among Afro–American writers, and who to-day, as Mrs. N. F. Mossell, is one of the leading women of a struggling race, whose brightest hope is that it can bring forth just such women.

Mrs. Mossell, *nee* Bustill, was born in Philadelphia of parents who were Philadelphians on both sides for several generations. Her parents were raised in the faith of the Society of Friends, and at a later date joined the Old School Presbyterian Church. It will thus be seen that Mrs. Mossell could hardly have escaped having those strong traits of character and that inclination to studious habits which distinguish her, if the law of heredity counts for anything. While still of tender age, death deprived her of a mother's care, and she and an older sister were boarded with friends until her twelfth year, when the sisters returned to their father's house, there to remain until they left it for homes of their own. The elder sister married Rev. Wm. D. Robertson, now pastor of the Witherspoon Presbyterian Church, at Princeton, N. J. The distinguished subject of this sketch became the wife of Dr. N. F. Mossell, of Lockport, now one of the leading physicians of Philadelphia, and one of the strongest and most progressive thinkers of the Anglo-African race.

The first ten receptive, impressionable years make the form and character of a lifetime, and those early years of Mrs. Mossell gave the keynote to all her future years. Deprived of the many influences that cling around a home life and a mother's care, the two little girls threw themselves into the company of books for their happiness. They both became omnivorous readers, and Mrs. Mossell has told me that often when her fund of books ran low, she would devour the encyclopædia or study the pages of a dictionary. Thus was laid the foundation of that store of general information and that fluency of language which have enabled Mrs. Mossell to achieve her present excellence.

After completing a course in the Roberts Vaux Grammar School, Mrs. Mossell taught school for seven years, a part of the time in Camden and later on in Frankfort. During all this time she kept up literary work, contributing a number of poems, sketches, etc., to the *Recorder*. Her marriage put an end to the school teaching, and for a time after it she ceased active literary work; but later on, she returned with redoubled vigor to her first love, and for a number of years contributed articles of special character to the leading journals of Philadelphia. She has edited at different times the woman's departments of the New York *Age*, *Echo* and Indianapolis *World*, and has assisted in the editorship of the Lincoln *Alumni Magazine*. Her contributions to the A. M. E. *Review* and other standard Negro journals would make, if collected, a volume of considerable size.

With so much that is calculated to attract the admiration of the public, the real woman can only be appreciated by one who sees her in her home life. Perfectly devoted to her husband's interests, and adopting herself to the increasing cares of his rapidly widening practice, Mrs. Mossell yet finds time to do her special work, and to surround her two interesting little daughters with the watchful care of a mother's love. The Mossell home is always open to those in need of encouragement and aid, and many a struggling student can testify to the beauty of its hospitality. Mrs. Mossell is intensely interested in anything that contributes to race progress. She has acted as agent and canvasser to several race publications, and has a well-stocked library of Negro literature of her own. She has in view a collection of her own writings and in actual preparation of work of value to the race.

When some future historian writes the history of the American Negro, it must be allowed that the Negro woman did a noble share in the race development, and when he calls over the roll of noble dames the name of Gertrude Mossell must be high on the list.   OLIVE.

We append the following as a sample of her merit as a writer and thinker:

OUR WOMEN IN MISSIONS.

It has been my intention for some time to prepare a paper on the above subject,—the editorial: Have we no Clara Bartons in our Race, that appeared in the last issue of Our Women and Children, led me to feel that my choice was felicitous. All other races have each in its history had noble women to rise from their ranks and stretch forth the hand opening the way for multitudes to follow, in good works of heroism, charity and benevolence. From the times of Joan of Arc down to Clara Barton of the present day, each race and era has been blessed in this respect—according to its needs. Shall we alone fail to find loving hearts, willing hands, and high inspiration in our midst? Do not fear that such will be the case. Dr. Crummel, in his beautiful tribute to " the Black Woman of the South," has shown what our women were capable of even during the debasing influences of slavery. Shall we not, in the light of great privileges and hence greater duties, prove worthy of still greater eulogy? We shall stand in the limits of this paper to glean here and there from what has already been accomplished, and encourage with counsel still greater effort in this most blessed and desirable work. Unfortunately I am not a traveler, so have but a limited field of observation to glean from, and do not know of any collected facts on this subject. Philadelphia, my birthplace and present home, has been blessed to some extent. The opening of public schools to the children of color was accomplished largely through the labors of Mrs. Mary M. Jennings and her daughter Cordelia, now Mrs. Atwell, of New York. Mrs. Ralls, of the A. M. E. Church, a woman of strong physique, noble in her appearance, with great love for humanity, established the

Sarah Allen Mission House. Boxes of clothing and books, food for the sick and such articles of use and instruction were collected and distributed. One summer a number of aged persons were taken care of in a pleasant country dwelling. A mission school of fifty pupils was carried on for several years, and a Christmas dinner to 500 aged poor is now among the permanent work of the Mission. A faith home for the aged was started at a later date by Mrs. Ralls for the care of the aged and infirm; it has some score of inmates, and has been very successful. Begun without a dollar and carried on with no income, its daily needs are met by the prayerful efforts of this God-fearing woman who collects from any source whatsoever what may be freely given for the support of the institution according to her faith and works it has been done unto her, no day has found a lack of the necessaries or many of the luxuries and nourishments needful for the life and comfort of the inmates. Mrs. Fanny Jackson Coppin, the great educator of the young of our race, has established, by persistent, persevering effort an industrial school that is daily proving itself of great value in the uplifting of the race. She has also partially secured the means to found a boarding house for pupils from a distance.

The first Sabbath-school in New York City on good authority was established by a colored woman named Happy Ferguson (how appropriate the name and the work). The fact is established in two publications, History of Sabbath-schools of New York by W. A. Chandler, and the Tribute to the Negro after the statement of the fact in his history. Says Mr. Chandler: "God bless the dusky hands that broke here an alabaster box, the perfume of which still lingers about the great metropolis." Hope some day our white friends of this hour in their great memorial meetings will take cognizance of this fact, and that the women of our race shall erect some monument or cenotaph to the memory of this noble woman. Amanda Smith, the African missionary; Sojourner Truth, the abolitionist, did good work in their day and generation. Mrs. Mary Barbosa, daughter of our late consul to Liberia; the Rev. Henry High-

...ct, D. D., established a mission for native girls in the West-Coast of Africa. A hospital fund is being secured by Mrs. Roberts, the widow of ex-President Roberts, of Liberia, to found a mission hospital at Liberia.

An orphanage for children has lately been secured by the earnest efforts of noble Afro-American women in the Southwest. The noble work being done by Miss Hallie Quinn Brown all show that working and waiting will bring about the desired result. All over this land different classes of the "submerged tenth" call for our aid and assistance. It does not need education, influence, wealth or power, although all of these may be of value. Mother Margaret, the orphans' friend of New Orleans, was a poor woman, yet she saved thousands from sin and misery. General Booth, of the Salvation Army, was not a millionaire, Jerry Mc. Auliffes Mission started in poverty, so it is not wealth that is the prime necessity, but a brave, loving heart, good health and persevering energy. Dr. T. G Steward wrote several years ago in the Christian *Recorder* a thoughtful paper on Our Women's Work and Place in the Church in the Present and Future. Women gave largely in their means, their time and their energy, but in an unsystematic way. He pleaded for their organization a larger recognition, and why not? Why not when two-thirds of the members of a church are women, and the means contributed by them swell the exchequer? Why not give them official credit for their effort? Why not learn a lesson from our sister church of the Catholic faith and establish an order having special work and costume, so they may not meet with obstacles while traveling about in the performance of the duties of the order? There are many ways in which two or three women may "lend a hand" in the work of reform. The ice water, flower, Chrismas card, Shut in Society, Working Girls' Union and dozens of other works come to our remembrance. Let us think on these things, and, like the people of the ancient town of Berea, have a mind to work and our duty will find us out.

MRS. N. F. MOSSELL, *in Ringwoood's Jurnal.*

"LOOKING BACKWARD"

Through the Spectacles of Jennie Jackson DeHart, the Famous Soprano of the Original Fisk Jubilee Singers.

BY A. E. W., CINCINNATI, O.

THE name of Jenny Jackson is one that for many years has been familiar in the homes of this country and Europe. For nineteen years she traveled from country to country with that famous band of Jubilee Singers, for the purpose of raising means to establish a permanent seat of learning for their race, in the land where they had so recently felt the lash of the master's whip, and where morally they are still enslaved by ignorance and crime. Gen. Clinton B. Fisk, in charge of the Freedman's Bureau in the Kentucky and Tennessee district, joined hands with the American Mission Association to establish a school at Nashville. Through his personal efforts the hospital barracks, formerly used by the Union Army, were secured, the purchase being made without it being known for what purpose they were going to be used. In 1866 the school was established and named Fisk University in honor of the man who did so much to make its establishment a certainty. To this Jennie Jackson came in 1868 to take advantage of the opportunity offered for an education, an opportunity heretofore denied her. In 1871 a crisis in the management of the school was reached, when it was found that the resources were inadequate to the demand, and the funds must be increased or the school must be moved to Atlanta. How to increase the funds was a perplexing problem, but one that was happily solved by Prof. Geo. L. White, instructor of music in the University. With him originated the idea of taking a band of singers from the school to the North and by singing in churches and halls raise the required sum of money. How well this plan succeeded is well known. In eight months they sent home $20,000, and when the company disbanded they had helped the University to the extent of over $150,000.

Their aim being accomplished, the members of this great band of singers (there were ten of the originals) scattered here and there, each (with one exception) a living monument of love and devotion to race elevation. One, his work being finished, has fallen asleep. Jenny Jackson is now the wife of Andrew J. DeHart, and resides on Walnut Hills, Cincinnati, O. Her devotion to her race is well worthy of imitation. While with the company she sent to the University for the education of poor students over two thousand dollars, collected from friends made in her travels, besides educating two girls out of her own private funds. Many valuable coins, stones and other curios have been contributed by her to the University's cabinets, while to her, also, its famous autograph album is largely due.

Thinking that something from this woman of such a wonderful experience might be of interest to the readers of "Ringwood," I, one cold, rainy day, not long since, donned my wraps and ventured over to her home. I found her in her cosy little dining-room, where burned a cheerful grate-fire, which, together with a very warm welcome, caused me to soon forget the cold stormy weather through which I had come. After making me comfortable in a large armchair and poking the fire a little she seated herself and—"So you want me to talk to you? All right, what shall I talk about?" "About yourself." "About myself? Why, my dear, there is nothing to say about myself that's worth saying." "Well, tell me something about the Fisk Jubilee Singers." "Very well, I'll just get my scrap-books and photographs, they may interest you more than I can." She brought out two large scrap-books and a large box of photographs and placed them on the table by my side.

The two scrap-books I found filled with newspaper clippings, programmes, letters, invitation cards, etc., and the box contained photographs of the singers, of friends connected with the school, of distinguished persons of this and foreign countries, of the school, of halls, churches and hotels. These, together with the many little reminiscences which they called forth from the madam, made a story that reads almost like a romance. That these emancipated slaves should have gone forth over the civilized world, the guests of the crowned heads of Europe, and returned with $150,000, with which to build an educational institution for the elevation of their race, seems little short of a marvel.

The story of their travels has been so often told, that it is no doubt familiar to the readers of this journal. A few clippings will, perhaps, still be of interest.

Mr. Beecher, one of their earliest and stanchest friends, in an address delivered in 1886, says: "I think there never was such a phenomenon as the building of Fisk University. We talk about castles in the air. That is the only castle that ever I knew to be built by singing, from foundation to top. That is a castle in the air worth having. They sang through our country, and it is one of the things that I cherish with pride that they took their start from Plymouth Church lecture room. Oh! those days after the war! My brother Tom wrote to me that this Jubilee band were trying to sing their way to the East and see if they could not raise a little money, and urged me to look after them. They called on me. I said, 'I do not know whether the folks will bear it or not, but come around Friday night, at the prayer meeting, and I will give you a chance.' Friday night they sat there, and after the service concluded I said to the people: 'There is a band of singers here, every one of whom has been baptized in slavery, and they are coming to the East to see if they can raise some little funds for their education and their elevation, and now I wish you would hear them sing a few pieces.' I called them upon the platform. There were about eleven hundred people there. The Jubilee band began to sing. It was still as death. They sang two pieces, tears were trickling from a great many eyes. They sang again and the audience burst forth into a perfect enthusiasm of applause, and when they had sung four or five pieces my people rose up in a mass and said: 'These folks must sing in the church.' I had them sing on Sunday morning, and on Wednesday night the church was crowded and crammed, and from that they went on, conquering and to conquer. They sang up and down our own country; they sang here ; they sang in the presence of the royal family ; they sang in Paris; they sang in Berlin; they sang before the Emperor William, and when they came back they had earned one hundred and fifty thousand dollars for the Fisk University."

BEECHER'S NEGRO MINSTRE

The great Plymouth preacher as an "End Man" is the heading of an article in the New York *Herald*, which says.— The Plymouth Varieties.—

Mr. Henry Ward Beecher, the eminent divine of Brooklyn, our sister city, is a man remarkable for many things. His great aim and chief object in life is never to be like anybody else. This achieved; and he is perfectly satisfied unto himself and his very peculiar congregation, or, as the irreverent term them, his "audience." But never before in his life has Mr. Beecher essayed to appear as a manager of Negro minstrels or as an "end man," as was apparent from the nature of the performances last evening at Plymouth church. A "Jubilee Singers' Concert," to be given by a band of nine Negroes, male and female, had been largely advertised among the faithful. Consequently, last evening, to answer this call upon the pious and meek and lowly congregation of Zion, about twenty-five hundred persons had assembled in Plymouth church, composed about equally of ladies and gentlemen. The Negroes went through a very monotonous minstrel performance. "Go Down, Moses," "Roll, Jordan, Roll," "The Old Folks at Home," "Home, Sweet Home" and other Negro melodies were sung just as they would be sung in a concert hall, and the behavior of the audience was just as it would be in a Negro minstrel hall, etc. etc. This same paper, two years later (1873), in speaking of a concert given by them, says : "The programme was mainly made up of those fervent and musical hymns that exactly reflect the enthusiastic, even ecstatic nature of the colored people, and which, having become wrought into their being during servitude, still holds sway over their feelings. The worthiness of their enterprise, though great, will have much less to do with filling the hall than the pleasing nature of the previous concerts."

The Rev. Newman Hall, after writing a very minute descrip tion of a breakfast party given to the singers by Mr. Gladstone, makes this apology :

"To English readers I should apologize for writing in this way. My description would be severely criticised as giving prominence to trifling courtesies, which, with us, are matters of course. No one here pretending to social refinement would make the least distinction between the guests he might meet merely on the ground of color, and no one would hesitate on that account to invite to his house anyone otherwise suitable. I am told there still exists in the United States some remnant of the old prejudice. This may be found, no doubt, among some of the ignorant and vulgar of our own land, and so also it would not be fair to infer that such prejudice is general in America, because exhibited by some low-bred, unrefined and narrow souls. I fancy some of these were at Surrey Chapel the other Sunday morning when the Jubilee singers did me the honor of taking a little luncheon with some of my friends of Rowland Hill's parsonage. Some Americans had come to take my hand and I asked them to join us. But when they entered the house, and saw our Negro friends sitting down to table, side by side with some English ladies, they looked sur- prised, stood awhile at the door, and then walked away down the street. I wish they had been present yesterday to see Mrs. Gladstone and her daughters, and noble lords and ladies present, taking their Negro friends by the hand, placing them chairs, sitting at their sides, pouring out their tea, etc., and conversing with them in a manner utterly free from any approach either of pride or condescension, but exactly as if they had been white people in their own rank of life."—*Ringwood Journal.*

MRS. SARAH GIBSON JONES.

SARAH EMILY GIBSON, daughter of Daniel and Mary Gibson, was born in Alexandria, Va., April 13, 1845. Her father, a man of unusual strength of intellect and will, was self-reliant and well-read in, at least, the English literature of the day ; and her mother, a quiet and practical woman, gentle, firm and efficient. She was the third of eleven children. Of these only four survive, Mrs. Josephine Ward, of Walnut Hills; Mrs. Louisa Davis, of New York, and Samuel Gibson, a young lawyer of Troy, New York. Soon after the birth of Sarah her parents, wishing to give their children better educational advantages, came to Cincinnati in 1849. Her first schooling was obtained in a pay school, taught by a Mrs. Hallam, afterward Mrs. Corbin, a white lady well remembered by old Cincinnatians. The free schools furnished the rest of her education, her principal instructors being Mrs. Corbin and Peter H. Clark. She began her career as a teacher, at Newtown, Ohio, in 1860. After leaving there became governess in a family near Oxford, O., then taught a private school at her own home until appointed to a position by the Cincinnati school board in September, 1863. Two years later she was united in matrimony to M. P. H. Jones, younger son of Rev. Samuel Jones, one of the pioneer Baptist ministers of the State of Ohio. At that time Mr. Jones was clerk of the colored school board, and was a gentleman of fine literary attainments, a pleasant and intellectual conversationalist and possessor of a wonderful memory. Although he was her senior by twenty years the marriage was a congenial one. Three children were the result of the union, two dying in infancy and one—Joseph Lawrence, surviving. This young man is as talented as one would naturally suppose the son of such parents would be. He graduated from Gaines school in, and is to-day one of the rising young men of Cincinnati.

Mrs. Jones taught in Mt. Healthy two years, Columbus, O., three years, and is now employed on Walnut Hills, where she has been for sixteen years. She is well known as a careful and conscientious instructor. Her first literary venture was in 1862, when she assisted J. P. Sampson, editor of *The Colored Citizen*, writing articles on various subjects. She has contributed to the *Christian Recorder*, and later she wrote regularly for the Indianapolis *World*, edited by the Bagby brothers. She is in constant demand by the different churches, literary societies, etc., to give readings and is seldom known to refuse. In 1883 she wrote a lecture which she delivered before large audiences in Dayton, Zanesville, Cincinnati, Walnut Hills and other places in the State, but was forced to retire from the lecture field because it interfered with her school duties. She was appointed a lady manager of the Col. Orphan Asylum in 1884 and holds the position at present. In early life she became a member of the Union Baptist Church, which position she holds to-day. She is not only a "church member," but one of the truest and best christians I have ever known. Her faith is in right living rather than in church creeds, and she looks forward to the time when all men shall believe in "one Lord, one faith and one baptism." She is the only one I ever knew who always urges something in favor of the erring, whether friend or foe, and who tries to see only the good in every one. Her religion is broad enough to cover with the mantle of charity every sinner in the land. She enjoys a good sermon whether delivered by one denomination or another, and is one of the most faithful of friends. Mr. Jones, whose health had been gradually failing for a number of years, gave up entirely in 1886. From that time until his death, which occurred Oct. 3, 1891, he was an invalid. For seven months he was bedfast, but was nursed with a tender patience that never even flagged for an instant. He bore his affliction through those long weary months with christian fortitude, and died in the triumphs of faith.

Mrs. Jones is one of the noblest of noble women. With discouragements of all kinds, she has kept on her way, a tender mother, a loving wife, a consistent christian and a faithful friend. Pure in heart, mind and conversation she has yet been misunderstood by many and has at times been the target for some evil minds, who would dare sully the brightness of the stars. But by those who know and appreciate her womanly qualities, she is dearly loved, and they all join in saying—
"May she live long and prosper."

"SISTER MARY."

TO the readers of "Ringwood" will be given a series of biographical sketches of Afro-American women who have done or are doing something to lift themselves and their race to a higher moral and intellectual plane. This will be done that the readers of this journal may not only become acquainted with what the women of the race are doing, but by their successes and achievements in the battle of life may be inspired to do even greater things, for Longfellow tells us :

Lives of great men all remind us
We can make our lives sublime,
And departing, leave behind us
Footprints on the sands of time.

It requires a number of flowers woven together to make a garland. It is the more brilliant and fragrant flowers of the garland, however, that attract attention. But sometimes we find under a leaf or peeping between petals, an humble little flower, and with careful touch we coax it from its hiding place and find that its tiny petals, delicate tints and sweet perfume add new beauty to our garland. To the list of women who will constitute the Ringwood garland, I send the name of Sister Mary. I send it not on account of any very brilliant achievements of hers, but as a souvenir to her many friends, who knew and loved her for her affectionate and sympathetic disposition and helpful and self-sacrificing spirit. To those who knew her not, I send it as an example of one who "learned the luxury of doing good." One of those to whom the Savior will say—" I was a hungered, and ye gave me meat : I was thirsty, and ye gave me drink : I was a stranger, and ye took me in : naked, and ye clothed me : I was sick, and ye visted me : I was in prison, and ye came unto me."

Mary Frances was the second of ten children of the Rev. Wallace and Mrs. Susan Sheldon. She was born in Cincinnati, Ohio, March 31, 1836. She was a delicate child and early became subject to severe sick headaches. This affliction followed her through life, but she was a most patient sufferer. She early developed such traits of character as not only endeared her to her mother, father, sisters and brothers, but to a very large circle of friends. While yet young, she shared with her mother the responsibilities of the care of the very large family. To her the father learned to look for assistance in entertaining the many who came to partake of his hospitality, and it was to " Sister Mary " the children would come for sympathy and help. She learned dressmaking and was soon self-supporting. At about the age of twenty-four she was married to James Buckner. Two children, a boy and a girl, were the fruit of this union. The boy died in infancy ; her daughter still lives. After her marriage she continued to follow the dressmaking business, and being a very skillful one she was always kept busy. Many times when help was hard to find and work was pressing, she would sew all night, and yet she was never so busy but what she could find time to go and minister to the sick. Often she has taken me with her on some errand of mercy, to see some poor one sick or in distress, and she never left them without doing something for their comfort and cheer. Strangers came to her, and on hearing the story of their misfortunes she would take them in and give them shelter and food. No one was ever turned from her door hungry or emptyhanded. I have known her to give and cheerfully too, the last cent of money she had to one in distress. There are many persons in this and other cities who remember with grateful hearts this woman who took them in, strangers though they were, and encouraged and helped them. Then there are many who when sick miss her gentle soothing touch, miss the nightly visits she would make them ; when all the world seemed wrapped in forgetful slumber, she would come and minister to their wants, comfort and cheer them. Many miss the sympathy that she so freely gave to the sorrowing or distressed. Her life was one of unceasing toil, toiling for others, thinking always of the happiness and comfort of others, always forgetting self. She wore her life away, and one night, the 22nd of May, 1888, the Master sent a hasty summons and her soul took its flight.

A. E. W., Cincinnati, O, *in Ringwood's Journal.*

SUSIE I. SHORTER, nee LANKFORD.

USIE ISABELLA was the eldest-born child to Whitten S. and Clarissa Lankford. She was born at Terra Haute, Indiana, January 4, 1859.

Her mother died when she was but fourteen, leaving her as the one who must care for and comfort a bereaved husband with five motherless little ones. She was attending Wilberforce University when her mother died.

Her father married soon afterward, and she went to Rockville, Indiana, where she was a successful teacher two years. Her third term as a teacher was spent at Richmond, Indiana—her home at that time—from which place she was married.

Soon after the death of her mother, the family moved to Baltimore, Maryland, where her father was pastor of Bethel A. M. E. Church. A little incident occurred which no doubt helped shape her future course. One evening near sunset a minister called to see her father. He had every look of a traveler; dusty, weary, hungry, almost forlorn. However, he was soon made presentable, and in the meantime Susie had spread a refreshing meal. He enjoyed it very much, he said, when he had finished; and pronounced the biscuit excellent (he had managed to consume eleven, though they were not very large). The young housekeeper was delighted that her father's guest—a stranger to her—had been made so welcome.

The minister was a professor of theology, and resided with his family near Xenia, Ohio. Chief among his friends there was a bachelor professor, to whom—as soon as they had welcomed each other—he related the little incident in Bethel parsonage, and recommended at once the little girl who could make such good biscuit as a suitable companion for a wife. Soon after this the second marriage of her father took place, and what with a new wife and fashionable hired girl, it was plainly seen that Susie was not needed; so she was allowed to return to Wilberforce, where, in spite of herself, she must come in contact daily with this bachelor professor, and he taught her all about the verb " love " and " to be " loved. They were married in 1878, by this same professor and minister who had enjoyed her hospitality so long ago—Dr. T. H. Jackson—assisted by Dr. B. F. Lee. It was many years afterward e'er Susie knew anything of this revelation, when the doctor mentioned it in her presence, in general conversation with Prof. Prioleau and wife, at their residence. Early in life she was inclined to write. She wrote a poem on the death of her mother, at the age of fourteen years, which was highly complimented. For many years she wrote occasional papers for the *Christian Recorder*, and is at present contributor to the news column of the same. She is possessed of a missionary spirit, and aids willingly any enterprise that has for its object the bettering of humanity.

HEROINES, BY MRS. SUSIE I. SHORTER.

Believing that much good can and will be derived from this amiable little book, we have asked the author's permission to republish a part of it in her column, " Plain talk to girls." (Editor.)

The crown and glory of man is woman, filling his very being with joy inexpressible.

Woman, beautiful being, grandest creation of earth, brightest star in Heaven !

Nothing is more lovely than a good woman; nothing more loathsome, more detestable than a vile woman.

The woman who lives a pure life, a Christian here and dies the Christian's death, is queen of earth and Heaven ; but what shall be the portion of the thousand and more women who live and die in degradation and sin ? Surely they will dwell in the lowest depths of utter darkness, where the sun of righteousness does not shine and where the wicked forever reap that they have sown.

Women occupy positions no other creatures can occupy— no others wield so great an influence for good or evil ; how necessary then that we have good women, pure, undefiled, pious, yea everything combined to make them fit for the end of their creation.

Who does not admire a beautiful woman! I do not mean beautiful because her face, form or general appearance may be fascinating or comely—but beautiful in thought, kind words, loving deeds, amiable in disposition, patient in everything, an example worthy of imitation.

Hands that are ever ready to assist the needy are beautiful hands, though they be rough from work or wrinkled with age.

The diamonds that sparkle in eyes of noble Christian women are far more precious than those which deck the crowns of royalties, or glisten on the throats of gaily dressed ladies of fashion.

The pearly tears, shed on account of a fallen woman, an orphan child, an ontraged or discouraged comrade, are more precious than rubies, they are but the outward sign of an inward sympathy, tender and true.

Those are lovely feet that go on errands of mercy to the hut of a poor widow, the haunts of poverty, even though they have only a cup of cold water to convey to the parched lips of some one slowly but surely dying.

Very much good is daily accomplished by other true women, who on account of some bodily affliction are not able to visit the sick, poor or distressed, but who prepare at home some little relish to tempt the appetite, some garment that will shut out the biting blasts of winter, perhaps a letter whose encouraging words may save some one from despair— for often timely words are the means of causing those who are cast down and those who resolve to go to the bad, to look up and see that life is not all shadows.

If ever the human heart needs sympathy and encouragement it is when crushed with sorrow, or heavy on account of a downfall, for when a woman (or man either) starts on the down grade very many are ready to give her a push, she is already conscious of her guilt, the sin gnaws continually, she feels to be an outcast, and if no kind spirit administers words of advice, she plunges hopelessly into the dark chasm beneath her, a ruined woman. But we thank God there are many noble women who are in His hands the instrument of doing much good for this class of individuals by their timely words, and for other needy ones whom they may not be able to visit in person, but to whom they send blessings by their children, not only benefiting the needy, but instilling within the bosoms of their children a spirit of true benevolence.

In all ages women have been leaders in good enterprises. Every truly great man owes his success in life to the careful training of his devout mother, who led him in the way of true greatness.

We speak of the nobleness of women of every age, of every clime—for every age and clime has produced noble women, *grand, good women*—but, the women of this busy, ever advancing age who shall claim our special attention are our women, the Negro women of America, the *Heroines of African Methodism.*

As far back as 1759 (more than a century ago) we find women leading in the cause of Christ, for the first black person baptized by John Wesley at Wordsworth, England, Nov. 30, 1759, was a Christian woman, and that same woman became the first black class leader in West India Isle.

In this, our beloved America, where the chains of slavery have long since been broken, where we can serve God north, east, south and west and fear no evil, two classes composed of Negroes were organized in 1766. Methodist class north by Phillip Embry, consisting of five members—a woman in the midst; Methodist class south by Robert Strawbridge, consisting of twelve members. One was a woman, Anna Switzer, who lived in a family of white Christians whose name she bore. They afterward moved to Brownsville, Penn., where Miss Bell Switzer, a descendant, taught in the Negro Sabbath-school. One of her bright-eyed boys—whose first teacher she was—was Poor Ben, who labored and ascended the ladder of true Christian progress, round by round, and is to-day before you one of the greatest of all men, black or white, of the century in which he lives. Bishop, leader, brother, friend, beloved by all on account of his pleasing manner, and yet, Bishop Benjamin W. Arnett owes all his true greatness, all his success in life to his dear mother, who led him in the right way. She lived to see her boy a noble, Christian man, then quietly fell asleep in Jesus.

When Bishop Wm. Paul Quinn went to the then far West to organize a church in St. Louis, Mo., he stopped at the home of one of our pioneer mothers, Mrs. Anna Baltimore. She was ever the friend of ministers, and showed the true courage of a brave woman by standing between the bishop and a cruel mob. Ever was she a faithful worker in the African Methodist Episcopal church, and God spared her to see a general conference in that place.

Phillis Wheatley was born in Africa and brought to Boston, Mass., in 1761. Though a slave she was allowed to improve her talent, and became a noted poetess. "She addressed a poem to the Earl of Dartmouth, who received it very kindly," also some complimentary verses to General Washington in 1776, during the War of the American Revolution. Like many other good women, she married a worthless man, and at last died in poverty. She has gone to the home of the soul where all is bliss, and in her beautiful compositions yet lives on earth.

Mary E. Ashe Lee, Lucretia Newman Coleman, Bertha B. Cook, Fannie Jackson Coppin, Josephine Silone Yates, Ida B. Wells, Josie D. Heard, Anna H. Jones, A. J. Cooper and Mary E. Church are but a few of the composers and poetesses of our times of whom we are proud, and very proud also are we that we have a Frances Ellen Watkins Harper, poetess and teacher, who was the first woman connected with the Union Seminary School, Columbus, Ohio, out of which grew our beloved Wilberforce.

We are proud of our women. Little as has been written concerning them, they are walking in all life's avenues successfully, daring and doing what the women of other varieties of the human race dare and do.

Listen to the strains of sweet music as they flow from the lips of Nellie E. Brown, Madame Selika, Harriet E. Freeman, Jennie Jackson, Lena Miller, Madam Dougan, Mattie E. Cheeks, Jennie Robinson Stewart, Cora Lee Watson, Anna S. Baltimore, Essie Fry Cook, Anna Jones Coleman, Hyers Sisters, and many others, and tell me, is any sound sweeter?

Hear the melody produced by Ernestine Clarke Nesbit, Gay Lewis, Bertha B. Cook, Hellen D. Handy (who so lately filled your courts with sweet music, but whose musical fingers are now still and cold in death), Mattie F. Roberts, Katie Stewart Bazel, Bertha Battles, Alice Richards, Gussie E. Clarke Jones, Mary E. Church, Dovie King, Anna L. Arnett, Ella Shepherd, and a number of others; listen, I say, as they ring sweet music from the piano, organ or violin, and tell me, is it not charming?

There was a time when we could not boast of women physicians and surgeons, but now we have S. B. Jones, Carrie V. Anderson Still, Consuello Clark, and others skilled in this profession.

Gaze upon the beautiful marble statue chiseled by the skilled hand of Edmonia Lewis, or behold a life-like portrait of your departed friend penciled by the artistic fingers of Mattie F. Roberts, and you behold work done by our women that will compare favorably with that done by women of other race varieties.

Sit in rapture and amazement at the feet of Hallie Quinn Brown, as in queen-like manner she personates every phase of life, and there acknowledge in woman an elocutionist who has few equals and fewer still superiors.

Visit stores managed and controlled by women like Kate Turner, Bell Johnson Highwarden, and Mary E. Williams, and be convinced that women can carry on business as successfully as men; indeed, we need not go North for examples of business women, for I believe the South is ahead. I remember reading in the *Southern Review* of April, 1890, published in this city, of a little mulatto woman, Jane Simmons, of Milledgeville, Ga., who is said to be the first woman in the South to become a butcher by profession. She can kill, clean and cut up more hogs in a day than any man in the country.

We have women also said to be successful lawyers, who can plead at the bar as earnestly and successfully as men.

The name of Amanda Smith has long been sung as a great benefactor, teacher and preacher, who, like Mrs. Mossell, Mrs. Bishop Campbell, and others, has a missionary spirit, laboring that those who sit in darkness may receive the light of this blessed gospel day.

Who shall estimate the worth of the band of faithful women who are teachers in our Sabbath-schools, day-schools, high schools, seminaries, colleges, and universities? All over this broad, free land of ours, wherever there is a hamlet, town or city, we find these earnest, faithful workers. Toil on, noble band, yours is the greatest of missions given to women (save the sacred mission given to mothers) however humble or obscure.   Susie I. Shorter, *in Ringwood's Journal.*

MRS. ROSA D. BOWSER.

WHEN revolutionary ideas shake society, and the condition of affairs in church or state calls for leaders, the demand is usually met. This is no whim of the mind, but a fact which history will establish beyond the shadow of a doubt. He who reads history with the eye of the philosopher will readily see the hand of Providence in the historic development of the race. This fact is very patent in the life of the one of whom we now proceed to give a brief pen picture. Rosa D. Bowser (*nee* Dixon) was born in Amelia county, Virginia. When she was but a child her parents moved to the city of Richmond, Va. Early in life her thirst for knowledge was great, hence as soon as an opportunity for attending school offered itself, she availed herself of it, entered school and began at once. She enjoyed her school life very much, and made rapid progress in her studies, and soon won the affection and esteem of her instructors and fellow pupils. Her design in acquiring a good education was to qualify herself for usefulness in a higher degree. She recognized the fact that much would depend upon the foundation laid in this the formative period of life, therefore she regarded it her duty to have a definite aim, to select for herself a vocation. The importance of this was seen from the simple and evident fact that the usefulness of every person depends wholly upon his own labors. This idea led the subject of our sketch onward, and as each new obstacle was surmounted she saw her fond object nearer her grasp, until finally, as a reward for her diligent labor, she had the gratification of gaining her coveted object, and the satisfaction of knowing that it was a recompense for her masterly exertion in the pursuit of knowledge. She pursued the course of study laid down in the various grades and finally graduated with distinction from the Normal School. Mrs. Bowser's makeup fitted her for work of teaching, therefore she began to teach soon after she got through with her course of study. If we are to decide from her work and the success attending her efforts, we are forced to conclude that she is a born teacher. She has in herself the element of a true teacher. That element is sympathy, a sympathy not merely intellectual in its nature, but a sympathy which flows from a community of life. This shows itself that she endeavors to help her pupils to become something in the world. This very effort upon her part has done much to enshrine her name in the hearts of hundreds of pupils whom she has taught. If the life she so nobly lives be lived again in souls she has moulded, it will be to her a monument more enduring than any art can devise. She taught school for seven successive years, and then was married to James H. Bowser, Esq., a scholarly gentleman, and a man of most upright Christian character. Mrs. Bowser's married life was brief, but it was full of pleasure and happiness ; and this was true because of the fact that she carried into this new relationship the same devotion and noble characteristics that she had exhibited all through her career.

Since the death of her husband, Mrs. Bowser has taught nine years in our public schools and has done her work in the same acceptable manner as in former years. Mrs. Bowser also taught very acceptably in a Summer Normal Institute, several summers ago, at Lynchburg, Va. Her course has been different from that of many of our young people who graduate from the schools. She gives herself to study and thus endeavors to advance in knowledge and to acquaint herself with the most improved methods of imparting information to others. Mrs. Bowser not only writes well, but she speaks with an ease and freedom of which many a man who regards himself something of a speaker would be proud. We would not close this sketch without calling attention to the fact that Mrs. Bowser became a Sunday-school scholar very early in life and soon saw the need of a personal Savior. She accepted Christ in the days of her youth, and began at once to make herself useful. She is found in all good work, whether it is the Church, Sunday-school, Y. M. C. A., or Missionary Society. The success which has come to Mrs. Bowser is largely due to this, that she recognizes the fact that the changes of earth are constantly occurring and they depend altogether upon the power that one has to do good or evil! She is strong in mind, in heart and in life, and day by day she is impressing the people with this fact. Mrs. Bowser is serving the second year as president of the Richmond Normal School Alumni and also of the Virginia Teachers' Association which meets at the V. N. & C. I. Petersburg, Va., in July. She is president of the Woman's Educational Convention of Richmond, Va.

Dr. Jos. E. Jones, in Ringwood's Journal.

Richmond, Va.

M. BELL JACKSON.

Singer.

THE subject of our sketch was born February 24, 1864, in Xenia, Ohio. She early convinced her parents, as well as all who came in her way that, no matter how well she might become fitted for other things, music burned its mellifluous incense upon her heart. Indeed, the appellation of

Jackson's singing girl was applied to her even before she could walk. The whole trend of her genius was given up to the fate which seemed to devour her, and hence, as early as eleven years of age she became a member of the Second Baptist

Church choir, of Springfield, Ohio, and there for a number of years demonstrated that, in the realm of song, the recipient of such a marvelous voice was worthy of the gift.

In 1889, she joined the Anthony Musical Concert Company, and traveled with them one year as the soloist. Soon after she was summoned to contract for the season of 1890 and 1891, to travel in the above capacity with the Nashville Students. Her press notices have been showered in profusion upon her. She is thoroughly awake

M. BELL JACKSON.

to the necessity of competency in her art, and is working with all the energy of her soul to rank among the greatest of our closing century.

MARIA BECRAFT.

MARIA BECRAFT was among the pioneer colored Catholics of America, a brilliant light. Her religious devotion and wonderful intelligence, as well as piety and refinement, marked for her a footprint "upon the sands of time," a paragraph in the history of her race.

She was born, 1805—attended school in Washington, 1812, and later attended the school taught by Mrs. Billings until

1820, when she, restless to do good for the race, opened a school and achieved marvelous success. In 1827 she was given new duties, more becoming the high place to which she had by dint and push elevated herself. Her beauty and high character inspired Father Vanlomen, the erudite priest, who transferred her to a larger house opposite the convent where she opened a boarding and day school for colored girls, which she conducted for four or more years. Later, she became a sister of a convent at Baltimore, where she was noted as a high teacher. Her name as a sister of Providence was Sister Aloyn.

ANNA ZINGA.

African Queen.

" A more odious spirit, licentious, blood-thirsty, and cruel, never inhabited the form of woman," says Mrs. Hale, " and yet she is deserving a place alongside of the great women of the world; for she, in understanding and ability, stepped far beyond her countrymen, and the circumstances under which she lived."

ZINGA was born in Matamba, in Africa, in 1592. Her father was what the European travelers and writers chose to term a king. What state or elevation could be assumed by a chief of Negroes and cannibals, it would be difficult to define; but, at all events, he was the principal personage of his tribe. Nothing can be said about a throne where a bench or chair was a rare and inappreciable luxury. Zinga manifested a craft and management by which she soon got the better of her brothers; and upon the death of her father, investing herself with the sacred character of priestess, became the leading spring of the people. At that time the Portugese and Dutch were attempting a rival influence on the coast of Africa, for commercial purposes; religious difficulties became involved in this rivalship; there were no doubt many missionaries of high and pure motives, while others, forgetting their message of peace, served to exacerbate the opposition among Christians. Zinga had the good sense to appreciate the advantages she could derive from the Christians; she visited the

Portugese settlement, ingratiated herself with the Governor, and was baptized. With their aid she soon made herself predominant among all the tribes of the neighborhood ; and as soon as she had destroyed all whom she might have feared, she abjured her new faith and returned to her idols. For some time she lived feared and respected among her own people ; but perpetrating acts of despotic cruelty too terrible for detail, she soon became wearied of reigning over a race of trembling savages. Her intercourse with the Portugese had taught her the advantages of civilization, and her own sagacity perceived that the introduction of Christianity could alone improve her nation. She sent for priests, and again became a nominal member of the Christian church. She was now sixty-five years old, and determined to remain faithful to the injunctions of the missionaries. Her example was followed by those who surrounded her ; and had she lived, the spirit of the gospel might have tempered this savage race, but a sudden illness put an end to her existence in 1663.

Her courage and vigor were remarkable ; she was naturally formed for government, and her native capacity and energy would, in a different country and with suitable education, have made a great queen ; while her extreme hardness of heart must have rendered her hateful and repulsive as a woman , still, she exhibited better dispositions than any king of her race had ever done, and she was the first of her tribe who made any attempt to adopt Christianity. Had she been born and brought up under its blessed light, how different would have been her character and her destiny ! When such instances of the capacity of the colored race are brought before us, we should be awakened to the importance of sending the gospel and the means of instruction to the wretched millions of women and children in Africa.

MISS ELIZABETH TAYLOR GREENFIELD.

The Famous Songstress (The "Black Swan").

IT is very difficult for the historian to say a few words of one that has so nearly reached perfection in the art of music and song, hence, the danger of saying too little, when so much fitting and appropriate should be said, but as Mr. Trotter's Music and Some Highly Musical People, also her complete biography, are at our command, we take the liberty of plucking such as we hope may not prove burdensome to our readers. As they will see further along in this sketch that the press, critics and music lovers have gone into ecstasies, captivated and completely captured when even prompted by a spirit of curiosity to hear the African nightingale, the peer of Patti, Nilsson, Jenny Lind or Parodi.

She was not of vanity, nevertheless a child of nature, a *vis a tergo* controlled her being and taught her the true lessons of sublimity. Notwithstanding she knew the power of her voice, and the perfection of her attitude to command through curiosity, because of her formidable color, she heeded her inmost natural feelings and stood fair with all mankind.

She was better known as the "Black Swan" in both America and Europe. Her career in song and music having almost annihilated her Elizabeth Taylor Greenfield cognomen.

"She was born of slave parents, in Natchez, Miss., in the year 1809. When but a year old she was brought to Philadelphia by an exemplary Quaker lady by whom she was carefully reared. Between these two persons there ever existed the warm affection that is felt by mother and daughter. In the year 1844 this good lady died. In her will, the subject of this sketch was remembered by a substantial legacy. The will was contested however, and she never received the bequest. Her family name was Taylor; but, in honor of her benefactress and guardian, she took the latter's name—Greenfield. Previous to the death of this lady, Elizabeth had become distinguished in the limited circle in which she was known for her remarkable powers of voice. Its tender thrill-

ing tones often lightened the weight of age in one who was
beloved by her as a mother."

By indomitable will she surmounted difficulties almost invincible. At first she taught herself crude accompaniments to her
songs, and intuitively perceiving the agreement or disagree-
ment of them, improvised and repeated until there was heard
floating upon the air a very 'lovely song of one that had a
pleasant voice, and could play well upon a guitar.'

"There dwelt in the neighborhood of Mrs. Greenfield a
physician, humane and courteous; capable too, of distinguishing and appreciating merit and genius under whatever prejudices and disadvantages they were presented. His daughter,
herself an amateur in the science of harmonious sounds, heard
of Elizabeth's peculiar structure of mind. Miss Price invited
her to her house. She listened with delighted surprise to her
songs. She offered to accompany her upon the guitar. This
was a concurrence of circumstances which formed the era of
her life. Her pulses quickened as she stood and watched the
fair Anglo-Saxon fingers of her young patroness run over the
key-board of a full toned pianaforte, eliciting sweet, sad,
sacred, solemn sounds. Emotion well-nigh overcame her; but
the gentle encouragement of her fair young friend dissipated
her fears and increased her confidence. She sang; and before
she had finished she was surrounded by the astonished inmates
of the house, who, attracted by the remarkable compass and
sweetness of her voice, stealthily entered the room, and now,
unperceived, stood gathered behind her. The applause which
followed the first trial, before this small, but intelligent audience, gratified as much as embarrassed her, from the unexpected and sudden surprise. She not only received an invitation to repeat her visit, but Miss Price, for a reasonable com-
pensation, undertook her instruction in the first rudiments of
music. The progress of genius is not like that of common
minds. It is needless to say that her improvement was very
rapid."

"But the lessons above mentioned were taken quite
privately and without, at first, the knowledge of her guardian.

Elizabeth was rapidly acquiring an acquaintance with music, when some one maliciously informed Mrs. Greenfield, with the expectation of seeing an injunction laid upon the pupil's efforts.   The old lady sent for Elizabeth, who came tremblingly into her presence, expecting to be reprimanded for her pursuit of an art forbidden by the Friends' discipline. 'Elizabeth,' said she, 'is it true that thee is learning music and can play upon the guitar?' 'It is true,' was her reply. 'Go get thy guitar and let me hear thee sing.' Elizabeth did so; and when she had concluded her song, she was astonished to hear the kind lady say: 'Elizabeth, whatever thee wants thee shall have.' From that time her guardian was the patroness of her earnest efforts for skill and knowledge in musical science. She began to receive invitations to entertain private parties by the exhibition of the gift which the God of nature had bestowed."

Upon the death of her patroness, in consequence of the contested will she found herself thrown upon her own resources for a maintenance. Remembering some friends in the western part of New York, she resolved to visit them.

While crossing Lake Seneca, en route to Buffalo, there came sweetly stealing upon the senses of the passengers of the steamer her rich, full, round, clear voice, unmarred by any flaw. The lady passengers, especially the noble Mrs. General P., feeling that the power and sweetness of her voice deserved attention, urged her to sing again, and were not satisfied until five or six more songs were given to them. Before reaching their destined port she had made many friends. The philanthropic Mrs. General P. became her friend and patroness. She at once invited Elizabeth to her splendid mansion in Buffalo, and, learning her simple story, promptly advised her to devote herself entirely to the science of music. During her visit a private party was given by this lady, to which all the elite of the city were invited. Elizabeth acquitted herself so admirably that two days after a card of invitation to her through the public press, signed by the prominent gentlemen of Buffalo, requested her to give a series of concerts.

In October, 1851, she sang before the Buffalo Musical Association, and her performances were received with marks of approbation from the best musical talent in the city. That established her reputation as a songstress. "Give the 'Black Swan,'" said they, 'the cultivation and experience of the fair Swede or Mlle. Parodi, and she will rank favorably with those popular singers who have carried the nation into captivity by their rare musical abilities. Her voice has a full, round sound and is of immense compass and depth. She strikes every note in a clear and well-defined manner, and reaches the highest capacity of the human voice with wonderful ease and apparently an entire want of exertion. Beginning with G in the bass clef, she runs up the scale to E in the treble clef, and gives each note its full power and tone. She commences at the highest note and runs down the scale with the same ease that she strikes any other lower note. The fact that she accomplishes this with no apparent exertion is surprising, and fixes at once the marvelous strength of her vocal organs. Her voice is wholly natural, and, as might be expected, lacks the training and exquisite cultivation that belongs to the skillful Italian singer. But the *voice* is there, and, as a famous maestro once said, 'It takes a hundred things to make a complete singer, of which a good voice is ninety-nine.' If this be so, Miss Greenfield is on the verge of excellence, and it remains for the public to decide whether she shall have the means to pursue her studies."

"To several gentlemen in Buffalo belongs the credit of having first brought out Miss Greenfield in the concert room. The Buffalo papers took the matter in hand and assured the public they had much to expect from a concert from this vocalist. The deep interest her first public efforts elicited from them gave occasion to the following certificate:

BUFFALO, Oct. 80, 1851.

MR. H. E. HOWARD.

Dear Sir: At your suggestion, for the purpose of enabling Miss Elizabeth T. Greenfield to show to her Philadelphia friends the popularity she has acquired in this city, I cheerfully certify as follows:

The concert got up for her was unsolicited on her part and entirely the result of admiration of her vocal powers by a number of our most respectable citizens, who had heard her at the residence of General Potter, with whose family she had become somewhat familiar. The concert was attended by an audience not second in point of numbers to any given here before, except by Jennie Lind, and not second to any in point of respectability and fashion. The performance of Miss Greenfield was received with great applause, and the expression since, among our citizens generally, is a strong desire to hear her again.

Respectfully yours, etc.,

G. REED WILSON.

Rochester next extended an invitation for her to visit that city, which we copy :

The undersigned having heard of the musical ability of Miss Greenfield, of the city of Buffalo, and being desirous of having her sing in Rochester, request that she will give a public concert in this city at an early day, and feel confident that it will afford a satisfactory entertainment to our citizens.

(Signed by a large number of the most respected citizens in Rochester.)

ROCHESTER, December 6, 1851.

This evening in Corinthian Hall, the anticipated entertainment is to be presented to our music-loving citizens. Curiosity will lead many to attend, to whom the performance of a colored prima-donna is a phenomenon at once wonderful and rare. Miss Greenfield has received from all who have heard her the name of being a vocalist of extraordinary power.

Speaking of her concert in Rochester, *The Express* says:

On Monday, Parodi, in all her splendor, sustained by Patti and Strakosch, sang at Corinthian Hall to half a house. Last night Miss Greenfield sang at the same place to a crowded house of the respectable, cultivated and fashionable people of the city. Jenny Lind has never drawn a better house, as to character, than that which listened with evident satisfaction to the unheralded and almost unknown African Nightingale. Curiosity did something for her, but not all. She has merit, very great merit ; and with cultivation (instruction) she will rank among the very first vocalists of the age. She has a voice of great sweetness and power, with a wider range from the lowest to the highest notes, than we have ever listened to ; flexibility is not wanting, and her control of it is beyond example for a new and untaught vocalist. Her performance was received with marked approbation and applause from those who knew what to applaud.

Another city paper says:

Much has been said and written of this personage since she was introduced to the public as a musical prodigy. All sorts of surmises and conjectures have been indulged in respecting the claim put forth of her merit, and generally the impression seemed to prevail that the novelty of ' color' and idle curiosity accounted more for the excitement raised than her musical powers. Well, she has visited our place, and given our citizens an opportunity of judging for themselves. We are ignorant of music and unqualified to criticise. But a large audience was in attendance at Ringueberg Hall last evening. Among those present were our musical amateurs, and we heard but one expression in regard to the new vocalist, and that was wonder and astonishment at the extraordinary power and compass of her voice ; and the ease with which she passed from the highest to the lowest notes seemed without effort. Her first notes of " Where are now the hopes? " startled the whole audience, and the interchange of glances succeeded by thunders of applause at the end of the first verse showed that her success was complete. She was loudly encored, and in response sang the baritone, " When stars are in the quiet sky," which took down the whole house.

We have neither time nor space to follow her through her different pieces. Suffice it to say, that there never was a concert given in this town which appeared to give more general satisfaction, and every person we met on leaving the hall expressed their entire approbation of her performance. No higher compliment could be paid to the "Swan," than the enthusiastic applause which successfully greeted her appearance, and the encore which followed her several pieces.

There was a very general expression among the audience that the sable vocalist should give another concert, and at the earnest solicitation of several of our citizens, Colonel Wood, her gentlemanly manager, has consented to give another entertainment to-morrow evening, when the "Black Swan " will give a new programme, consisting of some of Jenny Lind's most popular songs.

The concert on Thursday evening was what in other cases would have been called a triumph. The house was full, the audience a fashionable one, the applause decided, and the impression made by the singer highly favorable.

We can safely say that Miss Greenfield possesses a voice of remarkable qualities ; singular for its power, softness and depth. She has applied herself with praiseworthy perseverance and assiduity to the cultivation of her extraordinary powers, and has attained great proficiency in the art which is evidently the bent of her genius. By her own energy and unassisted, she has made herself mistress of the harp, guitar and piano. We are informed that the proceeds of the entertainment this evening are to be wholly appropriated to the completion of her musical education in Paris under the world-famed Garcia. We predict for Miss Greenfield a successful and brilliant future.

The Rochester *American* says :

Corinthian Hall contained a large and fashionable audience on the occasion of the concert by this new candidate for popular favor on Thursday evening. We have never seen an audience more curiously expectant than this was for the *debut* of this new vocalist. Hardly had her first notes fallen upon their ears, however, before their wonder and astonishment were manifest in an interchange of glances and words of approval ; and the hearty applause that responded to the first verse she sang was good evidence of the satisfaction she afforded. The aria, " O native scenes !" was loudly encored ; and in response she gave the pretty ballad, " When Stars are in the Quiet Sky. "

The Buffalo *Commercial Advertiser* says :

Miss Greenfield is about twenty-five years of age, and has received what musical education she has in the city of Philadelphia ; she is, however, eminently self-taught, possessing fine taste and a nice appreciation, with a voice of wonderful compass, clearness and flexibility. She renders the compositions of some of the best masters in a style which would be perfectly satisfactory to the authors themselves. Her low, or properly *bass* notes, are wonderful, especially for a female voice ; and in these she far excels any singing we have ever heard.

We learn that this singer (soon to become celebrated, we opine) will give a concert in this city on Thursday next. There is no doubt that the novelty of hearing a colored woman perform the most difficult music with extraordinary ability will give *éclat* to the concert. All representations unite in ascribing to Miss Greenfield the most extraordinary talents, and a power and sweetness of vocalization that are really unsurpassed.

The *Daily State Register*, Albany, Jan., 19, 1852, said :

THE "BLACK SWAN'S " CONCERT.—Miss Greenfield made her *début* in this city on Saturday evening, before a large and brilliant audience, in the lecture room of the Young Men's Association. The concert was a complete triumph for her ; won, too, from a discriminating auditory not likely to be caught with chaff, and none too willing to suffer admiration to get the better of prejudice. Her singing more than met the expectations of her hearers, and elicited the heartiest applause and frequent encores. She possesses a truly wonderful voice ; and considering the poverty of her advantages, she uses it with surprising taste and effect. In sweetness, power, compass and flexibility, it nearly equals any of the foreign vocalists who have visited our country ; and it needs only the training and education theirs have received to outstrip them all.

The compass of her marvellous voice embraces twenty-seven notes, reaching from the sonorous bass of a baritone to a few notes above even Jenny Lind's highest. The defects which the critic cannotfail to detect in her singing are not from want of voice, or power of lung, but want of training alone. If her present tour proves successful, as it now bids fair to, she will put herself under the charge of the best masters of singing in Europe ; and with her enthusiasm and perseverance, which belong to genius, she cannot fail to ultimately triumph over all obstacles, and even conquer the prejudice of color— perhaps the most formidable one in her path.

She plays with ability upon the piano, harp and guitar. In her deportment she bears herself well, and, we are told, converses with much intelligence. We noticed among the audience Governor Hunt and family, both Houses of the Legislature, State officers and a large number of our leading citizens. All came away astonished and delighted.

A New York paper says:

MISS GREENFIELD'S SINGING.—We yesterday had the pleasure of hearing the singer who is advertised in our columns as the "Black Swan." She is a person of lady-like manners, elegant form, and not unpleasing, though decidedly African features. Of her marvellous powers she owes none to any tincture of European blood. Her voice is truly wonderful, both in its compass and truth. A more correct intonation, so far as our ear can decide, there could not be. She strikes every note on the exact centre, with unhesitating decision. . . . . She is a nondescript, an original. We cannot think any common destiny awaits her.

The *Evening Transcript*, Boston, Feb. 4, 1852, said:

Miss Greenfield, the "Black Swan," made her *debut* before a Boston audience last evening at the Melodeon. In consequence of the price of the tickets being put at a dollar, the house was not over two-thirds full. She was well received, and most vociferously applauded and encored in every piece. She sings with great ease, and apparently without any effort. Her pronunciation is very correct, and her intonation excellent. Her voice has a wonderful compass and in many notes is remarkably sweet in tone.

From The *Daily Capital City Fact*, Columbus, Ohio, March 3, 1852:

Last evening proved that the "Black Swan" was all that the journals say of her; and Miss Greenfield stands confessedly before the Columbus world a swan of excellence. She is indeed a remarkable swan. Although colored as dark as Ethiopa, she utters notes as pure as if uttered in the words of the Adriatic.

From The Milwaukee *Sentinel*, April, 1852:

What shall we say? That we were delighted and surprised? All who were present know that from their own feelings. We can only say that we have never heard a voice like hers—one that with such ease and with such absence of all effort, could range from the highest to the lowest notes.

Said a Rochester (N. Y.) paper of May 6, 1852:

The magnificent quality of her voice, its great power, flexibility, and compass, her self-taught genius, energy and perseverence, combine to render Miss Greenfield an object of uncommon interest to musicians. We have been spellbound by the ravishing tones of Patti, Sontag, Malibran and Grisi; we have heard the wondrous warblings of the *nightingale*, and we have listened with delight to the sweet melodies of the fair daughter of Erin, but we hesitate not to assert that, with one year's tuition from the world-famed Emanuel Garcia, Miss

Greenfield would not only compare favorably with any of the distinguished artists above named, but incomparably excel them all.

The *Globe*, Toronto, May 12–15, 1852, said :

Anyone who went to the concert of Miss Greenfield on Thursday last expecting to find that he had been deceived by the puffs of the American press, must have found himself most agreeably disappointed. . . .

After he [the pianist] had retired, there was a general hush of expectation to see the entrance of the vocalist of the evening; and presently there appeared a lady of a decidedly dark color, rather inclined to an *embonpoint* and with African formation of face. She advanced calmly to the front of the platform, and courtesied very gracefully to the audience. There was a moment of pause and the assembly anxiously listened to the first notes. They were quite sufficient. The amazing power of the voice, the flexibility and the ease of execution, took the hearers by surprise; and the singer was hardly allowed to finish the verse, ere she was greeted with a most enthusiastic applause, which continued for some time. The higher passages of the air were given with clearness and fullness, indicating a soprano voice of great power. The song was encored and Miss Greenfield came back, took her seat at the piano, and began, to the astonishment of the audience a different air in a deep and very clear bass or baritone voice, which she maintained throughout, without any very great appearance of effort or without her breaking. She can in fact go as low as Lablache or as high as Jenny Lind— a power of voice perfectly astonishing. It is said she can strike thirty-one full clear notes; and we could readily believe it.

From a Brattleborrough (Vt.) paper, June 23, 1852 :

The "Black Swan," or Miss Elizabeth Greenfield, sang in Mr. Fisk's beautiful new hall on Wednesday evening last to a large and intelligent audience.

We had seen frequent notices in our exchanges, and were already prepossessed in favor of the abilities and life purposes of our sable sister; but, after all, we must say that our expectations of her success are greater than before we had heard her sing and conversed with her in her own private room. She is not pretty, but plain. . . . Still she is gifted with a beauty of soul which makes her countenance agreeable in conversation, and in singing, especially when her social nature is called into activity, there is a grace and beauty in her manner which soon make those unaccustomed to her race forget all but the melody. . . .

Nature has done more for Miss Greenfield than any musical prodigy we have met, and art has marred her execution less.

But the limits of this book are such as to preclude my giving all or even a hundredth part of the testimonials and criticisms pertaining to the singing of this wonderful Negro woman, that filled choice spaces in the American newspapers during her captivating career in the United States.

Doubtless our readers are buoyant as well as enthused over what they have already read. The few excerpts in commendation of her abilities are simply fair words of praise as compared to others too lengthy to publish here.

After singing in nearly all the free States, she resolved to carry out her long entertained purpose of visiting Europe, in order to perfect herself in the technique of her art. Learning of her intentions, the citizens of Buffalo, N. Y., united in tendering her a grand testimonial and benefit concert. The invitation was couched in terms most flattering, and signed by many of the most distinguished residents.

The concert took place on March 7, 1853, and was in all respects a grand success.

Leaving Buffalo, she went to New York, where, after singing before an audience of four thousand persons, she received the following complimentary note:

NEW YORK, April 2, 1853.

MISS ELIZABETH T. GREENFIELD.

Madam: By the suggestion of many enthusiastic admirers of your talent, I have been induced to address you on the subject of another and second concert, prior to your departure for Europe. Your advent musical in Gotham has not been idly heralded among the true lovers of song, and admirers of exalted genius, of which your unprecedented success on Wednesday evening must have sufficiently convinced you; while all are eloquent in the commendation of your superior powers and engaging method.

Confiding, madam, in your reported magnanimity and generosity to oblige, I will divest myself of tedious circumlocution, and fervently exhort you to make a second exhibition of your skill, which, there can be no doubt, will be highly successful to you, and as interesting to your admirers.

THE PUBLIC.

Miss Greenfield embarked from New York in a British steamer for England, April 6, 1853, and arrived in Liverpool the 16th of April, 1853; rested over the Sabbath, and proceeded Monday morning to London, in which metropolis she became safely domiciled on the evening of the same day. But painful trials awaited her from a quarter the most unexpected. The individual with whom she had drawn up the contract for this musical tour was unfaithful to his promises, and she found herself abandoned without money and without friends in a strange country.

She had been told Lord Shaftesbury was one of the great, good men of England, and she resolved to call upon him in person, and intreat an interview. His Lordship immediately granted her request, listened patiently to her history, and directly gave her a letter of introduction to his lawyer.

It may perhaps be considered a providential concurrence that Mrs. Harriet Beecher Stowe was in London this same time with Miss Greenfield. We notice in her " Sunny Memories," under the date of May 6th, the following remarks : ' A good many calls this morning. Among others came Miss Greenfield, the so-called " Black Swan." She appears to be a gentle, amiable, and interesting young person. She has a most astonishing voice. C. sat down to the piano, and played while she sang. Her voice runs through a compass of three octaves and a fourth. This is four notes more than Malibran's. She sings a most magnificent tenor, with such a breadth and volume of sound that, with your back turned, you could not imagine it to be a woman. While she was there, Mrs. S. C. Hall, of the " Irish Sketches," was announced. I told her of Miss Greenfield, and she took great interest in her, and requested her to sing something for her. C. played the accompaniment, and she sang " Old Folks at Home," first in a soprano voice, and then in a tenor or baritone. Mrs. Hall was amazed and delighted, and entered at once into her cause. She said she would call with me, and present her to Sir George Smart, who is at the head of the Queen's musical establishment, and, of course, the acknowledged leader of London musical judgment.

"In the course of the day I had a note from Mrs. Hall, saying that, as Sir George Smart was about leaving town, she had not waited for me, but had taken Miss Greenfield to him herself. She writes that she was really astonished and charmed at the wonderful weight, compass and power of her voice. He was also as well pleased with the mind in her singing, and her quickness in doing and catching all that he told her. Should she have a public opportunity to perform, he offered to hear her rehearse beforehand. Mrs. Hall says: "This is a great deal for him, whose hours are all marked with gold."

Again Mrs. Stowe says: " To-day the Duchess of Sutherland called with the Duchess of Argyle. Miss Greenfield happened to be present and I begged leave to present her, giving a slight sketch of her history. I was pleased with the kind and easy affability with which the Duchess of Sutherland conversed with her, and betraying by no inflection of voice, and nothing in her air or manner, the great lady talking with the poor girl. She asked all her questions with as much delicacy, and made her request to hear her sing with as much consideration and politeness as if she had been addressing any one in her own circle. She seemed much pleased with her singing and remarked that she should be happy to give her an opportunity of performing in Stafford House as soon as she should be a little relieved of a heavy cold which seemed to oppress her at present. This, of course, will be decisive of her favor in London. The Duchess is to let us know when the arrangement is completed.

"I never so fully realized," continues Mrs. Stowe, "that there really is no natural prejudice against color in the human mind. Miss Greenfield is a dark mulattress, of a pleasing and gentle face, though by no means handsome. She is short and thickset, with a chest of great amplitude, as one would think on hearing her tenor. I have never seen in any of the persons to whom I have presented her the least indications of suppressed surprise or disgust, any more than we should exhibit on the reception of a dark-complexioned Spaniard or Portuguese.

"Miss Greenfield bears her success with much quietness and good sense.

"Her Grace, the Duchess of Sutherland, afterward became her ever unfailing supporter and adviser.

"The piano-forte which previously had been furnished Miss Greenfield to practice upon was taken from her. The Duchess of Sutherland, upon learning the fact, immediately directed her to select one from Broadwood's.

We cannot refrain from quoting Mrs. Stowe's description of the concert, after dinner, at the Stafford House:

The concert room was the brilliant and picturesque hall I have before described to you. It looked more picture-like and dreamy than ever. The piano was on the flat stairway just below the broad central landing. It was a grand piano, standing end outward and perfectly banked up among hot-house flowers, so that only its gilded top was visible. Sir George Smart presided. The choicest of the *elite* were there, ladies in demi-toilet and bonneted. Miss Greenfield stood among the singers on the staircase and excited a pathetic murmur among the audience. She is not handsome, but looked very well. She has a pleasing dark face, wore a black velvet headdress and white Cornelian ear rings, a black moire-antique silk made high in the neck with white lace falling sleeves and white gloves. A certain gentleness of manner and self-possession, the result of the universal kindness shown her, sat well upon her. Chevalier Bunsen, the Prussian ambassador, sat by me. He looked at her with much interest. "Are the race often as good looking?" he said. I said: "She is not handsome compared with many, though I confess she looks uncommonly well to-day." The singing was beautiful. Six of the most cultivated glee singers of London sang among other things, "Spring's Delights are now Returning," and "Where the Bee sucks, there lurk I." The Duchess said, "These glees are peculiarly English."

Miss Greenfield's turn for singing now came, and there was profound attention. Her voice, with its keen, searching fire, its penetrating vibrant quality, its *timbre* as the French have it, cut its way like a Damascus blade to the heart. She sang the ballad, "Old Folks at Home," giving one verse in the soprano, and another in the tenor voice. As she stood partially concealed by the piano, Chevalier Bunsen thought that the tenor part was performed by one of the gentlemen. He was perfectly astonished when he discovered that it was by her. This was rapturously encored. Between the parts, Sir George took her to the piano and tried her voice by skips, striking notes here and there at random, without connection, from D in alto to A first space in bass clef. She followed with unerring precision, striking the sound nearly at the same instant his finger touched the key. This brought out a burst of applause.

Lord Shaftesbury was there. He came and spoke to us after the concert. Speaking of Miss Greenfield, he said:

I consider the use of these halls for the encouragement of an outcast race a consecration. This is the true use of wealth and splendor, when they are employed to raise up and encourage the despised and forgotten.

TUESDAY, May 31, 1853.

Miss Greenfield's first public morning concert took place at the Queen's Concert rooms, Hanover square. She came out under the immediate patronage of her Grace, the Duchess of Sutherland ; her Grace, the Duchess of Norfolk, and the Earl and Countess of Shaftesbury. It commenced at three o'clock and terminated at five.

The London *Morning Post* says :

A large assemblage of fashionable and distinguished personages assembled by invitation at Stafford House to hear and decide upon the merits of a phenomenon in the musical world, Miss Elizabeth Greenfield, better known in America as the "Black Swan," under which sobriquet she is also about to be presented to the British public. This lady is said to possess a voice embracing the extraordinary compass of nearly three octaves, and her performances on this occasion elicited the unmistakable evidence of gratification

The London *Times* said :

Miss Greenfield sings, "I know that my Redeemer liveth," with as much pathos, power and effect, as does the "Swedish Nightingale," Jenny Lind.

Again, the London *Observer* remarks :

Her voice was at once declared to be one of extraordinary compass. Both her high and low notes were heard with wonder by the assembled amateurs, and her ear was pronounced to be excellent.

The London *Advertiser*, of June 16th, contained the following comments :

A concert was given at Exeter Hall last evening by Miss Greenfield, the American vocalist, better known in this country under the sobriquet of the "Black Swan." Apart from the natural gifts with which this lady is endowed, the great musical skill which she has acquired, both as a singer and an instrumentalist, is a convincing argument against the assertion so often made, that the Negro race is incapable of intellectual culture of a high standard. Her voice is a contralto, of great clearness and mellow tone in the upper register, and full, resonant and powerful in the lower, though slightly masculine in its *timbre*. It is peculiarly effective in ballad songs of the pathetic cast, several of which Miss Greenfield sang last night in a very expressive manner. She was encored in two, "The Cradle Song," a simple melody by Wallace, and "Home, Sweet Home," which she gave in an exceedingly pleasing manner. The programme of the concert was bountifully drawn up, for in addition to the attractions of the "Black Swan," there was a host of first-rate artists. Herr Brandt, a German artist with a remarkably sweet voice, sang Professor Longfellow's "Slave's Dream," set to very beautiful music by Hatton, in a way that elicited warm applause. Miss Rosina Bentley, a fantasia by Lutz, very brilliantly, and afterward assisted by Miss Kate Lorder (who, however, must now be known as Mrs. Henry Thompson), in a grand duet for two pianofortes, by Osborne. M. Valadares executed a curious Indian air, "Hilli Milli Puniah," on the violin, and Mr. Henry Distin, a solo on the sax-tuba. The band was admirable, and performed a couple of overtures in the best manner. Altogether, the concert, which we understand was made under the distinguished patronage of the Duchess of Sutherland, was highly successful, and went off to the perfect gratification of a numerous and fashionable audience.

In July, she gave two grand concerts in the Town Hall in Brighton, under the patronage of her Grace, the Duchess of Sutherland; her Grace, the Duchess of Norfolk; her Grace, the Duchess of Beaufort; her Grace, the Duchess of Argyle; the Most Noble, the Marchioness of Ailesbury; the Most Noble, the Marchioness of Kildare, the Most Noble, the Marquis of Lansdowne; the Earl and Countess of Shaftesbury; the Earl of Carlisle; the Countess of Jersey; the Countess of Granville, the Countess of Wilton; the Viscountess Palmerston; the Lady Constance Grosvenor, and Mrs. Harriet Beecher Stowe.

Vocalists.—Miss E. T. Greenfield (the "Black Swan"), Madame Taccani, Countess Tasca, Mr. Emanuel Roberts (Queen's Concerts).

Instrumentalists.—Piano-forte soloists, Miss Rosina Bentley (pupil of Miss Kate Lorder); violin, M. de Valadares (pupil of the Conservatoire, Paris); accompanist, Mon. Edouard Henri; conductor, Mr. F. Theseus Stevens.

She gave a series of concerts at the Rotunda, in Dublin, Ireland.

In October, 1853, we find her again at the Beaumont Institution, Beaumont Square, Mile End, London, at Mr. Cotton's concert, supported by Miss Poole, the Misses Alpine, Miss Alleyne, Mr. Augustus Braham, Mr. Suchet Champion, Mr. Charles Cotton, the German Glee Union, and the East Indian violinist, M. de Valadares; conductor, Herr Ganz.

These testimonials are a few of the one thousand at our command, but since it is the desire of the author to please as well as to portray, we must close this sketch here. The music people of both continents have been startled with wonder and amazement time and time again, when confronted by the proofs of indwelling genius which seems to be inherent in the Negro race.

White, the violinist, had pleased two continents with his violin, Blind Tom had done as much with his piano, Elizabeth Taylor Greenfield, the wonderful musical nightingale, with her voice, drew unto her the kings, queens and nobility of the Old as well as the New Continent.

Her return from London to America was attended with flattering ceremonies and grand circumstances. Her trip resulted in much benefit, intrinsical as well as artistical, adding decided *éclat* to her professional reputation.

MRS. FANNIE JACKSON COPPIN.

Founder of a College, Teacher, Lecturer, Writer, Great Scholar.

PROF. GEO. W. WILLIAMS, in his "History of the Negro Race in America," says: Fanny M. Jackson, at present Mrs. Fanny Jackson Coppin, was born in the District of Columbia, in 1837. Though left an orphan when quite a child, Mrs. Sarrah Clark, her aunt, took charge of her and gave her a first-class education. She prosecuted the gentlemen's course in Oberlin College, and graduated with honors.

Deeply impressed with the need of educated teachers for the schools of her race, she accepted a position at once in the Institute for colored youth at Philadelphia, Pa. And here for many years she has taught with eminent success, and exerted a pure and womanly influence upon all the students that have come into her classes. Without doubt she is the most thoroughly competent and successful of the colored women teachers of her time.

Her example of race pride, industry, enthusiasm and nobility of character will remain the inheritance and inspiration of the pupils of the school she helped make the pride of the colored people of Pennsylvania.

Says *Ringwood's Journal:*

Mrs. Fannie Jackson Coppin has probably attained more fame as a teacher than any of the noble Afro-American women of the age. There are many whose work has been as noble in conscientious efforts as hers, but few and probably none have been as conspicuous as hers, nor as long. The opportunities that presented themselves to her in her early life were presented to but few Afro-American women forty years ago. That she grasped them has been made evident by her pre-eminent life of highest usefulness. If the capability of Afro-American women to govern were questioned, her wonderful achievements as the principal of the Youth's Academy of Philadelphia would establish it beyond question. Mrs. Coppin's fame has been won by her success in a colored school. There are others, probably not so extensively known, but whose success as teachers in white schools has been quite as effective in establishing the ability of Afro-American women. Miss Richards, of Detroit, Mich.; Mrs. Rev. George Booth, *nee* McGlin, formerly of New Haven, Ct.; Miss Sarah Mitchell and Miss Dever, of Cleveland, Ohio, have done effectual work in the establishment of our ability.

Their accumulative work has given Afro-American women an enviable reputation with the educators of the country. The primary work of these ladies was attended with the greatest difficulties. They met race prejudice, and successfully vanquished it, at least to so large a degree that in the cities in which they teach no Afro-American woman is denied a position as teacher on account of her race connection.

The exquisite qualities of these five women have justly won them the affectionate regards of the race.

Says *The Colored American:*

THE WOMAN'S LEAGUE.—ITS QUARTERLY MEETING A GRAND SUCCESS IN EVERY WAY.—AN OVATION TO MRS. FANNIE JACKSON COPPIN BY HER MANY ADMIRERS.—A PEN PICTURE.

The quarterly meeting of the Colored Woman's League, held last Monday evening in the Fifteenth Street Presbyterian

Church, was largely attended by members and friends of the organization, which promises to be a great power for good. After the transaction of business the speaker of the evening was introduced by the president, Mrs. John F. Cook, who reminded us that Mrs. Coppin is a Washingtonian by birth, spoke in glowing terms of her worth and achievements, and recalled the fact that at Oberlin, where she graduated with high honors, she was a classmate of the present president of Wellesley College.

Mrs. Coppin, whose integrity of heart, purity of life, vigor of faculties and extent of attainments are acknowledged by all, was warmly greeted by the audience, whom she promised to address in an informal manner.

Mrs. Coppin's stature is commanding, her face strong, but kindly in expression, her manner pleasing but dignified. Without manuscript the speaker proceeded to pay a beautiful tribute to the women of past generations whose many deeds of heroism, though not recorded, are nevertheless facts of unwritten history. By the thoughtlessness and unreasonableness of those who ignore the services of these women pioneers, many of whom worked early and late to buy the babes they bore in their arms, a great injustice has been done, for these noble souls fought their part of the battle successfully and heroically.

The necessity of building up a strong character was earnestly and eloquently urged upon us. The invincible quality of character, said the speaker, is the prerequisite of a race striving to progress and prosper. Teachers play an important part in solving the problem. First-class pupils are possible only when we have first-class teachers, who are the great soul artists in the school-room, the makers of men and women. The graduates of Howard University have done great service, and have been powers for good all over the country. The father of the Black Prince, when urged to send assistance to his son who was hard pressed in battle, refused to do so and insisted that he should win his spurs. Like the Black Prince we are sore-pressed in the battle of life, but our Heavenly Father insists that we win our own spurs. What we do for ourselves is that which ennobles and enlarges.

Men have their part to perform, for they must see to it that the fifteenth amendment has its face-value. The right of petition is a powerful weapon of defense. Lawlessness, insubordination and hatred are the bloody angle of our race battle.

According to Mrs. Coppin, the Colored Woman's League is not a sudden outcropping of a wild idea. Fifteen years ago she, herself, and others, were earnestly inquiring how our battle should be fought, and were advocating organization. Mrs. Coppin then proceeded to a rhetorical annihilation of young writers who give gratuitous advice to their elders, making sweeping statements concerning what was not, but should have been done in the past, and fancy they are originating plans which are older than the youthful enthusiasts themselves.

Many of our young women, tenderly reared and carefully educated, who go down South as teachers, succumb to the hardships and privations to which they are not accustomed. We cannot make martyrs of all the young women who may acquire an education. Mrs. Coppin then related how a beautiful young woman of her acquaintance taught in the South, where her health was destroyed by the long walks she was obliged to take in all sorts of weather, and the bad fare to which she was not accustomed. At the expiration of two years she returned home and died. "I once visited an organization of white women who were seated in a magnificent building of their own, when a petition to commute the sentence of a murderess was brought to them, and they were requested to sign it. They were terror-stricken that they should be asked to sign such a petition." "But," said Mrs. Coppin, "I thought of the beautiful young woman who was obliged to go South, because she could find no employment at home and I asked myself if these women were wholly guiltless of her murder. I then asked myself why we have not an organization of our own. A hundred men can lift a log together very easily, but when only a few take hold at a time very little is accomplished. So no one of us can promise to find employment for our young women, but when we combine our forces it becomes an easy matter.

" First, a building must be secured, and it must be as large as possible. Then classes must be formed in art, needle-work, book-keeping, dress-making, Latin, German, French, millinery, cooking, in short instructions must be given in every trade and avocation in which women may engage."

Mrs. Coppin laid great stress upon the necessity and importance of paying special attention to the household department. Our girls must be taught how to cook on rational and scientific principles; they must be instructed in housekeeping, so that their houses may be economically managed and tastefully arranged.

Cooking has been lifted far above the station it formerly occupied and is now considered a dignified avocation. Learned professors are engaged to instruct cooking classes. They show the human stomach, explain its organization and lecture on chemistry and hygiene as it relates to food. Women must learn how to cook to suit men, who are such artists in all that pertains to eating. Mrs. Coppin assured us that a good cook could eventually convert a democrat into a republican and an atheist into a Christian by tickling their palates with tooth-some dishes.

We need statistics and statisticians, who shall record what we do. We need facts to answer arguments of those who underrate us. We possess much talent and genius of which we are not aware. A young woman who is a successful com-poser of music, but who is buried in obscurity, recently came to Mrs. Coppin's notice, and there are doubtless others equally talented of whom we have not heard. We must know what strength we possess. The proposal to uniform Roman slaves was once rejected because, said a philosopher, they would thus learn their numbers and know their strength. When people are conscious of possessing strength, they rapidly grow stronger. The Colored Woman's League will thus supply a long-felt want in gathering and disseminating statistics. Mrs. Coppin reminded us that there had been many abortive attempts at organization which has ended in windy declamations and inflammatory speeches.

After imploring women who have the leisure to devote themselves earnestly to the work in hand, and encouraging the League on what had already been accomplished, Mrs. Coppin concluded her address.

ESSIE FRY COOKE.

Musician, Talented Contralto Singer.

THIS favored young lady was born in Indianapolis, Ind., in 1868. At quite an early age she manifested an unusual talent for music and most especially that instrument that so beautifully adorns the parlor and whose tones remove the greedy gloom from so many hospitable homes, viz. the pianoforte.

Her parents, thoughtful of her future, very highly respected that wish uppermost in her heart and without hesitancy procured both piano as well as teacher worthy of the name, and started her on toward the high mark she has reached. In 1881 Essie was placed under the instruction of that distinguished teacher, Prof. Frank N. Scott, and he, becoming so charmed by her matchless range of voice, advised her to sing contralto; this she did for four years, convincing as well as establishing an enviable reputation as a contraltist.

Later Mr. Scott organized a troupe of singers, and offered Miss Cooke the greatest inducements to travel, which she accepted, and soon the F. N. SCOTT INDIANIAN's became quite famous. Weary of travel and the footlights, as well as the seas of faces, she retired from the stage until 1888, when she joined Milton A. Boyer's Troupe, traveling all over the West. But so unprepared did she feel herself for life's duties, that she could no longer restrain the principles within and her eagerness of advancing to a finish, that she again retired in 1890 and was placed under the tutelage of Prof. Gill, of Chicago. There she made such progress in music and song that she elicited the greatest plaudits from both press and people.

ESSIE FRY COOKE.

On returning to Indianapolis the aristocratic churches of the white race offered her special inducements for her services as soloist in their choirs, but, owing to the dismay engendered by feelings of having to decide which congregation she would serve, she did the next best thing and went again on the stage, singing with the Fisk Jubilees.

At this writing Miss Cooke is pursuing the higher rudiments of music in Philadelphia, under the instruction of Prof. Gouldezer, of Germany.

Though young, with only a portion of her latent genius at work portraying the sagacity and erudition of many twice her age, we shall watch her career with much interest, fully believing that when all the dormant energies of this heart, mind and soul are set in motion, great will the outcome be.

NELLIE E. BROWN MITCHELL

NELLIE E. BROWN MITCHELL, of Dover, New Hampshire, who in a very few years has, by the great beauty of her voice, and the exhibition of many noble qualities of heart and mind, won a name of which she and all of her admiring friends may justly be proud.

To Miss Caroline Broċkett our subject is indebted the *admonition* which has in later years made her famous. Then at quite an early age the rhythm of nature, as much as the musical notes which reached her ear, convinced her youthful mind of dearest *love*, fondest but not impatient desire to startle the music-loving world with a correctness of the human voice, and demonstrate that untrammeled opportunities could for her, as for Patti, Parodi and Jennie Lind, make her at last appreciative and much admired, if not famous.

She sailed out upon the broad billows of life with hoisted sails and banners unfurled, having inscribed thereupon Excelsior.

She says : " My motto is ' Excelsior.' I am resolved to give myself up wholly to the study of music, and endeavor, in spite of obstacles, to become an accòmplished artist." It may be observed that none but those actuated by the most noble motives, and who give utterance to such inspiring words as these, do become "accomplished artists."

The following have reference to Miss Brown's appearance in Boston during the musical season 1874 :

Said The Boston *Traveler*, April, 16th :

Miss Nellie E. Brown has for some months been the leading soprano at Grace Church, at Haverhill, Mass., which position she has filled with eminent acceptance, and with marked exhibition of artistic powers."

At another time above named paper said :

Miss Brown possesses a very fine voice of excellent culture, and gave with much taste several solos. Noticeably good was her rendering of Torrey's "La Prima Vera." In all her selections she exhibited excellent style and finish.

The *Globe*, March 31st, said :

Miss Nellie E. Brown showed a particularly well-modulated voice, trained study and appreciative method, which served her well in the pleasant rendering given by her so gracefully and unaffectedly.

The same paper, after alluding to her rendition of " Del Criel Regina," said :

This lady is fortunate in her exceedingly sweet and well-trained voice, which, in conjunction with her fine personal appearance and stage manners, rendered her reception unusually enthusiastic.

Speaking of an entertainment given at Parker Memorial Hall, a musical writer said:

Miss Brown has a charming voice and sings with intelligent expression and good taste. Two of her songs, " Beautiful Erin " and " Bonnie Dundee, " were rendered with great sweetness."

The Boston *Advertiser*, March 31st, said:

She has an exceptionally pure voice which has been carefully trained.

The *Transcript* April 16th, said:

A soprano of good voice and cultivation.

The *Journal*, June 13, 1874, said:

A talented vocalist, with a well-cultivated voice of a remarkably fine quality. She pleased very greatly in several selections.

Said The *Post*, Nov. 13th:

An artist of exceptional merit, possessing a voice of rare compass, flexibility and sweetness. In the solo, " Land of My Birth," by Operti, she received enthusiastic applause.

Mr. Trotter says: " Miss Brown has sung in quite a number of the large towns and cities of Massachusetts, in which State she is scarcely less a favorite than in New Hampshire. She has appeared in company at concerts with some of the most eminent artists of the country (such as, for instance, Prof. Eugene Thayer, J. F. Rudolphsen, Myron W. Whitney, Mrs. Julia Houston West, Mrs. H. M. Smith, and others), and always with fine success. In her own city and State she enjoys a popularity unequaled by any other cantatrice, her beautiful voice and many excellent traits of character winning her the warmest esteem of all. The people of Dover are very proud of her, and greatly delighted that one of their number is received with such marks of enthusiastic favor in other States. The Dover people always readily recall these triumphs, and proudly speak of her as ' our prima donna.'"

MISS MARY PROUT.

Eminent Pioneer Teacher.

MISS MARY PROUT is celebrated as one of our early teachers in Baltimore. She was beloved for her piety and religious devotion. Bishop Paine says she was born in 1800, and was still living in 1882. She was a prominent member of Bethel, and was considered one of its shining lights.

MRS. C. W. MOSSELL.

Missionary Christian Martyr.

MRS. REV. C. W. MOSSELL takes a prominent place in the history of our race as a daring missionary giantess. She is gone from her labors to reward. Her work still lives. Her monument lives in the hearts of all Haytians. Like the great Rock of Ages, her memory towers in the mind of those to whom she carried the missionary light.

MRS. C. W. MOSSELL.

The bread which she cast upon those West India waters are being gathered by the grand A. M. E. Church, after many days. Her eulogy expressed by Hon. Jno. M. Langston, is so splendid in rhetoric, so touching with love and a sacrifice of life, that we can find no words fitting with which to approach its sublimity and truth.

She laid her life upon the missionary altar that the truth might be known concerning Jesus. She held a light to guide the wanderer, and left a footprint as an emblem, announcing the birth of a Christian era upon the West India Isles. In her death our sainted brother lost a noble, true and sublime helpmate. Rev. C. W. Mossell, as others, mourns the death of a saint, for she was a Christian.

MISS FLORENCE RAY.

Eminent Teacher.

BISHOP DANIEL A. PAYNE, in the footnotes of his "Recollections of Seventy Years," says: "Rev. C. B. Ray is the father of three daughters now living, of whom he

has great reason to rejoice, because they have been well educated in the homestead as well as in the public schools of New
York.

Their sound and wholesome education has been manifest
to all acquainted with them, both in the school-room and in
the social circle.   All their lives, since the attainment of
mature womanhood, have been spent in the training of children—than which neither man nor woman can be more hon-
orably employed.   Miss Florence, second in age, has always
distinguished herself by her studious habits, and made commendable progress in German literature.   I can truly say it
was a real and a solid enjoyment to spend an evening in the
hospitable and refined home of this sainted man.   He has
left behind him a sweet, noble-hearted widow, and three interesting daughters, whom we have reason to believe and to
hope will honor his memory as they have adorned his life."

ANNIE MARIA HALL.

Pioneer Teacher of Washington, D. C.

MRS. ANNIE MARIA HALL ranks among the pioneer teachers of the Negro race.   Having conducted
successfully a school first started on Capitol Hill, she moved
after ten years to a more commodious structure, and continued
her labors until finally she moved to a house still standing on E.
Street, North, between Eleventh and Twelfth, West, and there
taught many years.   Prof. G. Williams in his history says of
her:

"She was a colored woman from Prince Georges' county,
Maryland, and had a respectable education which she obtained
at school with white children in Alexandria.   Her husband
died early, leaving her with children to support, and she
betook herself to the work of a teacher, which she loved and
in which for not less than twenty-five years she met with uniform success.   Her schools were all quite large, and the many
who remember her as their teacher speak of her with very
great respect."

EARNESTINE C. NESBITT.

Writer, Musician.

MRS. EARNESTINE C. NESBITT (*nee* Clark), daughter of Prof. Peter H. Clark, is a sweet and scientific singer, as well as a talented pianist and instructress. Mrs. Nesbitt has the distinguishing honor of being editress of the MOTHERS CORNER in Ringwood's, Journal of Fashion, an illustrated magazine, really edited and published by the women of the Negro race; the most brilliant attempt and most successful literary journal of the present day displaying the genius of our women.

DR. CONSUELLO CLARK.

Physician, Musician.

DR. CONSUELLO CLARK is a sweet singer and pianist. Quite early in life she inculcated the ideas of *Similia similibus curantur*, and nothing, not even the musical gift possessed by her which would have in many overthrown any apparently foreign desire to be anything else, yet man had not only set the example in the classics, he had said, "Come, follow," and thus in the professions, as few have made their advent, Miss Clark, feeling that fruits ripened to an abundant harvest, but for her sex there were no footprints of discovery, felt it her duty to explore those untrodden solitudes and gather those rich fruits and bring them as votive offerings to the profession. She is a gifted scholar, a practical as well as theoretical physician, a close student and stands out in bold relief reflecting credit on the profession of medicine and showing the capacity of women to follow in the occult avenues of thought, science and fine arts wherein men lead.

RANAVALONA III.

Queen of Madagascar.

THE Queen of Madagascar, Ranavalona III., who is a dignified, sensible woman, mounted the throne and was crowned in 1883, succeeding her aunt, Queen Ranavalona II., being chosen by her predecessor to succeed her, but was also formerly elected to the office.

According to the custom of the country, the queen on her accession married Ramalalarivond, the prime minister of the

QUEEN OF MADAGASCAR.
Ranavalona III.

kingdom, who had also been the husband of the last queen. The present queen has always been eager to forward the development of the people. She has embraced Christianity for herself and made it the State religion. The Hovas are a good fighting race, and their experience in repelling the recent French invasion has developed them greatly in a military. way.

Their civilization, also, has been advanced in spite of the war, during the past few years under the wise administration of the present queen. The queen has a council of advisers, but the royal will is supreme in every case.

The French minister, resident in Madagascar, has advised his government to confer the decoration of the Legion of Honor on the queen, regarding her friendship worthy of the gift.— *The Biographical Review.*

MARY S. PEAKE.

First Teacher at Fortress Monroe, Abolitionist, Christian Worker.

OF the many teachers employed to train the colored youths of the Southland, Mary S. Peake has merited the highest encomiums from the lips of an orator, the praise from the pen. The immortal Mrs. Hannaford says, in her *Daughters of America :*

The American Tract Society has issued a little volume as a deserved tribute to one Christian woman—a free colored woman, whose father was a white man, Mary S. Peake, who was the first teacher at Fortress Monroe. After long years of silent and, as many felt, unrighteous ignoring of the question of slavery, the American Tract Society at last gave the medal of praise to Christian effort without regard to race or color.

CHARLOTTE E. RAY.

Judge, Practices in the Supreme Court of the District of Columbia—Gifted Scholar—First Lady Lawyer of Washington.

UNDER the extensively treated subject, Women Lawyers, in *Daughters of America*, by Mrs. Phœba A. Hannaford, is found this glowing tribute to our own Charlotte E. Ray :

In the city of Washington, where a few years ago colored women were bought and sold under sanction of law, a woman of African descent has been admitted to practice at the bar of the Supreme Court of the District of

Columbia. Miss Charlotte E. Ray, who has the honor of being the first lady lawyer in Washington, is a graduate of the Law College of Howard University, and is said to be a dusky mulatto, possessing quite an intelligent countenance. She doubtless has also a fine mind and deserves success.

Her special endowments make her one of the best lawyers on corporations in the country ; her eloquence is commendable for her sex in the court-room, and her legal advice is authoritative.

SOJOURNER TRUTH.

Abolitionist, Anti-Slavery Agitator, Writer, Lecturer and Race Champion.

DURING the close of the 18th century a Negro girl became as much by blood as by circumstances an adapted daughter of genius and fame, but it remained for the 19th century, with its civilizing influences, to apply the finishing touch to make her what indeed and in truth she was, a woman and very forcibly so a rare specimen of the female kind. Though black and disfigured by force of circumstances and surroundings, yet within a capacious breast beat a heart which had a place for every unfortunate being, a head which contained a brain full of thought and grand knowledge characteristic of the oddity of her name.

Her life was all her name implies, and if nothing more could be said, her distinction is already gained, but does Sojourner Truth claim greatness? We think so, but for the thrilling appeals of this grand woman in many a public hall throughout the North and East we doubt not that a sad condition of affairs would to-day be the lot of every Southern Negro. Her work as an antislavery giantess commends itself, and fastens us in praise of her with bands of steel.

On one occasion Hon. Frederick Douglass was making a public address to 5,000 people, in which he made some disparaging remarks concerning the Negro's condition in America, in this fashion :

" We are doomed to go down, doomed to extinction, etc. " Sojourner Truth, then a very old lady, hobbled up the aisle toward the speaker. shouting: "Stop, Frederick; stop, Frederick, don't say that, does God live? He is not dead, neither has He gone off on a journey."

ANTI-SLAVERY LEADERS.

Mrs. Harriet H. Robinson, in her book entitled, "The Woman Suffrage Movement," does not hesitate to give our subject justice, for she says, In speaking of the Anti-slavery society which met in Worcester, Mass., Oct. 23 and 24, 1850: "Representative men and women were present from the different States, among whom were the following conspicuous speakers: Wendell Phillips, William Lloyd Garrison, C. C. Burleigh, W. H. Channing, Stephen S. Foster, Abby Kelly Foster, Lucretia Mott, Sojourner Truth" and many others whose names are too numerous for mention in this brief sketch.

Mr. Fairbanks, in his book entitled " How the War was Prepared," says of Sojourner Truth : " We were standing in the great East room, when she came walking in, and approaching the marshal said : "I want to see President Lincoln." " Well, the President is busy, I think, and you can't see him now." " Yes, I must see him. If he knew I was here, he'd come down and see me." Finally the marshal went to the President's room with a statement of the case, when the President said : " I guarantee she is Sojourner Truth. Bring her up here."

And here she came, and we just approached near enough to catch the glimpses, and hear the words of greeting : " Sojouner Truth, *how glad I am to see you.*" The President bought her book; then handing him her photograph she said : "It's got a black face, but a white back, and I'd like one of yours with a *green back.*"

That was too good. The President laughed heartily; then putting his fingers into his vest pocket, and handing her a ten-dollar bill, said : "There is my face with a green back."

NOTE: For further information concerning Sojourner Truth read in another place in this book Sojourner Truth, Amander Smith and Frances E. W. Harper compared.

MRS. JENNIE E. SHARPE.

A Returned Liberian Missionary.

MRS. JENNIE E. SHARPE, who has been in Western Africa since 1883 as a teacher sent out by the Boston Board of Control of Liberia College. and is now in St. Louis, gives some interesting facts with regard to the civilization of African tribes.

" There is no country in the world," said she, " more misrepresented than Western Africa. The situation there is thoroughly misunderstood. From the accounts in books one would be led to suppose that the natives were very ignorant and degraded. This is far from the fact. While the tribes are largely illiterate, they are usually bright and capable of a high degree of cultivation. There is one tribe in the interior of which I wish particularly to speak—the tribe of Mandingos, nearly all of whom, by the way, are Mohammedans. They are very skillful in the working of brass, gold and iron. Three young girls of this tribe were sent to me to attend my school in Liberia. They came in their savage state, clothed only in a string of beads, but had the culture and acuteness of children of good families in this country. By this I mean that they were disposed to gentleness and refinement and were capable of learning rapidly. The Veys are another tribe of considerable culture. They have a written monosyllabic language, the only written language of Interior Africa.

" It is just here the missionary societies make a mistake. They think that all Africans are ignoramuses, and that therefore ignoramuses are good enough to send to teach them ; while the fact is the natives are astute and it requires a good deal of tact to reach them. The missionary societies have so far done comparatively little good. Their emissaries seem to go at their work in a half-hearted sort of way and present the most unlovely side of the cause to which they expect to make converts.

" But there is an important field to work and I think it must be reached through Liberia. Liberia has already done more than all the foreign missionaries together to civilize the tribes of Interior and Western Africa, and if good schools were established and good teachers trained in the African Republic, there is no limit to the possibilities in the direction of civilization. I think that Africa must be civilized through the descendants of Africa. Let the best educated of the race in this country there seek a field for their labors. The resources of the African republic are vast and awaiting development. Schools, churches and colleges are awaiting founding and support. The work is a grand one. I believe that Liberia can be made a beacon light to illuminate Africa.

" To be sure, those who emigrate from here to Liberia must be prepared to endure hardship, as the first settlers did here, but there are no obstacles which cannot easily be surmounted. They must not take words of disgusted, lazy colonists, nor yet squeamish missionaries, but go with a purpose and judge for themselves. I have no patience with those who fight over the race problem here. Let the descendants of Africa raise themselves by culture and they cannot fail to command respect. There is a field for their best energies in Liberia."

Mrs. Sharpe is in the country to recuperate lost health and intends returning to her labors among her race in Liberia in about six months. In the meantime she will enlighten Americans on the condition of the civilization problem there, and try to arouse a sentiment in favor of her views.

MISS IDA B. WELLS (IOLA).

IT would in our judgment, should we attempt to say over every good thing that has been said of Miss Wells, indeed fill a volume, consisting of the grand and noble experiences as well as the hardships through which she has passed in the South. Since " there is a tide in the affairs of men which, taken at the flood, leads on to fortune." Miss Wells' position and responsibility actuated and prompted by the highest motives to be a benefactress to her race, were very similar to that of Frederick Douglass, when it is taken into consideration that distinc-

tion and fame are the result of the efforts put forth, and the
manner in which she braved the tide. Her forcible pen, her
caustic oddness, have disarmed the disputing South as to
women's ability and set up a sign-post portraying their power
with the pen, where the tombstone of doubt had so long remained. A symbol of Negro genius becomes the proud boast
of Southern contemporaries.

She was born in Holly Springs, Mississippi, where was

MISS IDA B. WELLS.

offered her the best educational advantages. At quite
an early age the dreams and
aspirations of her youth were
placed at a disadvantage,
owing to the early death of
her parents and the assump-
tion of unexpected responsibilities—that of not only
caring for number one, but
for her five brothers and
sisters. To say that she discharged her new duties as
two-fold-guardian, as not
only sister but parent, was
quite enough to inspire her
young life, as indeed for
this alone she is a heroine,
but what a world of good-
ness the harmony of that
useful and sacrificing life
fortells. We believe that Miss Wells possesses the greatest
love for woman in her realm, and chooses her profession
for no other reason than helping to improve our status in
journalism. Felicia Hemans to her is the portrayal of male
mockery, the Amazons are pictures of horror. She is teaching
the nation that sublime lesson of *modesty unchanged* even at
the severest test.

For several years she was editress of the Memphis *Free*

Speech, a paper which for news and circulation was the pride of the cultured Negroes of Tennessee.

Many Negro newspapers have been honored by her and more liberally patronized consequent of her ready articles touching the many phases of Negro progress. Among them the New York *Age*, the Indianapolis *World*, *Gate City Press*, the Detroit *Plaindealer*, Little Rock *Sun*, the A. M. E. Church *Review*, the Memphis *Watchman*, have all spoken editorially touching her ability. Our subject possesses that dignified pluck, which Webster fails to define, and being protected by the respect which man endeavors to possess for woman she has been able to touch as well as treat at length articles upon which our man editors have shown the greatest reluctance. In this respect Miss Wells left locality out of the question, and wrote what was wanting, naming persons, places, things.

Having by her tireless efforts for the good of the Negro race been "lead on to fortune" after braving the tide (not of adversity) for so many well-spent years in Memphis where she was a noted teacher, she contrived to do what she knew would be perilous. Looking danger full in the face she wrote a series of articles which for force are seldom equaled upon the outrages perpetrated upon the Negro, read the proof and started for New York City, her then future home. These treats to loyal lovers of liberty came out and started a wave of indignation, and for the wrongs done the Negro the gap which of late had become narrowed by Southern cupidity and deceit grew spontaneously into a broad abyss, and so terrible was the spark set to inflame and engender activity on the part of the Negro that the State of Tennessee suffered severely from the shock.

Previous to going to New York she in person visited Oklahoma, as she had so long read of it as a haven of rest free from depredations upon the Negro, and after spending a few days there learning all that she could of the Territory she painted the *dwarf State* in its proper colorings. Thousands of persons who had resolved upon what they should do, the following year, at once relaxed the feelings of departure, and

reasoned as Hamlet, " Better to bear the ills we have than fly
to those we know not of." Later, as we have already stated,
owing to outrages and depredations Miss Wells "took up arms
aginst a seat of trouble," that by opposing might endthem.

She is now a *citoyenne* of New York by adoption. As
formerly with her Southern friends she remains to-day, only a
sufficient distance which, being the metropolis city and State,
lends enchantment around the world. Her readers remain the
same, only the magnetic force of her pen enjoys a broader
scope. Before her audience was a multitude. Now it is the
nation. Ten thousand minds fly out to her in their adoration and
praise. Ten thousand hearts throb with exaltation in witnessing her triumphs. The New York *Age* is possibly made better by
reason of Miss Wells' association on the staff, for those who
know Mr. Fortune credit him with being one of our greatest
men, and great men adopt only such means as will improve
and make sure their success.

Miss Ida B. Wells continues as heretofore to dignify herself, her calling and prove the wonderful depth of her powers
of conception of right. She concedes to the fact that a certain
class of American citizens are Negroes, but because of that
fact it does not necessitate that such a class should be made a
"side show" at the World's Fair. Her paper before the
literati of Boston was forcible, logical and full of meaning ;
yet calm as a summer's stream, and wonderfully sublime. She
demonstrated the fact that it is adverse to the thought and
feeling of the Negroes of the South to be *set apart* on the
occasion of the World's Fair, and womanly denied the attachment of her name to the World's Columbian Jubilee Day Circular. The Negro of the South, as well as the Negro of the
North, has in her a champion for their cause.

This world indeed would be very queer if all could judge
alike. Some capable writers differ in opinions, just as men differ
in politics. The *Freeman* mildly expresses it when it says that
the editorial below is "How some women reason:"

Miss Willetta Johnson, of Boston, secretary of the " Colored
Jubilee Day " committee, is " all put out " at Miss Ida B. Wells,

because she had head enough not to indorse the "Jubilee
Day," and without writing her down a "horrid old thing!"
for the simple reason that Miss Wells is young and comely she
says several little spiteful things, which reminds us, laughingly,
how some women reason. Addressing our good brother of
the Boston *Courant,* she drops such pearls as these, referring
directly to Miss Wells.

*   *   *   *   *   *   *   *   *

I desire to express my surprise that one of our own people should not
appreciate the great benefit to the colored race if the World's Fair management will but accord them the honor of a day's recognition.

*   *   *   *   *   *   *   *   *

In a dignified and comprehensive way seek to mark an epoch in the history of the colored race that shall go down with the other great and worthy
results of the Fair

*   *   *   *   *   *   *   *   *

Why Miss Wells in particular should attack this committee, which is
just as legally constituted as any committee, and the people of Massachusetts
who have rallied round and supported her in her hour of sorrow and need is
strange to say the least.

*   *   *   *   *   *   *   *   *

The first two "pearls" may speak for themselves, and of
the last we have no apprehension that Miss Wells took
umbrage at the inoffensive "committee" or cared a straw
whether it was legally constituted or not, but at the foolish
block-headed thing it seemed anxious to persuade the race to
do. But the most womanly retort of the whole pronuncia-
mento, and quite inexcusable, if not coarse, is the reference to
what "Massachusetts" had done for Miss Wells "in her hour
of sorrow and need." We don't suppose that this good lady
speaks for the colored people of Massachusetts, when she thus
holds forth, but if she does so much the worse for Massachusetts. Only very womanly women, and "queer" men
reason like that. Because Massachusetts, in a burst of race
fealty and enthusiasm, chose to honor herself by honoring
this plucky little race lady from the South, what then did it
follow, that in the act of becoming the guest of the "Old Bay
State," and its soulful hospitality, she gave up her right to
opinion on matters affecting her people?—*The Freeman.*

MISS WELL'S CONGRATULATIONS.

EDITOR FREEMAN :

Accept my congratulations on the editorial in current *Freeman* against the Afro-American Jubilee Day at the World's Fair. It is in the nature of things that we cannot always agree on matters affecting race interest, but this is one in which every self-respecting person, it seems to me, can agree. I am more than gratified to find the *Freeman* in line. The Afro-American press is a gradually growing power and rightly used it will at last win the race's victory.   Respectfully, IDA B. WELLS,

NEW YORK, Feb. 25.

Among those who are doing lasting and beneficial work for the race, the name of Miss Ida B. Wells is entitled to high consideration. Born to the end of the high calling to elevate and defend her race from internal and outside adversaries, her life has been marked by a steadiness of aim and consistency of endeavors which seldom fail to attract the attention of posterity, to say the least. Whether in the schoolroom, behind her pen or before the public, her blows have been as nails driven in sure places. For years the press and teacher's desk have been her native field, until routed by the enemy, who little thought that though successful in driving this heroine from her sectional strongholds, they were conducting her footsteps to higher vantage grounds.—*The Christian Recorder.*

The action of the Memphis (Tenn.) *Commercial*, in using grossly insulting language toward the brilliant and self-sacrificing Miss Ida B. Wells, is indeed reprehensive and deserving of the severest censure.

The article does more to show up the coarseness and vulgarity in the editor that it does in reality injure Miss Wells. No gentleman would be guilty of such language, and it is to be regretted that a newspaper of the standing of the *Commercial* should be disgraced by such a person as the one who occupies the editorial chair. Southern spite and hatred are exercised upon the innocent and the defenseless.

Miss Wells need feel in no wise embarrassed or cast down. That God who has shielded and protected her thus far will stand by her to the end.

In the meantime our people owe it to themselves to aid this young lady by doing all in their power to strengthen her in her mission, that the American people may be aroused to the enormity of lynch-law and its kindred ends.—*Richmond Planet.*

Miss Ida B. Wells has been invited by the Moral Educational Association to read a paper before the Ladies' Physiological Institute, at Boston, Mass., Jan. 26, 1893.

From an editorial from the pen of Dr. H. T. Johnson concerning the Philadelphia Conference, we clip the following tribute to Miss Ida B. Wells:

Among the most prominent visitors to the Conference were Bishops B. F. Lee, Turner, Grant and Ward; General Officers Embry, Coppin, Green, Armstrong, Johnson, (editor); Drs. Seaton, Sampson, Morgan, Hannah, and Editor Ida B. Wells. But few made speeches. Those worthy of note were Bishop Lee, who said some wise witty things; Bishop Grant, who lifted the conference out of its boots, to speak elegantly; Bishop Turner, who was himself, and at his best; Dr. Emory, embrionically dull and droll, but who woke things up as he warmed in process; Dr. Green, the leonine disputant and tripod spokesman of the *Southern Recorder.* Dr. Coppin made some happy hits on the race question, the climax of which was capped by the dauntless but exiled "Iola," whose unique and inimitable speech won the conference, and so excited sympathy in her behalf that it were well for her Memphian adversaries that they were in their distant safety in the lower regions of the Mississippi Valley.

While our book is in the press, Miss Wells sojourns among the good and patriotic people of Scotland. At the solicitation of friends to outraged humanity, she has crossed the Atlantic to affiliate with them, to confer as to the best plans to be laid, to reach some conclusion in the attempt of setting forth a remedy for the evils practiced by one class, and adopt methods to lift our people out of many of the shameful conditions consequent of two hundred and fifty years of serfdom. The Constitution provides certain amendments, fostered by the chivalry of the republican party, but the rights that these amendments set forth have not been protected nor subserved for the good of those of our race who live in the South. We truly hope that the desired end and aims of this conference may be duly met. It will be the noble response to a people yet grateful, whose hearts and minds are ever prayerful for deliverance, and an ensign forever reminding all ·future generations that there still lives a just God, a generous people, who will lift up an appealing and grateful race. God is guiding Miss Wells.

MISS SARAH FORTEN.

MISS SARAH FORTEN, another one of our brainy women, is deserving especial mention here, from the fact that her conspicuous efforts to reform the depraved sentiment of the country concerning the human tie was not in vain. She addressed the following lines to the White Anti-slavery Women's Convention, soliciting their co-operation :

> We are thy sisters, God has truly said,
> That of one blood all nations He has made.
> O Christian woman! in a Christian land,
> Canst thou, unblushing, read this great command;
> Suffer the wrongs which wring our inmost heart
> To draw one throb of pity on thy part;
> Our skins may differ, but from thee we claim
> A sister's privilege and a sister's name.

After this, the whites and the free Negroes met in the same conventions, and mutually exchanged their opinions, and together ever afterward dealt their terrific blows at the foundation of America's disgrace, and, as we all gladly realize, drove the dreaded monster from this virgin land.

MRS. NATHANIEL SPRAGUE.
Agitator and Author.

MRS. NATHANIEL SPRAGUE, daughter of Hon. Frederick Douglass, who resides in Washington, D. C., is one who has done very much to ameliorate the Negro's condition in this country, a woman of purpose, an exponent for the equal rights, a restless agitator for the cause of humanity.

Mrs. Sprague is at present engaged in writing a book set-ting forth the deeds of the Negro women of the present century. She is an able writer, and the world may expect from her caustic pen a priceless addition to Negro literature.

PROF. MARY V. COOK, A. B.,

KNOWN extensively, and especially for literary and journalistic fame, as Grace Ermine, was born in Bowl-ing Green, Kentucky, in those dark days when the gloom of terror pervaded our virgin country, and laid desolate and bare the hopeful hearts of a much depraved people. Her education has fitted her especially for the art of teaching, but indeed, aside from the genius so necessary for school work which she possesses to no moderate degree, she has taken quite a step since 1886, when first she made her initiatory bow to the read-ing world, to the front. ranks of journalism.

She is bordering on sublimity as a Christian, and is devoted to Christian charity and temperance. Any one that is fortu-nate enough to see the inner life of Miss Cook at once becomes "a loyal lover" with humanity.

Of her writings to the Negro press, many and varied have been her articles, shedding therefrom a gleam of light where-ever found. Biographers delight to honor, as well indeed they might, some of her sayings; and feel elated when once inspired by her elegance and ease, her sparkling thoughts, her erudi-tion. Whatever post she has been called to fill in her eventful life, the position has fully participated in the honor with her; for with her, as with Josephine, a Napoleon could not fail. Mar-velous indeed is it when we take into consideration the fact that such women are indeed living realities, after only a few years isolation from slavery and only a few years of freedom to will and to act, now to think. But, as we believe in a God, we are mindful of the prayers commingled with tears, which then was the only comfort to the mothers and fathers of the now men and women, and we doubt not to-day the sorrows of thraldom will be fully compensated, for, when we hear such

papers before conventions, read such articles as Miss Cook
contributes to the press, our confidence in Jehovah reaches its
human limit.

These papers have had a wide sweep.   In August, 1887,
Mobile citizens turned out on the occasion of the National
Baptist Convention to hear this able scholar and writer upon
the theme of " Woman's Work in the Denomination."

At other times and on similar occasions she has discussed
subjects and read papers with the grace characterizing her
talent and power :

" Female education," " Is juvenile literature demanded on
the part of colored children ? "   " Woman a potent factor in
public reform."

Among the articles she has written for the press, none
seem to have won for her more hearts and minds than " Nothing but Leaves."

Indeed her life would comprise a history, if on journalism
alone the historian might dwell.   For the *American Baptist*
and the South Carolina *Tribune* have for years been the battle-
ground upon which she has crossed swords with our man
editors, in fact she may be styled the equal of many of our
boasted editors.

As an educator she seems to have adopted her own ideas,
instructing with the pen those who unfortunately do not
come under her direct tutelage.   This mode of life lifts one up
gradually into the channel of reflecting the goodness of
others, to the extent that they become so charged with the
absorbed reflection that the rays of light shines out impar-
tially to all.   A journal styled *Our Women and Children,*
published in Louisville, has participated largely in her writings, and what the future holds in store for this talented unit
of *Woman Fame* depends largely upon her own progressive
efforts in the behalf of her race.   To become great depends
upon the ease of losing sight of self to accomplish good for
others.

LUCRETIA NEWMAN COLEMAN.

Writer.

WHATEVER is high and ennobling in human beings largely depends upon their opportunities in early life, transmitted through years of restless anxiety to become what was most forcibly reflected upon their young minds. Some people are born great, some become great through years of active but patient toil, others have it thrust upon them.

LUCRETIA NEWMAN COLEMAN.

From early life, dealing with responsibilities, the spirit of usefulness seized upon Mrs. Coleman, and guided by the unshadowed Christian lives of her parents, who died while she was quite young, ever kept the precepts uppermost in her mind which were to characterize her daily life. Dresden, Ontario, is the city of her birth, and being early associated with the intelligence of the place, she as others felt the spirit on her to go through college. She attended Lawrence University, finishing the scientific course. Her experience as a teacher is the realization of some of her youthful hopes. Her experience as clerk adds to her grace and dignity, and most especially her relation as secretary and accountant for the financial department of the A. M. E. church, where she showed the pureness and beauty of an inner life, blessing and brightening the once unhallowed girls of Nashville.

During her connection with the financial department of the A. M. E. church, Mrs. Coleman contributed spicy philosophical literature to many Negro journals of the country, always portraying the usual fascination for saying things in her own way.

She has written many valuable poetic lines. Indeed the sublime is the counterpart of her adorable easy life. Many indeed are the comments from the press and its editors. Her poetic effusions reach such a depth of thought and meaning which at once establishes her claim to the title which critics have been liberal in bestowing.

MISS LILLIAN LEWIS.

Writer,

MISS LILLIAN A. LEWIS ranks among the literary leaders of Boston. Those who have read her articles in the Boston *Advocate* have long ago attributed to her the title she so justly claims (*Bert Islew*). The above named paper reflects very great credit on Negro journalism, and much of its power and potency is due to the unceasing efforts and well applied tone she has given it. Her association with the foremost men and women of the race has, coupled with her indomitable will, brought her in touch with the reading world. Her articles, teeming with brightness, characterizing the productions of the grand and great thinkers, have caused thousands to misjudge her race, identity and age. Her pen, as the sword, is ever drawn in defense of her race, and those who have had the honor of crossing weapons with her generally retire from the combat feeling that they have been vigorously fought. A journalistic career, though brief, is full of honor and deserved merit. What awaits her in the future none can say. The historian records the past and present; a speculation is therefore beyond the limit of our imagination; but if Miss Lewis continues in the path she has learned to tread so well, grand indeed must be the landscape from the lofty summit of her goal.

Among the host of women writers of the Negro race we could not conscientiously conclude this chapter without mentioning Miss Georgia Mabel De Baptiste, who inherits her journalistic taste, and who, like the worthy ones mentioned, is destined to shine as a full-grown meteor upon our cultured realm.   Miss Katie D. Chapman, Miss Alice E. McEwen, Miss Lucy Wilmot Smith, Miss Ione E. Wood, Miss Lavinia B. Sneed, Miss Mary E. Britton, Miss Meta E. Pelham, Mrs. A.

E. Johnson, Mrs. M. E. Lambert, Mrs. Frank Grimke, Miss Adina White, Mrs. Susie I. Shorter, Mrs. B. F. Lee are all deserving journalistic lights, brightening their several homes with that becoming intellectuality, proving the fathomless capacity that startles the reading world which woman possesses to a remarkable degree.

It is no wonder that a race progresses in spite of its obstacles when it is remembered that such women bedeck the bright escutcheon of our editorial prow.   The efforts of these brought to bear for the furtherance of the Negro cause in a very few years of activity

MISS LILLIAN LEWIS.

has told wonderfully for the great accomplishments within the possibility of the Negro race.   Each as well as all seems forced upon the arena, there to play well her part, not honor-seeking, but inspired by the mandates of DUTY.

JOSEPHINE TURPIN WASHINGTON.

Educator and Writer.

TO Augustus A. and Maria V. Turpin was born July 31, 1861, a daughter whose marriage name is Mrs. Josephine Turpin Washington, who was destined to shine even in the great State of her birth.   The State of Virginia has long been the land of the free and the home of the brave, and where educational facilities were fostered, and especially by the erudition of the Negro race.

Goochland county was honored by her nativity and made prominent by her praise. Soon after moving to Richmond she matriculated to the Richmond Institute, having already passed through the all important high school. Having a strengthened belief in her power to master the classics, not satisfied with a diploma from the limited course taken in the Richmond

JOSEPHINE TURPIN WASHINGTON.

Institute, she matriculated at Howard University, finishing the college course in 1886.

The tendency women have at the present day is to show the men of the race that it neither necessitates a broken-down, worn-out body, nor a fond and fictitious supply of *ego* to *pose* as a sample of learning. Our women generally pass through the college curriculum in the same length of time as their male classmates, and we have very few instances to demonstrate that woman presumes too much in her attempts to master the sciences. Mrs. Dr. Washington has not only been honored by a position in Howard University ; Howard University has been honored by her, not only as a teacher, but as a pupil, for even as the latter her association and demeanor served as a blessing to all who were fortunate to be her friend in the institution.

As a teacher she has so favorably arrayed herself for the work, and so ably availed herself with what is expected of a teacher, that her usefulness has a wide range, and her services have for a goodly number of years been sought by the presidents of our Southern colleges. Her efforts to advance Selma

University are recognized, and the good she accomplished while connected therewith is being felt.

She possesses a special penchant for writing, as indeed her literary career, both as a scholar and newspaper correspondent, has demonstrated to the world the power of thought when produced from the pen of such a talented woman. Many, and indeed varied, are the periodicals she has promoted by her lofty thought and able articles. Newspapers that have the support of the best writers are the ones most eagerly sought, and most readily patronized, hence the magnetic force of her pen found a host of avenues (newspaper columns) open wherein the race agitations and momentous questions were duly met by the readiness of her genius. Her will has been to answer back whenever the lover of Southern pride attacked the unfortunate race with which she claims identity—thus when Annie Porter, with concentrated infamy, threw down the sacred altars of Negro greatness, and played her hostile hand of treachery, in Miss Turpin (which then was her name) she more than met her match. The calumny occurred in the *Independent*—the dignified reproof of Miss Turpin in the New York *Freeman*. All of the prominent Negro newspapers have stood by her in her bold assertions, and applauded her achievements, have shared her joys and are made happy by her accomplishments.

She is the author of many high and ennobling subjects which have engaged the attention of the many eager and anxious searchers after truth, but our space dictates brevity. Dr. S. H. H. Washington, of Birmingham, Ala., took Miss Turpin's hand in marriage, thereby stamping the seal of success for all his future life.

The woman, great as she is, her intellect is greater. God is demonstrating through such women as Mrs. Dr. Washington some useful lessons, is writing upon the wall of TIME that which requires no interpretation, words which stand out as in blocks of fire, famous for simplicity, and all who see may read.

LUCY WILMOT SMITH.
Writer.

MISS LUCY WILMOT SMITH is a native of Lexington, Ky., and from Prof. I. Garland Penn's sketch we learn some facts (which time and space are not to be considered), as to her worthiness among the leading Negro women of America. She was born Nov. 16, 1861. Her mother, Mrs. Margaret Smith, the very embodiment of ambition, exerted herself arduously and unselfishly to place every advantage for education in her way, she being her sole support.

LUCY WILMOT SMITH.

We learn that she began teaching in 1877, serving under the Lexington, Ky., school board, and in 1887 graduated from the normal department of the State University. She was for a long time private secretary to Dr. William J. Simmons, by whose aid she was introduced to the world of thinkers and writers in newspaper life.

In every department of life she has officiated; whether as scholar, teacher, society worker, she has proven beyond the shadow of a doubt the competency of the female to be trusted with responsibilities.

She is now a member of the State University faculty.

She is a newspaper contemporary and has shown her peculiar fitness for her art in the demonstration of controlling special columns in *Our Women and Children,* one of the best magazines published by the Negro race. She has served on the staff of the *Baptist Journal*; in fact her newspaper career since 1884, though short, has been one full of rare experiences, and eliciting praise from the pens of the best writers of the country. Mrs. N. F. Mossell says: "Miss Smith writes compactly, is acute, clean and crisp in her acquirements and has good descriptive powers." "Her style is transparent, lucid, and in many respects few of her race can surpass her."

Her success proves the scope of her versatility and talent.

MISS A. L. TILGHMAN.

Editor of Musical Messenger, Musical Writer, Talented Vocalist.

THE subject of this brief sketch first saw the light of day in Washington City, District of Columbia. Her parents for uprightness and honesty have no peers in the race. Henry H. and Margaret A. Tilghman have always been the centre around which reveled the good and gay citizens of the national capital. In 1871 she finished the normal department at Howard University and thereafter taught fourteen years in the public schools of her native city. Her knowledge of instruction at once asserted itself, and made for her the reputation she justly won and merits.

Her musical as well as vocal talent has at all times won for her the greatest praise both from public and press.

She sang through New York State, at all times meeting the public expectations, delighting and captivating all who heard her with her melody in fact in 1881, the New York press styled her "The Queen of Song." In this same year she filled an engagement as leader of the Saengerfest, at Louisville, Kentucky, and two years later she was advised to travel, acting as the leading sopranist in the Washington Harmonic Musical Concert Troupe.

Her musical qualifications make her a marvel. Being a graduate from the renowned Boston Conservatory of Music, makes her less the foe and more the friend of critics, as for them their work becomes an easy as well as a pleasing task. She is a race lover and is restless in new adventures for the development of her people.

Her Queen Esther Cantata, a musical concert played under her management, is regarded by all by far the greatest musical effort ever carried to perfection in Montgomery, Alabama. Her instructions to the many young ladies of the race guarantees to us the realization of many accomplished pianists and singers in the South.

At Montgomery she published the *Musical Messenger*. On leaving the above named city by reason of her ability she was invited and accepted the duties of the musical department of Howe Institute, New Iberia, Louisiana. After one year of hard work she resigned her position and took up residence in Washington City, her home, where she, through God, is working in the field of music, teaching and editing the *Musical Messenger*.

LILLIAN PARKER THOMAS.

Local and Correspondent Editor of The Freeman.

LILLIAN PARKER THOMAS, correspondent editor of the *Freeman*, is a striking illustration of the triumph of perseverance over obstacles incidental to the experience of all who, unaided and alone, have hewn for themselves a place on life's rocky and untoward highway. Associated with her earliest remembrance has been an inspiration, now inviting, anon abating, to some time write her name among the galaxy of those whose sublime mission it had been to preserve for the edification and pleasure of coming generations the elevated and instructive in literature and thought. As if to test the validity and strength of this dominant aspiration, her lot was cast in a portion of the then new Northwest, where the chimes resonant from the halls of culture and art vied with the weird haloo of the untutored aboriginee. The members of her own race being few, the impetus afforded by association for rivalry played no part in developing her precocious talent. As best she knew and could, she builded. She "shunned delights, and lived laborious days" of application and study. The schools of Wisconsin, excellent and notably celebrated, offered superior facilities for her eager and inquiring mind. The School Lyceum had in her one of its most ardent devotees, as did the higher branches of the curriculum of the schools. Her bow to the public as a writer began with a strong, logical protest against the action of the United States Supreme Court, declaring the Civil Rights bill unconstitutional. Her protest appeared in the leading dailies of the State, and was the recipient of widespread and favorable comment. The succession of events, since that time, touching the interest of her race have been

LILLIAN PARKER THOMAS.

the animus to many and varied dissertations on this important theme. Coming to Indianapolis in 1885, she soon attracted the attention of the literati of the Hoosier capital, and was accorded that honest recognition due her sterling intellectual gifts and tastes. Her fame as a chaste and polished reader is far from being of the common " school-house elocutionary " order, and has long since ceased to be merely local. She has filled her present responsible position upon the *Freeman*, the race's greatest journalistic effort, for something over a year, and has filled it fully and exceptionally, not through favoritism or the chance of circumstances, but because her superior and exceptional qualifications and merit, pure merit, have enabled her to do so, she being the only lady of her race in this section holding a position of such journalistic importance. The special features of the *Freeman*, such as " Race Gleanings," " Church," " Stage" and " Friendly Reminders," are to be credited solely to her discriminating compilation and original creation. Her " Friendly Reminders," as given each week to the *Freeman's* thousands of readers, are solely and originally the children of her own thought and creation, and are worthy in many instances to be ranked with Tupper's Proverbial Philosophy. It may be said in a general way of this talented and growing race woman that what she has become to be, what she may yet become to be, if all signs do not fail and opportunity is not suddenly cut off, is and will be due solely or mainly to her own indomitable intellectuality and determination. She is a credit to her race, an ornament to her sex. The mantle of mental achievement, that belongs so properly to her was neither an accident nor a bequest, but one of her own weaving, with a filling thread of energy in warp and woof. She says:

"We believe that what should most interest women is woman; despite the glaring indication that her chief consideration, as well as chief glorification, is man. Woman's condition to-day, as compared with her condition in no far remote time, stands out in contra distinction in favor of the present. But even now she is environed with untoward odds which operate in many instances to stultify her aspiration or palsy her effort, and yet a number sufficient to wield telling influence have in the last few decades invaded, as one lord of creation has termed it, the ranks of the arts, sciences and industries, and have flung into the burning pile which is fast consuming the yokes of individuals and nations that theoretic weakling, *i. e.*, that woman is incapable of mastering economics outside the domestic realm. The loom, spinning wheel and quilting frames have been exchanged for the desk, the ledger, the brush and palette, the caligraph and the camera; churn, milkstool, soap kettle and lye hopper have each and all been relegated to dust-covered obscurity, whence they are only brought to do service as a corner-stone upon which some muse shall build his lore of "ye olden time," and yet woman has not abandoned the duties incumbent upon her as wife and mother, nor waived her claim to the coronet which bears the inscription 'Queen of home,' but has resolved the routine of household duties, which to our grandmothers were veriest meniality and which were often the bane of a cheerless existence, into a systematized series of domestic functions of which she is the proud promoter. If the broadening out of woman's mind by the leaven of science, philosophy and art bore no other beneficence than the per-meating of this earthly shrine, the home, with the aroma of culture and refinement and inculcating in the breast of the inmates of that home love for the good and the beautiful, the seeker after such knowledge had builded well. Nature mellows the heart, while the development of the mind creates a window through which the erstwhile mental captive may behold and appreciate the beauties of nature. But in this, a day of great possibilities, the feminine heart yearns for broader paths wherein to walk, an intellectual highway whereon all nations or sex may walk abreast. This granted, the son and daughter go hand in hand to the halls of learning and on common ground prepare for the arena of life and for the time when, should fickle fortune, whose mandate barrs no creed or sex, decree the undoing of their success, they have won alike a safeguard against wreck or ruin as a result of helplessness."

MRS. C. C. STUMM.

AMONG the women who have made for themselves names as writers and pioneer teachers, Mrs. C. C. Stumm ranks very high. She was born in Kentucky, is the daughter of Thomas and Eliza Penman, and the accomplished wife of Dr. Stumm, an able minister of Philadelphia. At quite an early age she matriculated at Berea College, where she procured a fair amount of learning, but by courage and thirst for knowledge she has studied her way to the top. Her experience as a teacher, as well as her reputation, has been won, not only in the public school-room, but in academies both in Texas and Kentucky. As a journalist her efforts have been frought with success. Her writings and editorial work cover many different States. In Boston the *Hub* and *Advocate,* in Kentucky the Bowling Green *Watchman,* each have found in her a ready exponent and versatile writer.

She is at present a resident of Philadelphia, where she is engaged in journalistic agency for the *National Monitor,* published at Brooklyn, N. Y., and *Our Women and Children* journal, published at Louisville, Ky.

MRS. SERENA LETITIA MOORE.

Artist.

BY JOHN C. DANCY.

THE subject of this sketch was born at Snow Hill, N. C. Nov. 11, 1863, and is the daughter of George Washington and Esther Suggs. At the age of three years she removed with her parents to Wilson, N. C., where she early began to attend school and continued therein regularly until she was 13 years old. Her principal during these years was the now distinguished Dr. J. C. Price, president of Livingstone College. At this age she entered the St. Augustine Normal and Industrial Institute, at Raleigh, N. C., under the presidency of Dr. Smedes and under the tutelage of such teachers as the now eminent teacher, essayist and speaker, Mrs. Anna J. Cooper, A. M.. Washington, D. C. After spending three years here, she spent one year at Scotia Seminary, Concord, N. C. After this she spent one year at St. Mary's Academy, Baltimore, Md.

Mrs. Moore professed religion when only eleven years old and joined the African Methodist Episcopal Zion Church at Wilson, N. C.

In the fall of 1879 the then young principal of Wilson Academy, Prof Edward Moore, Ph. D., now of Livingstone College, met her. He had just graduated from Lincoln University, and was recognized as a thorough scholar and brilliant young man. During that year relations began to grow between them, which finally terminated in their marriage Nov. 14, 1881, which has proven a very happy and fortunate union.

At school she was apt in all her studies, but from very early life she had a peculiar taste, aptness and fondness for drawing, which she has in later life cultivated, until she is now able to execute most excellent oil paintings, especially portraits. In her parlor can be seen life-size pictures of Dr. J. C. Price, Collector of Customs, John C. Dancy, Bishop C. R. Harris, and Mrs. Anna J. Cooper, which would do credit to many of our best artists. Her work in water colors and other forms of the painter's art does her great credit.

MRS. SERENA L. MOORE.

In 1883 she was elected one of the teachers of the preparatory department of Livingston College. She held this place till the increasing duties of the family made it necessary for her to resign in 1885. She is the mother of four interesting children and is always happy in instructing them, and marking out their pathway in life.

Mrs. Moore is of medium height, of a lively disposition, genial nature and beautiful face. Hers is a social nature, high-minded and ambitious. She always makes it pleasant for her friends. She delights to entertain, and is known for her characteristic hospitality.

MRS. A. E. JOHNSON.

Writer.

MRS. A. E. JOHNSON, we learn, was born in Maryland in 1859. Her education was obtained in Montreal, Canada, but for the reason that she might be of use to her race as an educator, she moved to Baltimore in 1874, where she has since resided. Her marriage with Dr. Harvey Johnson, an eminent divine, took place in 1877.

MRS A. E. JOHNSON.

A fine sketch of her appears in the *Afro-American Press*.

She began writing poetry at quite an early age, but published little till after her marriage. Since then she has written much for various reviews, and other miscellanies. In 1887 she launched upon the uncertain waves of journalism the *Joy*, an eight-page monthly, containing original poems and matters literary, in fact a symposium of stories, etc., by the best cultivated brain of the race.

Her writings are varied; she having a clear conception of what a poet means, she is reserved in her compositions, and so deep is her thought that her productions ward off the minnows in search for those who inhabit deep water. Her powers of imagination are so forcible that for every true disciple of her muses there is painted by the fairy a rare picture.

MRS. W. E. MATHEWS.

Eminent Writer.

MRS. W. E. MATHEWS (Victoria Earle) was born at Fort Valley, Georgia, May 27, 1861.

Those cruel days of servitude for our subject severed the parental tie, and by reason of cruelty and outrage perpetrated in those dark days caused many an unfortunate to seek refuge in the far North. Mrs. Caroline Smith, for that was her mother's name, after repeated attempts to flee, finally succeeded, making New York her home.

After a series of years, she returned and found living four of her children, our subject being one of the number, whom she freed legally from the clutches of the law, and took them finally to New York, where she might educate the little ones committed to her care.

Her opportunities at first proving to be not so smooth as anticipated, hence she was forced to work for maintenance. Possessing all of

MRS. W. E. MATHEWS.

the characteristics of a true disciple, she labored and studied arduously to make her way in the world. Such is the life of the mother; what of the daughter whose life engages the attention of the literary world?

By perseverance Mrs. Mathews has written her way into the hearts of America's best enlightened citizens. The wonderful fascination she has for the subjects her extensive writings embrace place her among the highest American female writers of the age.

More than a score of leading periodicals, daily and weekly, under the management of both white and Negro editors, demand the magnetic pulsation that her articles seem to give. For instance, she has been in demand on the following : The New York *Times, Herald, Mail* and *Express, Sunday Mercury,* the *Earth* and the *Phonographic World;* meanwhile acting as correspondent to the *National Leader,* Detroit *Plaindealer* and the *Southern Christian Recorder.* Her articles contributed to the A. M. E. Church *Review* have proven the force of her literary genius. The following leading Negro weeklies have always found her a ready exponent : The Boston *Advocate,* Washington *Bee,* Richmond *Planet, Catholic Tribune,* Cleveland *Gazette,* New York *Globe,* New York *Age,* and the New York *Enterprise.* She is as busy as a bee, for it has become an established fact that Mrs. Mathews' greatest pleasure is in the constant pursuit of her literary and journalistic duties.

Her high literary attainments abundantly fit her for achieving marvelous success in literature; her peculiar fascination for stories have added much to her grand attainments, as her *footprints* can be seen in the *Waverly Magazine* the New York *Weekly,* the *Family Story Paper* and *Ringwood Journal of Fashion.*

Her many literary achievements go to prove that merit is the watchword for the world. Of course the city wherein the most of her life has been spent, where she has proven herself a worthy scholar, meritorious in every way, and worthy of the reliance placed in her, naturally offered her the greatest inducements for her turn of mind. She is a success. The Negro race should be proud and more courageous in their boast of their greatest minds.

The Woman's National Press Association finds in her a worthy member, a giantess, the equal of any of her sex or society, and places the Negro race, from a literary standpoint, where it justly belongs in story writing and literature in general.

She is not only a novelist and press correspondent, she is an author of a series of text books and school literature.

Her wide scope with the pen proves the assurance of her versatility and talent, and demonstrates, as well as proves, the philosophy of industry, that he who would accumulate must work.

MRS. CHARLOTTE FORTEN GRIMKE.

Educator, Linguist, Writer.

IT is indeed a pleasure to record the deeds and usefulness of one who, by her dint and push, has made her name known to the literary world. She was born in Philadelphia, of honored parents, whose genealogy may be traced many generations; in fact, a grand-daughter of that venerable Mr. Forten, of Revolutionary fame, who was for many years the friend and adviser of America's great poet, John Greenleaf Whittier, though Mr. Forten was many years his senior. As soon as Miss Forten could conceive of the idea of what an education consisted, and the use of it, she determined to go where the very best training was to be gotten, hence she went to Salem, Mass., entered a school in which she, after graduation, taught for a number of years. Remarkable to say that in her department there was not a colored child, and she experienced no insinuations of disrespect on the part of the white children who were committed to her care. Her genius forced open higher avenues of learning year after year, and served as a convincing argument that the women of color with equal chances could do what white women could do. After teaching a number of years in Massachusetts, the call was made for volunteers to go South and carry the intellectual light to the boys and girls; the women and men of to-day. Miss Forten then, as now, being one of the best educated persons of the race, made her way to Port Royal, South Carolina, where she gave to the newly freedmen two of the busiest years of her young life teaching, working in church and Sabbath-school, and as forcibly as possible did she delineate upon their duties to their God, their fellow-men and themselves. The XIII., XIV. and XV. amendments to the Constitution found the Negro as void of under-

standing then, as the sudden issuance of the emancipation proc·
lamation found them almost incapable of the faith, to compre-
hend their deliverance. Much had to be accomplished, schools
and school-houses had to be erected, and, true to every instinct
of the genius she possessed, she returned to New England and
became correspondent for the New England Freedman's Aid
Society. This position was the responsive cord to the "even
tenor of her way." She had been South, studied the Negro's
rude conditions, taught their children, labored with them and
knew their wants. God really placed her there. Miss Forten is
an erudite scholar, a forcible writer, and, withal, a woman of
extraordinary powers who would do honor to any race. At
the solicitation of the poet Whittier, she corresponded with him
during her stay South, also while sojourning there she wrote an
article entitled "Life on the South Sea Isles," which occurred
in the Atlantic *Monthly*, a journal that needs no praise.

At the suggestion of Colonel Higginson, her knowledge of
the French language was brought to the severest test in the
translation of a book (written in the French language) into
English, copyrighted by Erckmon and Chatrian, and published
in Scribner's *Magazine*, for which she was long a correspondent. Unlike very many women writers, Miss Forten enjoyed
the reputation of being a costly correspondent in that a work-
man was worthy of his hire. She has contributed largely of
her talents and time to invigorate and make interesting many of
our newspapers, and all who have come in for a share of such
of her favors have shown it in their journalistic success. Her
association with such minds as Whittier and Longfellow has
been inspiring in effect, and given her an insight very keen to
appreciate the true, the beautiful; for this rare enjoyment, she
has been caused to feel and know the difference between the
exalted and the humble, and as compared with the literary
work of the exalted, she claims to have done very little; but
those who know her best freely assent in crowning her with
the laurels she has so beautifully won.

After leaving Boston, she came South to Washington, D.
C., where she spent a number of years in the cause of educa-

tion. The high school was her workshop, and the material turned out year after year during her activities there proved most wonderfully her fitness as a teacher—a leader—and it is the boast of the whites in Massachusetts, as well as the Negroes in Washington, D. C., that Charlotte Forten was their teacher. Here this lady met Rev. Dr. Grimke, and surrendered her life-work, leaning upon him, who became the mainstay of her eventful life. He is a husband, a model for men; she a wife, an example of purity and chastity; a teacher of Christian piety; yea, a copy for our girls, who can make for themselves a record.

LUCINDA BRAGG ADAMS.

Musician and Writer.

THE subject of our sketch is the accomplished daughter of Mr. and Mrs. Geo. F. Bragg. She was born in the Old Dominion, in the city of Petersburg, and so circumstanced that she could enjoy the advantages of becoming a musician, at quite an early age. Proficiency indeed seems to be her second nature. Her force of character and magical art seem to go hand in hand, and altogether fit her for the highest realms of music and song. She possesses every feature of the high art. Her compositions are full of her soul, portraying in every line the uppermost tenor of her soul.

She has won the meed of praise from the papers of Virginia and in an article on music, which appeared in the A. M. E. *Review*, she seems to have concentrated all her genius, as, indeed, her friends far and wide paid such glowing compliments that she has more than ever confined her talents and time to music. She is assistant editor of the *Musical Messenger*, of which Miss A. L. Tilghman is its accomplished editor. Mrs. Adams is the author of 'Old Blanford Church,' which she, for the friendship existing between her family and Hon. John Mercer Langston's, together with her high regard and conception of his rare ability, dedicated to him.

Prof. I. Garland Penn, in his *Afro-American Press*, says: "She is a woman of indomitable will, and a writer of superior ability. The *Messenger*, with Mrs. Adams' aid, will be a paper of commanding influence in Afro-American journalism."

MRS. MARY E. BRITTON (MEB).

THE subject of our sketch is an ardent student of metaphysics and a firm believer in phrenology, and had her phrenological character written out by Prof. O. S. Fowler. He describes her predominant characteristic as "ambitious to do

MRS. MARY E. BRITTON.

her level best." He speaks of her as "thoroughly conscientious, and actuated by the highest possible sense of right and duty; as frugal and industrious, adapted to business."

Her career as a writer began with an address prepared for her school exhibition.

Her next article was a race appeal, which appeared in the Cincinnati *Commercial*.

Mrs. Amelia E. Johnson says of her: "She has an excellent talent for comparing, explaining, expounding and criticising, and has made no small stir among the city officials and others for their unjust discriminations against worthy citizens." We say of her as others; many and varied have been her treatises on the race question. She is one of the leading women writers of the South. More than a dozen Negro journals have been forced onward toward the high mark, owing to the quality of her contributions. All Louisville, (Ky.) is alive to the fact that within its borders there is one plucky woman and she is our *Meb*. Her educational work in Louisville speaks for itself.

The citizens join in one unanimus voice in accrediting her with all the estimable qualifications of a noted lady, a useful and tireless worker and a model of our latter day civilization.

MISS PAULINE POWELL.

Eminent Pianist and Artist.

THE subject of this sketch was born in the city of Oakland, county of Alameda, June 27, 1872, and is the only daughter of the late William W. Powell and Josephine Powell, old and respected residents of the city of Oakland. She was educated in the public schools of Oakland and always stood very high in her studies. She graduated from the grammar school, and was promoted to the high school, where she remained one year, when she was taken out by her parents to pursue her studies in music and painting. Miss Powell has been studying music and the piano for seven years under the best masters of the profession, and among her most prominent teachers was the late Prof. McDougall, who took an extra interest in her progress in that particular study, and to his teaching

MISS PAULINE POWELL.

she owes the most of her success as a brilliant performer upon the piano and her knowledge of music, both vocal and instrumental. Although Miss Powell is well advanced in the musical profession, being one of the most brilliant performers upon the piano that we have in the city of Oakland, either white or colored, she still pursues her studies in music, and has for her instructor Miss De Gomez, lately of the Conservatory of Music at Berlin, Germany.   She has also pursued her studies in painting for five years, having a natural gift and taste for the profession.   Though she has never had a great deal of teaching in that profession from the great masters of the art, yet she has produced some as fine paintings as those who have ranked as prominent artists in the great studios of Europe and America. Miss Powell had several paintings on exhibition at the Mechanics' Institute fair in 1890 in this city, which received great praise from the committee of award and those who admired works of art amongst the thousands that visited the pavilion during the season.   They were the first paintings ever before exhibited by a colored artist in this State at any of the art exhibitions, and speak well for the push and energy exhibited by the young lady in showing the capabilities of the race in the arts and sciences.

Miss Powell resides with her mother, Mrs. Josephine Powell, at 579 Sixteenth street, corner of Jefferson, in the city of Oakland, who owns a handsome cottage of six rooms, of modern build and improvements.   The family consists of three—the mother and her son and daughter, Mr. William Powell and Miss Pauline Powell, who are bright examples for emulation, as far as refinement, love of mother and home are concerned. They are a blessing to their widowed mother.

Read what the San Francisco *Examiner* says of her performances :

Miss Powell gave a beautiful piano solo, after which Miss Winslow gave a recitation and another exhibition of Delsarte movements. The very excellent work done by the Misses Powell and Winslow has been one of the most attractive features of the assembly.   Miss Pauline Powell was born and educated in Oakland.   She has been making music a special study, and has given several recitals in San Francisco with great satisfaction to her friends.   She interprets classical music with fine taste and exquisite finish.   She has made a most happy success here by her refined and cultured performances, and all Chautauquans and their friends have generally bestowed their congratulations upon her, and prophesy for her a brilliant future as a pianist.

Another brilliant testimonial of her talents :

Miss Pauline Powell's piano performances were from memory, brilliant in execution and perfect in harmony.   Her "Fantasie Impromptu, C sharp minor," by Chopin, and " Rondo Brilliante," by Weber, were played in a masterly style, and evoked continued applause.—*P. G. Review*.

Miss Powell was born in Oakland, Cal., and as a native daughter reflects credit on the golden State. She has a natural genius for music, and interprets the classic music of the great masters with evidences of thorough instruction and rare natural genius. She invariably plays without her notes and entirely from memory, which is high proof of her talent.—*San Francisco Call*.

ASSISTED BY C. KELLOG, THE BIRD WARBLER, AND THE MISSES POWELL AND WINSLOW, PIANIST AND DELSARTIST.

(From Tuesday's Daily.)

The grand entertainment Saturday evening as per program was held at the M. E. Church, and really overreached the excellency of the merits claimed for it, Dr. Hirst presiding. At the conclusion of a few preliminary remarks by the Doctor, Miss Powell, who has won our hearts, was announced, and gave a " Rondo from Mendelssohn," the brilliant execution of which could not be well excelled.—*P. G. Review*.

MRS. OCTAVIA V. R. ALBERT.

Author of The House of Bondage.

OCTAVIA VICTORIA ROGERS, wife of the Rev. A. E. P. Albert, D. D., was born in Oglethorpe, Macon county, Ga., of slave parentage, December 24, 1853, and was educated at Atlanta University, in that State. She and Dr. Albert first met at Montezuma, Ga., where they taught school together, in 1873, and on October 21, 1874, they were united in holy wedlock. They had an only daughter, who survives her mother. She united with the African Methodist Episcopal Church under the preaching of Bishop H. M. Turner, at Oglethorpe, Ga., and was converted and united with the Methodist Episcopal Church, under the pastorage of the Rev. Marcus Dole, at Union Chapel, New Orleans, in 1875. Her own husband baptized her at Houma, La., in 1878, during the first year of his ministry. She was an angel of mercy whose loving spirit will long be cherished by all who knew her but to love her. Now she rests from her labors, and her good works do follow her. Peace to her precious memory!

THE COMPILER.

DR. ALBERT SAYS IN PREFACING.

The following pages, giving the result of conversations and other information gathered, digested, and written by Mrs. Octavia V. Rogers, deceased wife of the Rev. A. E. P. Albert, A. M., D. D., first appeared in the columns of the *Southwestern Christian Advocate*, some months after her death, as a serial story, under the name of *The House of Bondage.* It was received with such enthusiasm and appreciation that no sooner was the story concluded than letters poured in upon the editor from all directions urging him to put it in book form, so as to preserve it as a memorial of the author, as well as for its intrinsic value as a history of Negro slavery in the Southern States, of its overthrow, and of the mighty and far-reaching results derived therefrom.

No special literary merit is claimed for the work. No special effort was made in that direction ; but as a panoramic exhibition of slave-life, emancipation, and the subsequent results, the story herein given, with all the facts brought out, as each one speaks for himself and in his own way, is most interesting and life-like.

The conversations herein given are not imaginary, but actual, and given as they actually occurred. No one can read these pages without realizing the fact that "truth is often stranger than fiction." As such we present it to the public as an unpretentious contribution to an epoch in American history that will more and more rivet the attention of the civilized world as the years roll around.

An only daughter unites with the writer in sending out these pages penned by a precious and devoted mother and wife, whose angelic spirit is constantly seen herein, and whose subtile and holy influence seem to continue to guide and protect both in the path over which they since have had to travel without the presence and cheer of her inspiring countenance.

To her sacred memory these pages, the result of her efforts, are affectionately inscribed.

EDITORIAL ROOMS   A. E. P. ALBERT.
Southwestern Christian Advocate,   LAURA T. F. ALBERT.
NEW ORLEANS, LA., November 15, 1890.

THE INTRODUCTION TO HER BOOK, COMING AS IT DOES FROM ONE OF
AMERICA'S GREATEST CHURCHMEN, WE COULD NOT
REFRAIN INSERTING IT.

The story of slavery never has been and never will be fully
told. In the last letter that John Wesley ever wrote, addressed
to Wilberforce, the great abolitionist, and dated February 24,
1791, and this only six days before his tireless hand was quieted
in death, he wrote these words: "I see not how you can go
through your glorious enterprise in opposing that execrable
villainy (slavery and the slave trade), which is the scandal
of religion, of England, and of human nature. Unless God has
raised you up for this very thing you will be worn out by the
opposition of men and devils; but if God be for you, who can
be against you? Are all of them together stronger than God?
O, ' be not weary in well-doing.' Go on in the name of God,
and the power of his might, till even American slavery, the
vilest that ever saw the sun, shall vanish away before it."

It is because American slavery was "the vilest that ever saw
the sun" that it is, and will remain forever, impossible to ade-
quately portray its unspeakable horrors, its heart-breaking
sorrows, its fathomless miseries of hopeless grief, its intolerable
shames, and its heaven-defying and outrageous brutalities.

But while it remains true that the story can never be completely told, it is wise and well that the task should be
attempted and in part performed; and this for the reason that
there are some who presume that this slavery, "the vilest that
ever saw the sun," has been, and is still, of divine appointment;
in short, that from first to last it was a divine institution. It is
well to remind all such people that the Almighty Ruler of the
universe is not an accessory, either before or after the fact, to
such crimes as were involved in slavery. Let no guilty man,
let no descendant of such man, attempt to excuse the sin and
shame of slave-holding on the ground of its providential character. The truth is that slavery is the product of human greed
and lust and oppression, and not of God's ordering.

Then it is well to write about slavery that the American
people may know from what depths of disgrace and infamy

they rose when, guided by the hand of God, they broke every
yoke and let the oppressed go free. Finally, it is well to tell,
though only in part, the story of slavery, so that every man,
woman and child of the once enslaved race may know the ex-
ceeding mercy of God that has delivered them from the hopeless and helpless despair that might have been their portion if
the Lord God Omnipotent had not come forth to smite in divine
and righteous wrath the proud oppressor, and bring his long-
suffering people out of their worse than Egyptian bondage.

This volume, penned by a hand that now rests in the quiet
of the tomb, is a contribution to the sum total of the story that
can never be entirely told.

In her young girlhood the author had known the accursed
system, and she knew the joy of deliverance. With a deep,
pathetic tenderness she loved her race; she would gladly have
died for their enlightenment and salvation. But she has gone
to her reward, leaving behind her the precious legacy of a sweet
Christian influence that can only flow forth from a pure and
consecrated life.

May this volume go forth to cheer and comfort and inspire
to high and holy deeds all who shall read its pages !

WILLARD F. MALLALIEU.

BOSTON, MASS., NOV. 15, 1890.

To more fully demonstrate her powers as a writer, and to
prove the worth of her contribution to Negro literature we
insert the following :

CHAPTER XVIII.

NEGRO GOVERNMENT.

Kuklux—Reign of terror—Black laws—Reconstruction—Colored men in
constitutional conventions and State legislatures—Lieutenant-Governor
Dunn—Honest Antoine Dubuclet—Negro problem—What the race
has accomplished since the war—Emigration and colonization.

If the Kuklux treated the missionaries in that manner you
must not imagine that they left the colored people and their
children unharmed. Thousands of colored men and women
throughout the South were in like manner whipped and shot

down like dogs, in the fields and in their cabins. The recital of some of the experiences of those days is enough to chill your blood and raise your hair on ends. The horrors of those days can scarcely be imagined by those who know nothing about it. Why, madam, you ought to have been down here in 1868. That was the year in which Grant and Colfax ran for president and vice-president, against Seymour and Blair. A perfect reign of terror existed all over the South; and the colored people who attempted to vote were shot down like dogs everywhere. There was such a reign of terrorism in many States of the South that the Congress of the United States refused to count the bloody electoral votes of several of the Southern States. Two years before that, in July, 1866, there was a constitutional convention in New Orleans, to frame a constitution whereby the State of Louisiana might be reconstructed and re-admitted into the Union. On the 30th day of that month, I believe it was, a fearful riot was instituted by those fire-eaters, and the result was that the streets of New Orleans were flooded with Negro blood. Hundreds of them were killed without any knowledge of the murderous intentions of their enemies. They lay dead on every street and in the gutter, and were taken out and buried in trenches by the cart-load in all the cemeteries. The children at school were also the object of the same murderous spirit. When we sent our children to school in the morning we had no idea that we should see them return home alive in the evening.

"Big white boys and half-grown men used to pelt them with stones and run them down with open knives, both to and from school. Sometimes they came home bruised, stabbed, beaten half to death and sometimes quite dead. My own son himself was often thus beaten. He has on his forehead to-day a scar over his right eye which sadly tells the story of his trying experience in those days in his efforts to get an education. I was wounded in the war, trying to get my freedom, and he over the eye, trying to get an education. So we both call our scars marks of honor. In addition to these means to keep the Negro in the same servile condition, I was about to forget to tell you of the 'black laws,' which were adopted in nearly all of the Southern States under President Andrew Johnson's plan of reconstruction. They adopted laws with reference to contracts, to the movement of Negro laborers, etc., such as would have made the condition of the freed Negro worse than when he had a master before the war. But, in the words of General Garfield upon the death of President Lincoln, 'God reigns, and the government at Washington still lives." It did live, and, notwithstanding Andrew Johnson, it lived under the divine supervision which would not and did not allow the Southern States to reconstruct upon any such dishonorable, unjust plan to the two hundred thousand Negro soldiers who offered their lives upon the altar for the perpetuation of the Union and the freedom of their country. And the whole matter was repudiated by Congress, and the States were reconstructed upon the plan of equal rights to every citizen, of whatever race or previous condition. It was then declared that, whereas the stars on our national flag had been the property of only the white race and the stripes for only the colored, now the stars should forever be the common property of both, and that the stripes should only be given to those that deserved them.

" Under this new plan of reconstruction many colored men entered the constitutional conventions of every Southern State; and in the subsequent organization of the new State governments colored men took their seats in both branches of the State governments, in both Houses of Congress, and in all the several branches of the municipal, parochial, State and national governments. It is true that many of them were not prepared for such a radical and instantaneous transition. But I tell you, madam, it was simply wonderful to see how well they did. And, although in the midst of prejudice and partisan clamor a great deal of the most withering criticisms have been spent upon the ignorance, venality and corruption of the Negro carpet-bag reconstruction governments inaugurated by our people, I believe time will yet vindicate them, and their achievements will stand out in the coming years as one of the marvels of the ages. Who of all the officers of any State government can compare with the unassuming, dignified and manly Oscar J. Dunn, Louisiana's first Negro lieutenant-governor, or with Antoine. Dubuclet, her honest and clean-handed treasurer for twelve years? His successor, E. A. Burke, a white man, representing the virtue and intelligence of our 'higher civilization,' is to-day a fugitive from the State for having robbed that same treasury of nearly a million dollars. Alabama has had her Vincent, Tennessee her Polk, Mississippi her Hemingway; Kentucky, Maryland, and nearly every one of the Southern States have had their absconding State treasurers, with hundreds of thousands of dollars of the people's money unaccounted for, since the overthrow of the Negro governments of the South. Such is the contrast that I like to offer to those people who are constantly denouncing the Negro governments of reconstruction times in the South.

"If our people did so well when only a few years removed from the house of bondage, wherein they were not permitted to learn to read and write under penalty of death, or something next to it, what may we not expect of them with the advances they have since made and are making?"

"I declare, colonel, I would not miss this interview I have had with you for a great deal. I was so young when the war broke out that I had no personal knowledge of many of the things that you have told me, and I assure you that you have interested me with their recital. I understand that you occupied several very important positions in State affairs during the period of 'Negro supremacy,' as the white people call it, and I know you must have made some valuable observations growing out of the downfall of those governments and the condition and tendencies of things since. Tell me just what you think of our future in this country, anyway. Tell me whether we are pro-gressing or retrograding, and whether you think it is necessary for us to emigrate to Africa, or to be colonized somewhere, or what?"

"Well, madam, I must confess that some of your questions are extremely hard to answer. Indeed, some of them are to-day puzzling some of the profoundest philosophers and thinkers in this country; and I doubt very much whether I could assume to answer them dogmatically. One thing, however, I can tell you, without fear of successful contradiction, and that is that no people similarly situated have ever made the progress in every department of life that our people have made since the world began. Why, just think of it! Twenty-seven years ago we did not own a foot of land, not a cottage in this wilderness; not a house, not a church, not a school-house, not even a name. We had no marriage tie, not a legal family—nothing but the public highways, closely guarded by black laws and vagrancy laws, upon which to stand. But to-day we have two millions of our children in school, we have about eighteen thousand colored professors and teachers, twenty thousand young men and women in schools of higher grade, two hundred newspapers, over two million members in the Methodist and Baptist churches alone, and we own over three hundred million dollars' worth of property in this Southern country. Over a million and a half of our people can now read and write. We are crowding the bar, the pulpit and all the trades, and every avenue of civilized life, and doing credit to the age in which we live.

"I tell you, madam, I am not much disturbed about our future. True, I cannot and do not pretend to be able to solve the Negro problem, as it is called, because I do not know that there is really such a problem. To my mind, it is all a matter of condition and national and constitutional authority. Get the conditions right and my faith is that the natural functions, security to 'life, liberty and happiness,' will follow. My advice to my people is: ' Save your earnings, get homes, educate your children, build up character, obey the laws of your country, serve God, protest against injustice like manly and reasonable men, exercise every constitutional right every time you may lawfully and peacefully do so, and leave results with God, and every thing will come out right sooner or later.' I have no faith in any general emigration or colonization scheme for our people. The thing is impracticable and undesirable. This is the most beautiful and desirable country that the sun shines upon, and I am not in favor of leaving it for any place but heaven, and that when my heavenly father calls, and not before. Of course, in localities where inhumanities are visited upon our people to such an extent that they cannot live there in peace and security I would advise them to remove to more agreeable sections of the country ; but never would I advise them to leave the United States. Another thing : I do not think we ought to ever want to get into any territory to ourselves, with the white people all to one side of us or around us. That's the way they got the Indians, you remember, and we know too well what became of them.

" My plan is for us to stay right in this country with the white people, and to be so scattered in and among them that they can't hurt one of us without hurting some of their own number. That's my plan, and that is one of my reasons why I am in the Methodist Episcopal Church. God's plan seems to be to pattern this country after heaven. He is bringing here all nations, kindreds and tongues of people, and mixing them into one homogeneous whole ; and I do not believe we should seek to frustrate His plan by any vain attempts to colonize ourselves in any corner to ourselves."

With this the colonel left, expressing himself delighted with his visit, as I am sure I was.

Between Mrs. Stowe's "Uncle Tom's Cabin" and Mrs. Albert's "House of Bondage" there is a most beautiful contrast ; the former dignifies the Negro as a fugitive and asserts his rights to be a fugitive ; the latter shows up the unrelenting patience of the Negro and his unrivaled faith in the Giver of all good. Again, the former is scenic, presenting a most beautiful as well as lasting, yet touching landscape ; while the latter is just what its title identifies—"The House of Bondage."

MADAM SISSIRETTA JONES.

The Black Patti of Her Race.

THE subject of this sketch was born in Providence, R. I. When quite a wee child she proved beyond the shadow of a doubt her fitness for the stage as a race representative, and has among other things maintained her ground, never weakening and giving down, but nourishing a faith fit only for the righteous, which has led her gently into the pleasant and peaceful paths of success.

Some say that greatness is sometimes thrust upon us; others, more liberal, say that it is inborn; others argue that it is acquired. We say that this is an instance where classical musical ability reigned uppermost, controlling and directing the possessor as the mainspring of all her infantile life; but on becoming cognizant of this state of affairs, she was advised by good Northern friends to turn her whole attention to the pursuit for which her heart and mind thirsted. Hence, after a few weeks with the classic masters, the whole Negro race was applauded for the advent of one among us, and sufficiently black to claim our identity, that was destined to move the world in tears. Year after year our subject has won new conquests, and in only a short season she is termed the Black Patti. Is this an instance of acquired greatness, thrusted greatness or inborn greatness? We loth to say inborn or thrust. For every achievement made by our race that seems to attract the attention of the world we are caused to feel that were it not for God's intervention, etc., etc. When

Negroes are smart, as a rule, a characteristic spirit seems to predominate in them when very small. Her career, while brief, is nevertheless full of bright successes. We append below a few press comments:

At the concert given by the World's Fair Colored Concert Company at New York, February 13th, Mme. Sissiretta Jones is said to have surpassed all former appearances. Among the boxholders were Judge and Mrs. Andrews, Colonel and Mrs. Ingersoll, Mrs. Jeannette M. Thurber, Mr. and Mrs. Henry Villard, Wallace C. Andrews, Mr. Morris Reno and Miss Reno, Daniel Bacon and R. W. G. Welling. Three rows of seats in the center aisle were occupied by a concert party from a fashionable girls' school, and there were musicians of fame in attendance who join with us in sentiment.—*The Freeman.*

A VALENTINE WORTH HAVING.

Tuesday afternoon, February 14th, Mme. Sissiretta Jones sang at the resi‑ dence of Judge Andrews, on Fifth avenue, New York, before a party of thirty ladies, among whom were Mrs. Hicks Lord, Mrs. C. Fields, Mrs. Van‑ derbilt, Mrs. Stevens and Mrs. Astor, at whose house Mme. Jones will sing next week. The Chief Justice of India, who was present, presented the singer with a valentine, which, when opened, contained a check for $1,000. She also received a solid silver basket filled with choice flowers. The ladies pronounced the singing superior to Patti's, and then sat down to lunch with Mme. Jones. Mr. Charles Anderson was a guest on this occasion. The pro‑ gram was a valentine souvenir printed on satin, and will be treasured by all as a memento.

"BROWN" AND "BLACK" PATTIS.

Their Singing—Selika the Best—Madame Jones a "Great Singer."

WASHINGTON, D. C.

Of Mme. Selika the world has spoken, and in her favor. Time nor rivals can wrest from her laurels so richly won ; but she is not the Selika of yester‑ day, and the fact is most apparent when she sings with another whose share to public favors is deserving because it is compensating. Selika is a finished artist who appeals to the technical society lights particularly, but they cannot support any first-class concert for the reason they are too few. In the rendi‑ tion of the staccato notes Mme. Selika has not been excelled, even by Patti, and her shading is so smooth and even that you cannot but commend it. Mrs. Jones is a great singer. She is not the "greatest singer in the world," nor is she a black, blue or green Patti. She is in no sense a Patti. If Mrs Jones would remember that Mrs. Greenfield, the Black Swan, made for herself a name without the need of styling herself the Black Jenny Lind, then she will know that she can succeed to as great an eminence without having to share the success with a white woman who would feel dishonored in wearing the title the White Black Swan. Afro-Americans need to impress their children that their race develops geniuses and heroes whose deeds can be emulated and perpetuated with everlasting profit, thus declaring our patriotism. We need more race pride! Our public men and women must exhibit it. Mme. Jones is a great singer ; Mme. Selika is the greatest colored singer. You hear Mme. Jones with pleasure ; you hear Mme. Selika with profit.—*J. E. Bruce* (*Bruce Grit*).

Mme. Sissiretta Jones' singing at the exposition at Pittsburg, Pa., saved the exposition management from bankruptcy.

MISS HALLIE QUINN BROWN.

Elocutionist.

A TRAVELER passing by a country farm house a few miles from Chatham, Canada, a few years ago, might, have seen a little girl of eight or nine summers, mounted upon a colt without bridle or girth, hair given to the winds to be tossed, dashing up a lane to the pasture. There he would have seen her dismount and hastily perform the duties of dairymaid, first calling each cow by name, and inquiring the health of each or making some playful remark. The milking finished, she now goes through the program that absorbs her whole attention, having risen before any other one of the household, so that she could not be seen. She jumps upon a stump or log and delivers an address to the audience of cows, sheep, birds, etc. Neither knowing nor caring what she says, she goes through her harangue, earnestly emphasizing by arm gesture, and occasionally by a stamp of the foot. She has a separate speech for the larger animals, and special addresses to the lambs, ducklings and any other juvenile auditors that happen to be near. Having exhausted her vocabulary, she begins a conversation in the language of the horse, cow, sheep, goose, rooster, or bird, until each is *imitated ;* then, bidding adieu to her pet auditors, she remounts her prancing steed and canters back to the house. This is her daily morning program. She supposed all along that her secret was locked in her own breast. But a farm hand saw her one morn by chance, himself unobserved, and 'twas a secret no longer. Nor did she realize her "ridiculous capers," as she has called it since, until she had grown to young womanhood. Who can say but that propitious Fate had her then in drill in order to develop the powers of her soul, so that she might make a portion of mankind happier by the instruction and amusement she should furnish. "Who was this little girl?" ask you. The subject of this sketch—Miss Hallie Q. Brown.

Hallie Quinn Brown is a native of Pittsburg, Pa. When she was quite small her parents moved to a farm near Chatham, Canada, Ontario West. At an early age, in the year 1868, she was sent to Wilberforce College, Ohio, to obtain an education

the country schools of Canada could not give, and where her parents subsequently removed and now reside, at Homewood Cottage. She completed the classical scientific course in 1873, with the degree of B. S. in a class of six. One of her classmates is the wife of Rev. Dr. B. F. Lee, ex president of Wilberforce, and now [1884] editor of the *Christian Recorder*; while another, Prof. S. T. Mitchell, A. M., has been elected president of Wilberforce.

MISS HALLIE QUINN BROWN.

Realizing that a great field of labor lay in the South, Miss Brown, with true missionary spirit, left her pleasant home and friends to devote herself to the noble work which she had chosen. Her first school was on a plantation in South Carolina, where she endured the rough life as best she could, and taught a large number of children gathered from neighboring plantations. She also taught a class of aged people, and by this means gave to many the blessed privilege of reading the Bible. She next took charge of a school on Sonora plantation in Mississippi, where she found the effort to elevate the minds of the people much hindered by their use of tobacco and whisky—twin vices.

But as she is an indefatigable worker she accomplished much, and at this place, as at all others where she is known, her influence for the better was felt. Her plantation school had no windows, but was well ventilated—too much so, in fact, for daylight could be seen from all sides, with no particular regularity, and the rain beat in fiercely. Not being successful in getting the authorities to fix the building—*shed*, we should have said—she secured the willing service of two of her larger boys. She mounted one mule and the two boys another, and thus they rode to the gin-mill. They got cotton seed, returned, mixed it with earth, which formed a plastic mortar, and with her own hands she pasted up the chinks, and ever after smiled at the unavailing attacks of wind and weather.

Her fame as an instructor spread, and her services were secured as teacher at Yazoo city. On account of the unsettled state of affairs in 1374-5, she was compelled to return North. Thus the South lost one of its most valuable missionaries. Miss Brown next taught in Dayton, Ohio for four years. Owing to ill health she gave up teaching. She was persuaded to travel for her *Alma Mater*, Wilberforce, and started on a lecturing tour, concluding at Hampton School, Virginia, where she was received with very great welcome. At the "Soldiers' Home" she was cordially greeted and kindly cared for by the sister of Dr. Shipman. After taking a course in elocution she traveled again, having much greater success, and receiving favorable criticisms from the press. For several years she has traveled with "The Wilberforce Grand Concert Company," an organization for the benefit of Wilberforce College. She has read before hundreds of audiences and tens of thousands of people, and has received nothing but the highest praise from all.

CRITICISM.

Miss Brown may be thought to gesticulate too frequently in some of her didactic selections; but right here is shown that she discards the rigid rules of the books and follows nature, for she possesses an ardent temperament, and nearly every sentence she utters in private conversation is made emphatic or impressive by a gesture or variation of the facial expression.

Miss Brown possesses a voice of " wonderful magnetism and great compass." At times she thrills by its intensity ; at times it is mellow and soothing. She seems to have perfect control of the muscles of her throat and can vary her voice as successfully as a mocking bird.

But we measure things largely by results. As a public reader Miss Brown delights, enthuses her audiences. In her humorous selections she often causes " wave after wave of laughter " to roll over her audience.

In her pathetic pieces she often moves her audience to tears.

In her didactic recitations she holds the listener spell-bound as she points out to him the shoals and quicksands or directs him to paths of right and truth.

But the public press speaks and it has a right to be heard.

The greatest compliment ever paid to Miss Brown, at least the one she doubtless appreciates the most, was received under the following circumstances. While at Appleton, Wis., she recited, among other selections, " How He Saved St. Michael's." After the concert a lady came forward, requesting to be introduced to the elocutionist. The Rev. F. S. Stein then introduced to Miss Brown Mrs. Dr. Stansbury, the author of " How He Saved St. Michael's." Madam Stansbury grasped the hand of the elocutionist and exclaimed : " Miss Brown, I have never heard that piece so rendered before." This, notwithstanding a famous reader a few weeks before, had given the same selection there, and advertised by announcing that she would render Mrs. Stansbury's famous poem. Miss Brown was confused. She did not even know the lady lived in the State, and did not dream of her presence in the house, hence she was taken completely by surprise, nor would she have attempted to give it had she heard of the presence of the authoress. The compliment was all the more appreciated because every elocutionist who visits that section renders " St. Michael's."

A CASKET OF LAURELS.

WON BY MISS HALLIE QUINN BROWN, OF WILBERFORCE.

Miss H. Q. Brown, the elocutionist, ranks as one of the finest in the country.—*Daily News*, Urbana, O.

The select reading of Miss H. Q. Brown is done to perfection. She has an excellent voice and has good control of it. She makes every piece sound as if it were the author speaking, and in many of them doubtless she excels the one she imitates.—*Neogo, Ill.*

Miss Hallie Q. Brown, a general favorite at Island Park, rendered in her inimitable style, "The Creed of the Bells." A prolonged encore followed.—Island Park "*Assembly.*"

Her style is pure and correct; her selections excellent. The "Fifty Miles an Hour" made one thrill, it was so very impressive.—Long Branch (N. J.) *News.*

Miss Brown displayed remarkable powers of pathos and dramatic elocution. * * * * Her excellent dramatic talent was displayed to the best advantage in the selection entitled, "The Sioux Chief's Daughter." The audience was the largest ever gathered at a public entertainment in that place.—Newport (R. I.) *News.*

The readings of Miss H. Q. Brown confer a histrionic glow upon the colored race. She is the superior of nine out of ten elocutionists before the public. Her description of "The Bells" is a masterpiece of elocutionary art which will withstand the severest and most cultivated criticism. Her prolongation of the tones of the bells is a wonderful representation of the poet's lines. Miss Brown's selections were all of a difficult order and exhibited great versatility and ability to reach in most of them a still better execution.—*Daily Republican*, Emporia, Kan.

Of the recitations of Miss Hallie Q. Brown too much cannot be said. As a reader she is the peer of any professional in the land.—Richmond (Ind.) *Paladium.*

Miss Brown in her elocution is unquestionably brilliant. Her "Fifty Miles an Hour," descriptive of Mrs. Garfield's ride to Washington when her husband was shot, was given with that generous touch of womanly feeling that made it the gem of the entertainment.—Miami *Helmet*, Piqua, O.

Most excellent was the dramatic reading of Miss Hallie Q. Brown, a graduate of Wilberforce College, and evidently a lady of much intelligence. * * * * Miss Brown is also at home in humorous pieces. The description of how a woman joined the Masons was received with almost continuous shouts of laughter, the members of that ancient and honorable order apparently appreciating it keenly.—Marion *Times* (Ia.).

Miss Hallie Q. Brown has but few equals as an elocutionist. She has a sweet, flexible voice. Her enunciation is distinct, her manner graceful and her gesticulations eminently appropriate to the character of her selections. Some of her humorous selections caused wave after wave of laughter to roll over the audience and were most heartily encored.—Red Oak (Ia.) *Express.*

The recitations and readings of Miss Hallie Q. Brown were simply superb. The magnetism, eloquence and wonderful compass of voice, as developed in "Uncle Dan'l's Pra'ar," "Farewell, Brother Watkins," and "Aunt Jemima's Courtship," might be equaled but could never be surpassed.—Richmond (Ind.) *Independent*.

The readings of Miss Hallie Brown were grand.—Urbana (O.) *Democrat*.

The elocutionary entertainment given by Miss Hallie Q. Brown, a graduate of Wilberforce, was worth double the price of admission. She has a wonderful voice, and a culture to match it. An educated and much-traveled gentleman who has listened to all the most noted elocutionists in this country and Europe was so enthusiastic over Miss Brown's rendition of the "Church Bells," that he declared he never saw or heard it equaled ; that her manner, voice and gesture were all superior to anything he had ever listened to or hoped to hear.—Richmond (Ind.) *Paladium*.

Miss Brown is quite tall, has auburn hair, a keen eye, a voice of remarkable compass and features of great mobility. Her selections were as follows : "The Last Hymn," "The Love Letter," "How He Saved St. Michael's" —a thrilling story in verse relating how this famous Charleston (S. C.) church was saved from fire by the daring act of a slave, " Jemima's Courtship," " Curfew Must Not Ring To-night,"—in which she exhibited intense dramatic power, "Ameriky's Conversion," "Uncle Daniel's Vision," "The Little Hatchet," and "The Creeds of the Bells." Miss Brown stands by far above the readers we are accustomed to hear.—Washington (D. C.) *Advocate*.

Several of our prominent citizens were present who were greatly delighted with the skillful and accomplished manner with which Miss Brown rendered the varied styles of elocution.—New Haven (Conn.) *Paladium*.

Miss Hallie Q. Brown, elocutionist of the Wilberforce Concert Company, has the distinguished honor of being the teacher in the department of elocution at the Monona Lake Assembly, and is meeting with great success.—Correspondence—Cleveland *Gazette*.

* * * Miss Hallie Q. Brown was decidedly entertaining in her efforts in elocution. She "brought down the house" on various occasions and had to respond repeatedly to the spontaneous calls of the vast audience.—"Monona Lake Assembly," Madison (Wis.) *Daily Democrat*.

Miss Brown is so well known in Xenia that one need not go into detail in praise of the good and even performance of this talented lady ; she will make friends for herself wherever she goes.—*Torchlight*, Xenia (O.).

Miss Hallie Q. Brown, the elocutionist, who has always been a great favorite with Xenia audiences, was cheered to the echo, and in some of her pieces was really interrupted by the continuous applause. She certainly excels in her character delineations and varied modulations of tone, three-fourths of the elocutionists on the stage.—*Daily Gazette*, Xenia (O.).

But the crowning feature of the company is the elocutionist, Miss Hallie Q. Brown. Nothing finer in elocution has been heard in this city, with no exception or reservation in favor of other eminent elocutionists, who have appeared in this city. She is capable of touching every chord of emotion, equally effective in pathos and humor. The intonations of her voice are as exquisite as those of an eolian harp, and as melodious as music itself, and in dramatic fervor and power of dramatic expression Miss Brown is inimitable. What for instance can be more melodious and touching than her recitation of the " Church Bells," or what more genuinely humorous than the recitation of the original piece called " The Apple?" Miss Brown cannot fail of establishing for herself a national reputation at no distant day.—*Republican,* Xenia(O.).

Miss Hallie Q. Brown, the elocutionist with the company, was loudly applauded. Many credit Miss Brown with being one of the best elocutionists before the public.—Indianapolis *Times.*

Miss Brown, the elocutionist, is a phenomenon, and deserves the highest praise. She is a talented lady and deserves all the encomiums that she receives.—The *Daily Sun,* Vincennes (Ind.).

The select reading of Miss Hallie Q. Brown was very fine. From grave to gay, from tragic to comic, with a great variation of themes and humors, she seemed to succeed in all, and her renderings were the spice of the night's performance.—*Monitor,* Marion (Ill.).

We must say the capacity of Miss Hallie Q. Brown to entertain an audience is wonderful. —*Tri-County Reporter,* Gosport (Ind.).

Miss Brown's recitals will compare favorable with many of the female elocutionists who are classed with Mrs. Scott-Siddons and others of lesser note. —Vincennes *Daily Commercial.*

MRS. LAVINIA B. SNEED.

Educator and Writer.

MRS. SNEED claims a very high place among the literary women of the race. For many years she has shown the trend of her genius as a writer, and though she is quite young, many a topic engaging the public mind has been treated at length with an erudite pen from her storehouse of thought. Happy indeed are they who live in the sunshine of Fate. Many Negro journalists have boasted of her favors, realizing the good of her articles gracing their columns. Her writing possesses that smoothness, clearness and fearlessness so often said of the great writers.

It is easily predicted that, should she live long, the race will be blessed with one other such woman writer as Mrs. Harper, one other such Christian as Mrs. Early, one other such chivalrous woman as Sojourner Truth.

IONE E. WOOD.

Educator and Writer.

MISS IONE E. WOOD ranks to-day among the foremost of our women; first, from the standpoint of acknowledged intellectual ability to write; second, as an earnest educator and race advocate. Not yet in the zenith of womanhood, but in the ascendency, she is unceremoniously climbing its rugged heights with the will of a Trojan. For her, as for others, God has destined to shine in the bright arena of American heroines, and she feels the spirit on her to quietly and noiselessly move unobserved into her place. Miss Wood does not make much noise, but howbeit she is heard in the press. The force of her genius, like the great power wheel of moving machinery, is ever asserting itself and keeping alive and uppermost in the minds of those who think the great topics agitating the Negro mind.

IONE E. WOOD.

MISS VALETTA LINDEN WINSLOW.

Elocutionist.

OUR race possesses many young ladies of ability who would prove powerful factors in demonstrating the possibilities of the race, if they would only exert themselves and apply their energies. Not seeming to realize our need of the highest intellectual advancement, they pass through the soft green meadows and flowing pathways of life, with no apparent aim. But, when we see a young girl, just budding into womanhood, in the face of many obstacles, making for herself a name that honors her and exalts the race, it is a pleasure to record her achievements. Such a one is the subject of this

MISS VALETTA LINDEN WINSLOW.

s'retch, Miss Valetta Winslow. She was born in Chicago, Ill., January 25, 1871, and is the eldest of three sisters, daughters of Elisha and Emma Winslow. She resided in her native city almost fourteen years, about half of which time she attended the public schools. Her father having taken up his residence in California, early in November, 1884, she, in company with her mother and sisters, departed for the far West, arriving in Oakland, Cal., on the ninth day of November. In this beautiful city, the Athens of the Pacific Coast, where the very best educational facilities are free to all, the family took up its residence. She began her school career there in January, 1885. She made excellent progress and attended regularly until February 14, 1890, when, owing to failing health, she was compelled to discontinue her studies. The possessor of commendable ambition, but, unfortunately, not of a robust constitution, she undertook too many studies, and the result was impaired health. However, she was able to complete her junior year in the High School, and did so very creditably. Miss Winslow had a special taste for elocution, and to this study she devoted much of her spare time while attending school.

Her teacher was Mrs. Carro True Boardman, one of the leading elocutionists of the Pacific Coast. After a short, but much needed and beneficial rest, she began studying again by taking up Delsarte and elocution as a specialty, and the progress she made was truly phenomenal. Possessed of a kind and generous nature, she gave unstintedly of her time and talents to every worthy cause, and, as a consequence, was a general favorite.

On the 16th of May, 1891, she was publicly presented with a handsome lace pin by the Masonic fraternity. The pin consisted of two pendants, a cross and the square and compass, significant of the best motives and resolves in the Masonic world,—a suggestive token of appreciation of her kind and generous qualities. In July, 1892, Miss Winslow filled a special engagement with the Chautauqua Assembly at Pacific Grove. And when we inform the reader that this Assembly is composed of some of the ablest men and brightest women on the Coast, that its entire membership is refined and of exalted tone, the importance of such an engagement is plainly evident. The following extracts from leading daily papers give an excellent impression of the talent and artistic ability possessed by Miss Winslow:

Miss Valetta L. Winslow, in all her public performances here, has shown most remarkable power, especially as a Delsartist, carrying her audiences by storm. Her facial expressions were a constant surprise, expressive of the various passions and emotions of the soul, while every movement was grace and beauty. She has made, without a doubt, a fine record at this assembly, and her future will be watched with increasing interest by the host of Chautauquans and the friends in attendance on these unusually attractive exercises. It is to be hoped that she will be engaged for assembly next year.—*Cor. San Jose Mercury, July 7, 1892.*

Miss Winslow's recitation, "Aux Italiens," was gracefully rendered and well received. Her portrayal of the different passions and emotions that ofttimes rack we poor mortals sore were true to the letter, particularly revenge, pain, abject fear, and entreaty. The lady is the personification of grace and ease, lithe as a panther and willowy as a reed.—*Pacific Grove Review, July 9, 1892.*

Then came the most pleasing event of the afternoon—Miss Valetta Winslow in Tableaux d'Art. She gave forty-nine different expressions, such as anger, horror, bashfulness, ridicule, etc., with appropriate gestures. The gifted young lady created great enthusiasm. The various expressions were to the life, and her gestures were full of charming grace and appropriateness. She was recalled, and recited "Sister and I," with powerful expression and gesture.—*San Francisco Call, Aug. 4, 1892.*

Among Miss Winslow's personal letters none are more highly prized than the two following:

"Miss Valetta L. Winslow, as Delsartist and elocutionist, was engaged for the Pacific Grove Chautauqua Assembly in July, 1892. Her work was artistic, and gave great satisfaction. As a Delsartist her movements were most graceful, and her delineations of the various emotions of the soul full of force and artistic power. I cheerfully commend her and her work."   A. C. HIRST, D. D.,
                              President Pacific Grove Assembly.
San Francisco, Cal., Oct. 4, 1892.

"I have had the extreme pleasure of hearing Miss Valetta Winslow as an elocutionist, and witnessed her rendition of the Delsarte system. I can conscientiously say that she surpasses any person in her line that I have met. I can cheerfully recommend her as an A No. 1 artist, both as a Delsartist and elocutionist."   A. WALTERS, D. D.,
                              Bishop A. M. E. Zion Church.
San Francisco, Cal., February 16, 1893.

In concluding this sketch, we appreciate the ability of the newspaper critics and the fine parts of the men whose testimony is herein recorded. When talented journalists and able divines of the dominant race use such glowing language to express their appreciation of a young colored lady's ability comment is unnecessary.

DR. IDA GRAY.

THE accompanying portrait is of Dr. Ida Gray, the only Afro-American lady dentist. Miss Gray resides in Cincinnati, and was one of the very many who received their educational start in Gaines High School. On leaving this school she entered the dental department of the University of Michigan, from which she graduated in 1890. On returning to her home she opened a very cozy office on 9th street, and has in these two years built up a large practice, having as many white as colored patients.

Miss Gray is a very refined lady, of whom the editor of the *Planet* says: " Her blushing, winning way makes you feel like finding an extra tooth any way to allow her to pull."

DR. IDA GRAY.

As a result of strict attention to business and the thoroughness of her work she is kept constantly busy. Cincinnatians are proud of their Afro-American lady dentist, and she in every respect proves herself worthy of their confidence and admiration.—*In Ringwood's Journal.*

SARAH G. JONES, M. D.

Virginia's First Woman Physician.

SARAH G. JONES, M. D., the first woman to be licensed to practice medicine in Virginia, is a daughter of George W. Boyd, the leading colored contractor and builder of this city. She was born in Albemarle county, Va., and educated in the public schools of Richmond, being graduated in 1883. She then taught in the schools of this city for five years. In 1888 Miss Boyd was married to M. B. Jones, who, at that time, was also a teacher, but now is G. W. A. Secretary of the True Reformers. Mrs. Jones entered Howard Medical College, Washington, D. C., in 1890, and was graduated this year with the degree of M. D. She appeared before the State Medical Examining Board with eighty-four others and received a certificate, which entitles her to secure a license to practice her profession. Mrs. Jones received over 90 per cent. on the examination in surgery. Out of the class of eighty-five twenty-one white graduates, representing several colleges, failed to pass. Dr. Jones and her husband are representatives of the best society of colored people in the State, and are well-to-do people. When a school teacher she was known as one of the brightest young colored women in the city. She will practice among her race.

MRS. N. A. R. LESLIE.

Pianist, Music Teacher.

THE biography of of Mrs. Leslie would necessitate a lengthy, but pleasing account of her busy life even in the realm of music. It is not our purpose to make the least attempt to say half that might be said in her favor.

For many years she has figured very conspicuously among the very best musicians of the race, in fact her field of usefulness takes in a wide scope of country not only many of the Southern States, but Indian Territory. She is now located at Corpus Christi, Texas, where she has started a musical conservatory wherein our ladies may pursue to completion the lyric art. For many years those of our race that were musically inclined were almost compelled to leave the State, travel over a wide stretch of country and under great expenses, in order to so fit themselves suffer the disadvantage of absence from the home circle. Mrs. Leslie finally concluded that Corpus Christi would be a good field for her activities, it being the home of her brother, Prof. Cole that erudite scholar from the classic Halls of Yale College, and hence moved there from Muscogee Indian Territory 1892. Since there her practical life has

added much to the social status of our race, and in molding public sentiment from the standpoint of music. Words seem indeed very dull when we attempt to give the slightest hint of the good she has accomplished. What Prof. Cole is, as a scholar, she is, as a musician. It has always been the disposition of this talented lady to excel in music, and those who have been under her painstaking instruction, or those who have had the pleasure of giving them-

MRS. N. A. R. LESLIE.

selves up to listen to the plaintive notes under her mellifluous execution, join in the universal verdict that the spell o'er cast is not only delightful, but entrancing.

Music indeed though termed easy of accomplishment, and considered not a task, is really one of the finest arts which if acquired becomes for the scholar one of the divinest arts, and made more noticeable in proportion to the complication of it. It has long been sorely abused especially when we consider the rude appelation applied to us as a musical race—Musical in the rough. Why not musical in the fine?

Mrs. Leslie is demonstrating wonderfully and well in a peculiar section of country, what our women can do in the art and science of music. She is not only talented as a reader and performer of her art, but is a composer of some prominence. Her fort however lies in the imparting to her pupil with ease, what she does and knows.

Aside from music, she is scholarly, gifted with force of character and the impress of her genius leaves the germ of ambition wherever it is stamped.

Hence the race, which has produced other great minds to shine forth proclaiming progress in various walks of life may feel proud of Mrs. Leslie who along with many more of her sex, is doing what she can to explode the doctrine of *inferior music* and the appellation, *musical race in the rough.* Much is accomplished with hard labor, and nothing without. With our subject as with all who succeed it is *labor omnia vincet.*

EDNORA NAHAR.

Elocutionist.

THIS talented lady was born in Boston, of high and well-known parents, in fact, the Howards possess a much envied family lineage, as indeed it reaches far down many generations. She is a cousin to Miss J. Imogene Howard, who is honored with the distinction of being a lady member of the New York World's Fair committee. Miss Nahar was educated in the public schools of Boston, and finished in the Fort Edwards Collegiate Institute, and soon thereafter spent a season at Boucicault's Madison Dramatic School, where she, on account of her genius, as well as being a favorite aspirant for stage honors, was not allowed to pay the customary $10 as an entrance fee.

Prior to finishing her education at Fort Edwards Institute, on account of her adaptability for reading, a class aspiring for elocutionary honors was placed under her charge. So well did she discharge her duties under that weight of responsibility that two of her pupils carried off two of the prizes offered at the end of the school year.

Since her *debut* she has not been idle by any means, but to the contrary, as her record will show. Thus it will prove to the youth of our race that nothing is accomplished without great labor. And those young ladies who desire to be known, which is to be admired, will look upon this record with Longfellow's Psalm of Life upon their pure lips; they can "make their lives sublime" only to the extent of the sacrifice they make in the world of pleasure, and strive with all their might to shine in the world of grand human accomplishment.

She has given sixty-eight readings in Boston. Her initial bow was made Nov. 16, 1886, and Nov. 2, 1887, she gave her first press concert in the famous Chickering Hall, being the second prominent woman of her race to appear behind its footlights. At two different times she has appeared before 5,000 people in her native city.

In 1890, Nov. 17, she read before 5,000 people in the

EDNORA NAHAR.

Academy of Music, Philadelphia, with the famous Marine band, from Washington. She has read in ten concerts in the British Provinces, read in thirty-one States, 300 cities and at over 800 concerts. Out of this vast number she has been her own manager. Indeed, she has so far exceeded the expectation of many of her compeers as a manager that she is awakening to the fact that she can not only manage for herself but for others. This new career dawned in her busy life with all its sweet and bitter vicissitudes on the 6th and 7th of February, 1893.

On the 27th and 28th of February she gave a cantata for children, at Bethel A. M. E. Church, in Chicago, and had packed houses each night. On the 7th and 8th of March she managed for Mme. Sisseretta Jones (otherwise known by the music lovers of this country as The Black Patti), and packed Zion Church (New York city) those two nights.

MISS NAHAR'S RECITAL.

The Chicago *Appeal* says: "A fair house greeted Miss Ed. norah Nahar, of Boston, at Bethel Wednesday evening, to listen to a very pleasing program. Miss Nahar, from point of grace on the stage, has very few equals, and to gaze upon some of her beautiful poses was alone worth the price of admission. Miss Nahar showed to best advantage in the 'Sioux Chief's Daughter,' and in her numerous selections she made a decided hit. The support of Miss Theodora Lee was very commendable. Miss Lee has a very sweet voice, and in her rendition of ' Snowflakes ' would have done credit to a professional. Miss Gertrude Washington, as accompanist, displaying her usual skill."

The Indianapolis *Freeman* says: " Miss Ednorah Nahar, the reader, is an assistant teacher of elocution at Fort Edward Collegiate Institute."

GREAT CONCERT AT BETHEL CHURCH.

Miss Nahar's all star aggregation renders excellent programmes to packed houses at Bethel Church Monday and Tuesday evenings. The " Black Patti" concerts at Bethel Church were great successes, both artistically and financially. They reflect credit on the performers, and especially on Miss Ednorah, who conceived the idea and brought it to successful issue. No entertainments ever given in Bethel Church have ever drawn such large audiences of Chicago's most intelligent and refined people.

WHAT THE PRESS SAY OF MISS NAHAR.

Miss Ednora Nahar is a reader of talent. Her gestures are easy, graceful, and to the point. While her stage presence would do credit to many a professional actress.—*Boston Daily Advertiser.*

Her general style is good, her manner pleasing, added to this she is most fortunate in the possession of a voice which is a marvel of sweetness and purity of tone.—*Boston Evening Traveller.*

Miss NAHAR's rendition of the " Chariot Race," from " Ben Hur " was a revelation, and too much can not be said in praise of it. With a clear resonant voice, full of fire and dramatic action she electrified her hearers and held them spell-bound to the end, She has a fine voice, and an earnest and expressive face.—*The Boston Pilot.*

Miss NAHAR in her description of the " Chariot Race," from " Ben Hur" showed a notable dramatic skill—*Boston Evening Transcript,*

Miss NAHAR has won for herself the title of " Boston's favorite elocutionist."—*Boston Advocate.*

Her art is no art, but nature itself. She is both elocutionist and actress.—*Newport (R. I.) Daily News.*

Miss EDNORA NAHAR, in her dramatic reading the "Sioux Chief's Daughter," made a strong hit, and her two ENCORE pieces showed a versatility rarely seen,—*Halifax(N. B.) Morning Herald.*

As a dramatic reader Miss NAHAR has few equals. Of her readings we can say nothing but words of praise.—*St. John (N. B.) Globe.*

Miss NAHAR as an elocutionist, is superb. Her voice is well modulated, her enunciation is very clear and distinct, and she possesses perfect control over her vocal organs. Her recitation of the " Organ Builder" and :" The Pilot's Story," were pathetic, while the curse scene of "Leah, the Forsaken," was a piece of stage work hard to be beaten. Miss Nahar's humorous pieces took the house by storm. " Aunt Jemimah's Courtship " and " The Lord's of Creation " were charming, while the rich Irish brogue she brought out in her rendition, "Low Back Car" was perfection itself.—*Danville Daily Register (Dem.)*

Miss NAHAR is an elocutionist of rare ability and power. Her diction is clear and her gestures full of grace. Her selections are the best. It is not saying too much of her to say, she reminds one very much in her stage movement and easy manner of Mojeska.—*Greensboro North Shore.*

Miss NAHAR's appearance here was a success in every particular. She made herself a favorite in her first piece. " The Pilot's Story," and the enthusiasm kept up during the entire readings. Her manner is decidedly easy and graceful on the stage. In the curse scene from " Leah " she not only sustained her reputation as a clear reader, but gave evidence of considerable histrionic power.— *Wash. Cor. of New York Age.*

Miss EDNORA NAHAR received a great amount of applause, and her rendition of the curse scene from " Leah, the Forsaken" was as fine a bit of acting as we have seen.—*Charlotte Chronicle.*

Miss NAHAR, of Boston, was particularly greeted to the echo, in her almost perfect rendition of dramatic selections.—*Norfolk Evening Telegram.*

"Aux Italiens" by Miss Nahar, was interpreted with a newer and subtile meaning than ever before, it was pathetic, tender, loving, firefull, fervid and dramatic, each following in place with a sequence that only comes with genius.—*The Philadelphia Weekly Sentinel.*

Miss Nahar is prepossessing in appearance, graceful in movement, and confident in bearing. She possesses decided dramatic powers has a fine voice, strong, pure, flexible and quite voluminous.—*Cleveland (O.) Gazette.*

In "Aux Italiens," Miss Nahar displayed original conception as well as extraordinary powers of execution, she has command of her voice, and her renditions are more like interpretations than recitations.—*St. Louis Advance.*

Miss Ednorah Nahar, as an elocutionist is superb.—*The Daily Record,* Columbia, C. S.

The honors of the evening were properly awarded Miss Nahar, who is a great favorite in St. John. Her "Chariot Race" from "Ben Hur" was a masterpiece of stirring power, while in Cleopatra in Egyptian costume she brought out fully the tremendous passion of that poem.—*Daily Telegraph*, St. John, N. B.

In the "Chariot Race" and "Cleopatra" an elegant Egyptian costume afforded every opportunity for displaying to the best her wonderful abilities.—*The Daily Sun*, St. John, N. B.

Her voice one always remembers with pleasure. It is said the charm of Booth's voice remains with one who has heard him, this is not much to say of Miss Nahar.—*Cincinnati Enterprise.*

Miss Nahar is a talented lady whose "Sioux Chief's daughter" given in Indian costume was finely rendered, while the "Chariot Race" from Wallace's "Ben Hur" was a revelation.—*New York Mail and Express.*

At the Hyperion Theatre about 1000 people attended the concert given by the Dixwell Ave. Church, besides the Yale Banjo and Apollo Club, Miss Nahar of Boston, a highly gifted elocutionist was received with great applause.—*The Paladium*, New Haven, Conn.

Miss Nahar is a reader of wonderful talent, very graceful and expressive; her selections are particularly refined ·—*Philadelphia Advance.*

Her gestures are easy and graceful and she possesse rare gifts and powers as an elocutionist.—*Durham (N. C.) Daily Sun.*

Miss Nahar is undoubtedly a genius, to equal her would be a task for many whose reputation is broader. "Aux Italiens" and the Curse scene from "Leah the Forsaken" were wonderful.—*Raleigh (N. C.) Chronicle.*

Miss Nahar captivated the audience with her vivacity, and the "Chariot Race" brought down the house.—*Hartford (Conn.) Telegram-Record*

Miss Nahar's dramatic readings were splendid and drew forth hearty applause.—*Detroit Free Press.*

"Aux Italiens" was magnificently rendered, but the climax was in the Garden scene from "Mary Stuart." In the character of Mary Stuart it is not too much to say her conception would have done credit to Charlotte Cushman, Jauneschek or Risbtori.—*Newport, R. I. Daily News.*

PRIVATE OPINIONS OF WELL-KNOWN PERSONS.

She is a genius.—Ex-Secretary Noble.

She has power and the sacred fire of genius, and ought soon to be at the top as an actress.—Dion Bouccicault.

She has power, force, talent and genius and should forsake the platform for the stage.—John Boyle O'Rielly.

She has given five readings at the Soldier's Home and has successfully entertained the theatre full of old soldiers. I consider her a reader of rare talent.—P. Woodfin, Governor Soldier's Home, Hampton, Va.

She is the finest I have ever heard.—Frederick Douglass.

Her " Chariot Race " from Ben Hur was magnificently rendered.—Col. Elliott Shepard.

Miss Nahar has plenty of talent.—Modjeska.

ELLA F. SHEPHARD.

Eminent Teacher, Singer, Pianist.

ONE of the most talented women of the race is Miss Ella F. Shephard of Fisk Jubilee fame, who for a number of years traveled through the United States, Europe and other foreign countries delighting with her company of singers the many thousands who flocked to hear them and even until now say lasting words of praise of them.

She is an intellectual model of most genial nature, ambitious; yea one, who has lived laborious days, and shunned delights, that she might do educational service for her race. For a number of years she served as lady principal of Prairie View Normal Institute of Texas, and resigned to recruit the *Old Jubilee Troupe.* Her qualifications as a musician, if the " fittest servive," may beconsidered a criterion, are par excellence. Those who have sat under the mellifluous music of her voice, have expressed their inspired admiration, with their greatest earnestness.

The greater portion of her useful life has been spent in the South where the greatest battles with ignorance have to be fought, as a teacher she has always been equal to the emergency and superior to the general rule. Wherever she has taught the whites as well as those of her race have become her faithful and lasting friends. Later in life she has filled very dignified positions as professor in some of our leading institutions of learning.

Her race affiliations are not contracted to a few teachers and ministers, but the broad field of her active life has brought her in social touch with the leading spirits of our 19th century civilization. Her worth cannot be estimated in words, she has lived in deeds, not the extended life of many, however, but the tireless activity of this noble heroine tell.

MISS A. E. McEWEN.

Essayist and Editor.

MISS McEWEN is one of the best essayists of the South. As a writer she is possessed with that grace and ease that is so noticeable among the great writers. She has, for a number of years, assisted her father in the publication of a very

MISS A. E. MC EWEN

able Baptist journal, and with both tongue and pen helped to make it a very newsy as well as flourishing newspaper. She is quite young, yet her ability with the pen gives her notoriety envied by many twice her age. A remarkable, a useful and illustrious life, full of good deeds and grand accomplishments in behalf of her race, beckon her on.

MRS. CORA L. BURGAN. (nee MOORE.)

Pianist and Teacher.

MRS. BURGAN is a graduate from one of the leading conservatories of music of America. She was educated in the public schools of Detroit, Mich., and at quite an early age showed the qualifications for which her father, grandfather,

and, in fact, her whole family for three or more generations back, have been famous—that of music.

Her father for many years was leader of the best orchestra of her native city.

For a number of years she taught music in the Texas Blind Asylum for colored youth; in fact, she was the first lady that was honored with a position in the Institute. Later she was appointed to a prominent position as teacher in the Paul Quinn College, by the affable Dr. I. M. Burgan, who in 1889 made her the mate for his useful career.

MRS. CORA L. BURGAN.

Mrs. Burgan is pleasing, courteous—in fact destined to be a grand and useful woman to her race.

MRS. JULIA RINGWOOD COSTON.

As a Journalist.

IN journalism, as in every other calling, women are occupying a very conspicuous place. We received on our exchange table last week *Ringwood's Afro-American Journal of Fashion*, edited by Mrs. Julia Ringwood Coston, of Cleveland, Ohio. It is a beautiful twelve-page journal, and the only publication of its kind on the market.   Every colored woman in America should read it.—*Lynchburg Counselor.*

Mrs. Coston says:

" The vibrations of our silent suffering are not ineffective.

MRS. JULIA RINGWOOD COSTON.

They touch and communicate. They awaken interest and kindle sympathies which arouse public consciousness and bid it to pity and revolt against the injustice of the oppression. They touch the keyboard of our human mind and convey through the nerve keys the sympathies of the intelligent, humane and Christian public a knowledge of our grievances in all parts of this broad land, which will at some time, we believe, not distant, secure to our children the protection of the Church and State. The cruelty of the treatment of African women in the South touched this keyboard in eighteen hundred and fifty-six. Our mothers had suffered long in hopeless endurance. But at last the keys moved and a Lincolnic voice spoke and they received the protection of the State. Through this board Lincoln spoke to the Church and State. By the editorials upon our barbarous treatment in the South and injustice of our treatment in the North we acknowledge an earnest desire for a humane South and Christian North. It will increase in potency, and secure for Afro-American women and children all the blessings of this great country."

As to women writers, and what she thinks, let the following speak for itself :

THE WOMEN WHO ARE LOVED ARE THOSE WHO ARE WOMEN.

They have a place in all our hearts ; the men adore them, and the women love them, yet they are essentially feminine. They know naught of woman's rights and universal suffrage ; they are not troubled with the affairs of State, nor are they agents of reform. They are women, adorable women, into whose minds has crept no vicious longing for publicity, no hunger to unsurp the sphere of men.

Would it not be well to make such women models for our girls ? Would it not be well to consider a little what are the deepest, truest, highest rights of womankind? Would it not be well to look ahead a bit and ponder, what sort of a world will it be when femininity shall be extinct?

Women have so many rights that are truly theirs, so many opportunities for influence upon the great world, that they may stop and consider, not how to obtain more, but how to make the best use of what already is theirs.

There pertains to true womanhood a sanctity and a purity without which the world must suffer. Politicians, lawyers and financiers can all be recruited from the ranks of men, but where are we to find the softening, refining influences of life if our women cease to be such ?

No one who comes in contact with homes that are happy and attractive can doubt the influence of her who is their inspiration. A truly feminine woman, one who is thoroughly in sympathy with great and noble thoughts, has a power so penetrating that our girls have need of careful training if they are to learn to wield it well.

Every true man has stored away in his heart an ideal woman such as would require all the strength and power of the real individual to realize. Surely the sphere can not be low or limited that possesses such possibilities, and surely the highest, most inalienable right must be that of realizing them.

Not for one moment is it meant to speak a light or disparaging word of that noble army of women who, finding themselves thrown on their own resources, have bravely taken up the burden and borne it through the thick of the fight. To these be all honor accorded.

It is not the silent army of workers who do harm, but the ostentatious seekers after notoriety. There is no good reason why a woman should cease to be feminine because she is compelled to work, but it too often happens that the girls who are forced to earn their own living become embued with a spirit of bravado.

Gallantry belongs to all strong, vigorous men ; their natural impulse is to protect and help the struggling woman? But what is to be done with an unsexed creature, a thing neither man nor woman ? In every situation in life, at home surrounded by luxury, or in the world struggling for preference, a woman's womanhood is her surest, strongest shield.

Recently there has appeared in the world of letters a certain class of women writers who have thrown off the veil of modesty, and who, in the name of reform, pose as martyrs, sacrificing themselves to a great work. To all such would-be missionaries it may be admissible to hint that the loss of one chaste womanly woman does more harm than any number of novels can ever do good. Also, it might be suggested that, inasmuch as books are read, not by a limited class only, but by a large public, there is danger that more minds become polluted than purified by their influence.

Only an utter lack of femininity could make it possible for a woman to stand before the world and proclaim its vice. The harm her example may do to the young and ignorant aspirants for literary honors is only paralleled by the cause she has given mankind to hold her womanhood in light esteem.

As to the worthiness of *Ringwood's Journal*, of which Mrs. Coston is the editress, we insert a few of the many comments from persons and presses :

WALNUT HILLS, O., March 1, 1892.

MRS. COSTON.

Dear Madam: I am much pleased with "Ringwood," and wish it a hearty success. Such a journal should be sustained by our people throughout the Union.

We have among us here and there women and men of considerable literary ability and sterling moral worth, of whom we may be proud, who have hitherto led lives of such seclusion that they are not known beyond the locality in which they reside by name, yet whose influence has been wielded for good, and who ould not be encouraged to remain in obscurity.

I can imagine what a great undertaking yours is ; but God is always on the side of the right, and "perseverance commands success."

Enclosed please find my yearly subscription. Hoping that I shall soon be in condition to send a short paper for the *Journal*, and bidding you God-speed in your noble work, I am, and hope to remain, yours for improvement,

SARAH G. JONES, 86 Chapel street.

Ringwood's Afro-American Journal of Fashion, edited by Mrs. Julia Ringwood Coston, Cleveland, O., the only illustrated journal of colored ladies in the world. Besides the latest Parisian fashions of ladies' gowns, etc., it contains biographical sketches of prominent ladies of the race and of promising young misses, edited by the Mrs. M. C. Church Terrel, Washington, D. C., with the following departments: "Plain Talk to our Girls," edited by Mrs. Prof. J. P. Shorter, Wilberforce University ; "Art Department," edited by Miss Adina White, Cincinnati, O.; "Mother's Corner," edited by Mrs. E. C. Nesbit, Cincinnati, O.; "Literary Department," by Mrs M. E. Lambert, Detroit, Mich.; "Home Department," by Miss S. Mitchell, Cleveland, O.

The current issue of *Ringwood's Ladies' Magazine* contains two very able articles from the pen of Mrs. Earnestine Clark Nesbit and Miss Adina White.—*Richmond Planet.*

631 PARK ROW, NEW YORK. May 22, 1892.

EDITRESS RINGWOOD'S JOURNAL.

Dear Madam: Through the kindness of some one, I have lately received a sample copy of *Ringwood's Journal* for April. I am *delighted* with it, and sincerely wish you positive and permanent success in establishing it. It is so pure, so womanly—positively agreeable in its every feature as reading for private home, instruction and guidance. Please find enclosed ($1.25) one dollar and twenty-five cents for yearly subscription, beginning with the May number Again wishing you every success, I am, very sincerely yours,

VICTORIA EARLE.

EDITRESS RINGWOOD JOURNAL.

Dear Madam: Through the kindness of Miss Mitchell I am made the happy recipient of your most satisfactory publication. Many of my patrons have expressed themselves concerning its value, its novelty and its force, and the belief engendered by such vehemence causes me to assure you of a subscription list in Waco.

Though your project be new and youthful as to age, you may freely dispel the delusion of failure, when taking into consideration the able associates at your command. Words, notwithstanding taking their poetical regularity, seem very dull when I attempt to say good of that which to me seems best— *Ringwood's Afro-American Journal of Fashion* possessing a multitude of boastful features is before me in fact a reality. Pure, yet simple, characteriz. ing the sublime force of education, of woman' prosperity, and portraying staying qualities in the field of journalism.

Respectfully,   M. A. MAJORS, M. D.

June 29, 1892.

Ringwood's Afro-American *Journal of Fashion* has made its appearance in this city. It is a likely journal, edited by Julia Ringwood Coston, of Cleveland, Ohio, a colored woman of more than ordinary literary ability. The illustrations are numerous and well executed. The many departments, especially those for boys and girls, are well edited by educated colored women Its success is assured.—Philadelphia *Recorder.*

A new fashion journal published in Cleveland, Ohio, is one that is sure to attract attention, as it is a well-conducted and bright bit of work. It is especially designed to be an Afro-American magazine, and is edited in its different departments by colored women, but the pleasing fashion articles, instructive talks with girls and mothers, and witty all-around paragraphs and interesting love stories make Ringwood's *Magazine* a welcome addition to any home, whether its occupants be black or white.—Philadelphia *Times.*

The November number of Ringwood's Afro-American *Journal of Fashion,* needle-work, reading, etc., is a handsome appearing work and reflects credit upon the publisher, Mrs. W. H. Coston, of this city, It contains much information of interest to the colored people of the city —Cleveland *World.*

Ringwood's Afro-American *Journal of Fashion,* published by Mrs. W. H. Coston, of Cleveland, Ohio, has reached our office. In appearance it is a typographical beauty and its matter is nicely compiled and interspersed with cuts dear to the feminine heart. It is the first publication of the kind, and should have the support of the Afro-American women of the land, as it is published by an Afro-American woman, and fully represents them " as they are intelligent, virtuous and beautiful." Rates $1.25 per year.—The *State Journal,* Philadelphia, Pa.

Ringwood's Afro-American Journal of Fashion, published in Cleveland, Ohio, is deserving first recognition by the race among our papers. We say this because of the peculiar make-up of this journal, *The Ringwood's Journal* is a combination of literary taste and modern fashion, and pre-eminently accepted in the families and homes of the most cultured and refined of Americans.

The journal is edited by Julia Ringwood Coston, Cleveland, Ohio ; associate editors are : Miss Sarah Mitchell, of the same place; Miss Adina E. White, Cincinnati ; Mrs. S. I. Shorter, Wilberforce ; Mrs. E. C. Nesbit, Cincinnati ; Mrs. M. E. Lambert, Detroit ; Mrs. Bishop B. F. Lee, Philadelphia, and Mrs. M. C. Terrill, Washington, D. C. The ladies are managing their respective departments with ability and literary tact. The illustration and fashion department in the current number for June is admirably arranged, and shows very conclusively that Afro-American journalism is advancing. This is the only magazine of the kind published in the world by our ladies, and for this reason alone it is suggestive of high appreciation that none can show more heartily than the race which these ladies so eminently represent.— *Florida Sentinel.*

PORT AU PRINCE, HAYTI, W. I., June 14, 1892.

Mrs. JULIA RINGWOOD COSTON,

> Publisher and proprietor *Ringwood's Journal,* Cleveland, Ohio :

DEAR MADAM : The sample copy of your journal, so kindly sent by you, has been received.

I perused it with great interest, and noted with pleasure the peculiar characteristics of its engravings. .

Strange as the fact may seem to you it will be the first journal of fashion issued in Hayti, and I am proud that the introduction be made by a lady of our race, for none other should have the precedence in a country of independent blacks.

Wishing my subscription to be entered at once I could not wait for it to appear here, but if possible it can be transferred later. I send you a draft of $1.50 (one dollar and fifty cents), the additional twenty-five cents to prepay postage.

Praying that all success may attend your efforts, I remain, dear madam,

> Yours sincerely,

> THEODORA HOLLY, Bishop of Hayti, W. I.

OAK ST., CHILLICOTHE, O., May 19, 1892.

Dear Mrs. Coston : Every succeeding issue of your journal makes advanced improvements on preceding numbers. It is an excellent periodical and one that every colored family ought to patronize. Mrs. Shorter's "Talks with Girls" are very practical and highly useful ; she is a *true woman* in the highest sense of the word.

I am yours truly,

MAMIE E. FOX.

COLUMBUS, IND., May 2, 1892.

MRS. COSTON — *Dear Friend:* I prize your journal very much. I have read it through and think I shall read it again, for its contents are not only good but great. I certainly did enjoy reading it. May God bless your effort and crown you with success. I will do all I can for you. There are a great many young ladies in this city that I trust will become as interested in your journal as I am, if so I know they will never be without it. You have my prayers through life as one who prizes your efforts highly.

Yours respectfully,

L. JOHNSON.

MRS. ALBERT WILSON, MRS. V. A. MONTGOM-ERY, MISS BLANCHE WASHINGTON.

MRS. ALBERT WILSON, MRS. V. A. MONTGOMERY AND MISS BLANCHE WASHINGTON, for music and song, are first among the lovers of their art. Worthy mention of this trio will be found elsewhere in this volume.

Indeed, a history could be written portraying the musical accomplishments of our women, dwelling alone in the realms of classic rythm, cadence and harmony. Suffice it ; these stand out in bold relief, proofs of our progress and mile stones along the intellectual highway of Negro accomplishments.

MRS. ELIZABETH KECKLEY.

Author, Mrs. Lincoln's Dressmaker, Teacher of Sewing at Wilberforce University.

ANYONE who has met Mrs. Keckley, conversed with, or read her book entitled "Behind the Scenes," cannot but exclaim, She is a good, grand, yea, a great woman. With a life so crowded with interesting incidents, it is no wonder that at the muses' dictation she has drawn the pen pictures and shelved them in a bound volume. Her most delightful narrative begins in 1868, and teems with soul-stirring, melancholic accounts, with just enough wit and humor to beautify and sweeten the whole story from beginning to end. Though apparently advanced in years, she still possesses remarkable personal charms, and, though she was educated in the school of experience, she is no less a teacher of maxims and underlying principles which go to make up character. With her array of ready words at the command of her doctrine, she argues with elegance and force, and gently convinces you in her persuasive manner.

She was born in Virginia, a slave, and notwithstanding opportunity, coupled with fate, said flee for your freedom, she could not bear the idea of being tracked by hounds or placed under arrest as a fugitive. While young she was taken to St. Louis, Mo., and from thence to Washington, in 1860, where she distinguished herself as a fitter and finisher of ladies' attire. Indeed, her successful art won for her the admiration of the ladies of the White House, and later she became Mrs. Lincoln's, Mrs. Seward's and Mrs. Jefferson Davis' dressmaker. Beyond this, she was beloved by Mrs. Lincoln for her unswerving principles. After the death of Mr. Lincoln, Mrs. Lincoln found in her the sympathizing friend, and, indeed, relied very much on Mrs. Keckley for advice and counsel. When Jefferson Davis was captured in disguise, Mrs. Keckley was taken before a notary and sworn that the dress found upon him was Mrs. Davis' dress, and that she was the maker of it.

For many years our subject has been a firm friend of Wilberforce University, and having been endowed with a goodly number of Mr. Lincoln's relics, she anticipated their bestowal to that institution, but on the account of delay on the part of the educational board of that school, her patience became exhausted, and she parted from them for a considerable sum, and they are now on exhibition at Libby (Prison) Museum, Chicago, Ill. She to-day wears a gold watch chain which Mr. Lincoln prized very dearly, and which Mrs. Lincoln gave to her.

Following is a list of the relics:

ARTICLES OF LINCOLN RELICS.

Comb and brush used by the president, during his entire administration. "Stock" (black silk" worn by the President prior to his administration.

One white kid glove, that the President wore at the last inaugural ball. One pocket-handkerchief taken from his pocket after his assassination.

One watch case of the President. One nut cracker that he used at his private table.

Piece of dress goods worn by Mrs. Lincoln at the last inaugural ball, and made by myself. Neck trimmings worn by Mrs. Lincoln.

Piece of dress worn by Mrs. Lincoln the night of the assassination. One pair of rubber over-shoes worn by the President during his entire term.

One bonnet worn by Mrs. Lincoln the night of the assassination. One black velvet circular worn by Mrs. Lincoln the night of the assassination and bespattered with the blood of the President.

One china candle-stick, held by Tad Lincoln while his father delivered a speech from the north window of the White House, the Tuesday night after the fall of Richmond.

One box containing three pieces of hair. One piece cut from his head, while he lay in state, the morning of the day that his body was conveyed to Illinois. The other piece was cut from the head at the tomb.

One white kid glove worn by Mrs. Lincoln. One piece of the carpet that was on the floor of the room that he was laid out in.

One box. This box contained a large wreath that was sent from (I think) some association in Philadelphia through the care of Mrs. James H. Vine, Willard Hotel, which was placed on the carpet when it was taken from the White House. This box has the address still on it.

One gold watch chain, the property of the President, and given to me by Mrs. Lincoln.

ELIZABETH KECKLEY.

Mrs. Keckley is at present instructor of the art of sewing at Wilberforce University, and is quite conspicuous in the Liberal Arts building at the World's Fair with her figures, posing as specimens of the work done by her pupils.

There can be seen on exhibition both plain and fancy dressmaking, the handiwork of her instruction.

THE AUTHOR.

MRS. JOSIE D. (HENDERSON) HEARD.

Poetess.

MRS. JOSIE D. (HENDERSON) HEARD was born in Salisbury, North Carolina, October 11, 1861. Her parents, Lafayette and Annie M. Henderson, though slaves, were nominally free, being permitted to hire their time and live in another city, Charlotte, North Carolina.

MRS. JOSIE D. HEARD.

At an early age Josephine displayed her literary tastes and aptness to perform on almost any musical instrument. As early as five years of age she could read, and was a source of general comfort to the aged neighbors, delighting to read the scriptures to them.

She received her education in the schools at Charlotte, and having passed through them with credit, was sent to the Scotia Seminary at Concord, North Carolina, spending several years there. Her desire was to reach even a higher plane, and she was next sent to Bethany Institute, New York, passing with honors from its walls. She commenced teaching in the State which gave her birth; then in the State of South Carolina, at Maysville, Orangeburg, and finally in Tennessee, at Covington, near Memphis.

In October, 1881, she became acquainted with the Rev. W. H. Heard, (now Presiding Elder of the Lancaster District, Philadelphia Conference) who was then in the U. S. R. Mail service, and they were happily united in the bonds of matrimony in the year 1882.

Mrs. Heard evinced a fondness for poetry, and during her school days contributed to several leading evangelical periodicals. After her marriage she was encouraged by the Rt. Rev. Benjamin Tucker Tanner, Rt. Rev. B. W. Arnett, and many other friends to give more time to it. At their solicitations she has ventured to bring to light these verses. She has some musical talent, having composed and written a piece of music which was played at the New Orleans Exposition, and which elicited much comment from the democratic press of the South.

W. H. H.

In giving our subject introduction to the public, Bishop Benj. Tucker Tanner says that he somewhat influenced the publication of " MORNING GLORIES," and gives the writer real pleasure, which is enhanced by the thought that he gladly accepted the invitation to write the introduction.

For quite a quarter of a century, he has had much to do with the literary life of the people with whom he is especially identified ; as that life manifested itself in the production of papers, of monthly or quarterly magazines, of pamphlets and of books. He rejoices in the great progress made, both in quantity and quality. When he may be said to have begun his public literary career, in 1868, there were scarcely more than two or three papers published by colored men. There are now quite as many hundred. Of magazines, there was none ; now there are four. Of pamplets, upon very rare occasions, one was now and then issued. Now they appear as do the leaves of autumn. And the same is true of books. A quarter of a century ago a colored author was indeed a *rara avis.* Not so now, however; such individuals are fairly numerous.

What is true of the colored literature of the country, as to quantity, is equally true as to quality. On this score the most rapid advancement has also been made, *incipient scholarship everywhere appearing upon the pages offered the public.*

On the line of Poetry, we as a people, give sufficient evidence to show that the Muse is indeed no respecter of persons. That he is equally an admirer of *shade* ; and although at times compelled in his approaches to us, to walk in unbeaten paths, yet he condescendingly comes, and inspires a music as sweet as is the wild honey of unkept hives. If any doubt, let him read, " MORNING GLORIES," to which these lines are to serve as an introduction. In rigid versification, the lines herein given, may here and there come short, but for brightness of imagination, for readiness of expression, and now and then for delicateness of touch, they are genuinely poetical ; clearly evincing a talent of no mean order.

We would wish that " MORNING GLORIES " might be received in the houses of our millions; showing thereby the party of the second part among us stands ready to support the party of the first part in all that tends to redeem the good name of the Race.

THE BLACK SAMSON.

The Product of Her Fertile Brain.

There's a Samson lying, sleeping in the land,
He shall soon awake, and with avenging hand,
In an all unlooked for hour,
He will rise in mighty power ;
   What dastard can his righteous rage withstand?

E'er since the chains were riven at a stroke,
E'er since the dawn of Freedom's morning broke,
He has groaned, but scarcely uttered,
While his patient tongue ne'r muttered,
   Though in agony he bore the galling yoke.

O, what cruelty and torture has he felt ?
Could his tears, the heart of his oppressor melt ?
In his gore they bathed their hands,
Organized and lawless bands—
   And the innocent was left in blood to welt.

The mighty God of Nations doth not sleep,
His piercing eye its faithful watch doth keep,

And well nigh his mercy's spent,
To the ungodly lent :
   " They have sowed the wind, the whirlwind they
      shall reap,"

From His nostrils issues now the angry smoke,
And asunder burst the all-oppressive yoke ;
When the prejudicial heel
Shall be lifted, we shall feel,
   That the hellish spell surrounding us is broke.

The mills are grinding slowly, slowly on,
And till the very chaff itself is gone ;
Our cries for justice louder,
'Till oppression's ground to powder—
   God speed the day of retribution on !

Fair Columbia's filthy garments are all stained ;
In her courts is blinded justice rudely chained ;
The black Samson is awaking,
And the fetters fiercely breaking ;
   By his mighty arm his rights shall be obtained !

" THEY ARE COMING."

Another of Her " Morning Glories."

They are coming, coming slowly—
They are coming, surely, surely—
In each avenue you hear the steady tread.
From the depths of foul oppression,
Comes a swathy-hued procession,
And victory perches on their banners' head

They are coming, coming slowly—
They are coming ; yes, the lowly,
No longer writhing in their servile bands.
From the rice fields and plantation
Comes a factor of the nation,
And threatening, like Banquo's ghost, it stands.

They are coming, coming proudly—
They are crying, crying loudly :
O, for justice from the rulers of the land !
And that justice will be given,
For the mighty God of heaven
Holds the balances of power in his hand.

Prayers have risen, risen, risen,
From the cotton fields and prison ;
Though the overseer stood with lash in hand,
Groaned the overburdened heart ;
Not a tear-drop dared to start—
But the Slaves' petition reached the glory-land.

They are coming, they are coming,
From away in tangled swamp,
Where the slimy reptile hid its poisonous head ;
Through the long night and the day
They have heard the bloodhounds' bey,
While the morass furnished them an humble bed.

They are coming, rising, rising,
And their progress is surprising,
By their brawny muscles earning their daily bread ;
Though their wages be a pittance,
Still each week a small remittance,
Builds a shelter for the weary, toiling head.

They are coming, they are coming—
Listen ! You will hear the humming
Of the thousands that are falling into line:
There are Doctors, Lawyers, Preachers;
There are Sculptors, Poets, Teachers—
Men and women, who with honor yet shall shine.

They are coming, coming boldly,
Though the Nation greets them coldly;
They are coming from the hillside and the plain.
With their scars they tell the story
Of the canebrakes wet and gory.
Where their brothers' bones lie bleaching with the slain.

They are coming, coming singing,
Their Thanksgiving hymn is ringing.
For the clouds are slowly breaking now away,
And there comes a brighter dawning—
It is liberty's fair morning,
They are coming surely, coming, clear the way.

Yes, they come, their stepping's steady,
And their power is felt already |
God has heard the lowly cry of the oppressed;
And beneath his mighty frown,
Every wrong shall crumble down,
When the *right* shall triumph and the world be blest!

NEWBURYPORT, MASS., March 24, 1890.

My Dear Friend:

Our mutual friend, Mrs. Higginson, has written me enclosing a poem which gives me credit for much more than I deserve, but for which I thank thee. It is a pleasant gift to express, as thee can, thy thoughts in verse among thy friends and acquaintances. In this way poetry is its own great reward —it blesses and is blest.

I am very glad to give the "token" asked for in thy little poem, by signing my name, with every good wish from thy aged friend;

JOHN G. WHITTIER.

REPLY TO WHITTIER.

PHILADELPHIA, PA., April 3d, 1890.

I now assume the pleasantest duty of my life, that of acknowledging the cordial receipt of your most inestimable favor of recent date.

Cognizant of the weight of years you bear, I will not burden you with a long letter, while my heart out of its fullness dictates to me faster than my fingers are able to trace; but my joy is *full;* my gratitude *unbounded.*

I should certainly have congratulated myself upon being so fortunate as to have obtained even your name from thine own hand, a *letter,* such as thee wrote me, freighted with rich advice and kindly recognition, is PRICELESS.

God Bless Thee, and may thy passage to the land of the blest be upon a calm sea, with zephyrs laden with the perfume of thy noble life's deeds to waft thy spirit's bark onward, and over Jordan. Gratefully Thine,

JOSIE D. HEARD.

OFFICE OF THE CHRISTIAN RECORDER, }
PHILADELPHIA, April 2nd, 1890. }

To MRS. JOSIE D. HEARD:

Dear Madam—Learning that you are about to publish in book form the poetic writings which from time to time you have contributed to the *Christian Recorder* and other journals, and others which have not appeared in print, I write to congratulate you, and to say that as " Snow Bound," "Maud Muller," " Evangeline " and " Miles Standish are now recited in the public schools, so in the future may be " To Whittier " and " Retrospect."

Already one of your poems has been selected from the *Christian Recorder* by an Afro-American youth to be read in a Pennsylvania school, whose teacher and a majority of whose pupils are white. I am

Very Respectfully Yours,

B. F. Lee.

Cromwell Houses, London, April 15, 1890.

Mrs. Josie D. Heard :

I thank you and answer you that we appreciate most deeply the expression of your sympathy in our great affliction.

Very Truly Yours,

Robert T. Lincoln.

SOLACE.

To Minister and Mrs. Lincoln, on the death of their son A. Lincoln.

As o'er the loved one now in grief ye bendeth,
A Nation bows with thee, its sorrow lendeth,
That ye, grief-stricken should's not weep alone,
Above the shrouded form of thy dear one.

But, as we shed with thee our silent tears,
For him who bore himself beyond his years,
Hope bids us cease and banisheth our pain,
And pleads your loss, his soul's eternal gain.

The reaper cuts the grain and lovely flowers,
Transplants them in a fairer land than ours.
The path to heaven rendered thus more plain,
Weep not, press on, ye all shall meet again.

He nobly lived nor feared the shad'wy vale,
Defied the white horse with it's rider pale ;
The grave no terror hath, and death no sting,
For him who fully trusts in Christ the King.

Mrs. Heard's knowledge is extensive and various, but true to the first principles of her nature, it is poetry that she seeks in history, scenery, character aud religious belief poetry that guides all her studies, governs all her thoughts, colors all her imaginations and conversation.

MRS. J. J. ROBERTS.

Lecturer, Educator, Philanthropist.

THEY who know this grand woman, are always eager to emphasize the fact, by relating some of her acts of charity, reiterating some of her grand sayings, or dwelling at length upon her activity in behalf of the oppressed. During the many long years of her eventful life, she has never lagged, to pause, or loiter, something remained to be done, as she could see clearly, and possibly better backed by her enthusiasm, and reinforced by the strength of her indomitable will.

When Liberia declared her independence President Roberts became one of her active statesmen, later its President, and through the co-operation of this great woman, the Republic grew and flourished as the green Bay tree.

Mrs. Roberts is the only Negro woman that has dined with President and Mrs. Cleveland at the White House. During her stay in Washington, the Hon. ex-Minister of Liberia, John H. Smythe, took an active interest in this deserving woman, and her honors, as well the introduction to the President and Mrs. Cleveland is due this race man, of whom the citizens of the District of Columbia are proud.

She came to America soliciting funds for the erection of a building to be used as a hospital for Liberian and American seamen, at Monrovia in Liberia, as a memorial to her husband ex-President Roberts.

With Longfellow , Mrs. Roberts reasons, when he says :

> " No endeavor is in vain ;
> Its reward is in the doing,
> And the rapture of pursuing
> Is the prize."

She will more than likely build her hospital, the result of an earnest, fruitful life, and the happy result of a patient endeavor to make lasting her husband's name among his bemoaning countrymen.

SUSAN McKINNEY, M. D., PH. D.

Member of Brooklyn College of Pharmacy.

IN the professions, possibly no Negro woman has distinguished herself more than has Dr. Susan McKinney, of Brooklyn, N. Y., who takes a leading part in the medical life of that city. She is strictly a race woman, and most fully portrays that becoming interest in her philantrophic spirit to help the poor. She is the most successful practitioner of medicine of her sex and race in the United States.

Located as she is, and capable as she must be, her practice is not confined to the lowly of any particular nationality, but among all classes and conditions—the high, the low, the rich and the poor. Her splendid achievements are answers to the questions and doubts of the many who question through pride, and who doubt with curiosity. She is a full-fledged, high-toned lady physician, worthy of the mission of doing good, because in this special field she can serve the greatest number of her fellow sufferers. She is being blessed with some of the goods of this world as she is blessing others in her daily life.

Woman is proving to man that God is no respector of persons, and is taking her place in all the leading movements upon which the progress of the age depends, and is refuting the doc. trine of incapacity, and is rapidly approaching the summit of intellectual equality. The old time ideas of Negro unfitness has become worn threadbare, being so continuously lashed by the waves of sentiment concerning their intellectual growth upon the turbulent sea of endeavor, and the once depraved opinion has become a new-born popular issue subserving the qualifications of all, regardless of race.

The women are actually entering every avenue of learning, reflecting credit not only in the forum, the pulpit, the press, but are adding dignity in the university chairs, where alone sage once sat, and many lead in the classics, the professions wherein once they were not allowed to follow.

Dr. McKinney, by the force of her genius, the calmness of her life and beauty of her character, has set the seal of high accomplishments upon the pages of history, leading in a field of usefulness, where many of our young, capable women are sure to follow. She is a worthy member of the Brooklyn College of Pharmacy, which honor "was not attained by sudden flight."

MADAM GLOVER.

Leading Dressmaker of Boston.

FOR energy, pluck and patience, no Negro woman is the equal to this talented industrious woman. Her business for many years has given employment to more than a score of women, who through the instruction, attained under her service, have made for themselves marks in the world. Her fortune is not the only special proof of her success in the art of dressmaking and fitting, but the persistency as well as the high-toned patronage from the best ladies in Boston and vicinity, as much demonstrate her merit, as other of her qualifications. Every year she goes to Paris for her styles.

The field of industry is broadening for the girls of the present and future generations, most especially sewing schools are being established all over this civilized country, and the sex feel less keenly the necessity of book inculcation and more the demand of the spirit of the age, *not only to know, but to know how to do* sewing, painting, sketching, telegraphy, stenography, etc., are all coming into custom, as in these the women monopolize. The art of dressmaking as Madam Glover represents it, holds up very grand inducements for the generations of girls growing up in our race. *Knowing how,* attention to business systematically arranged, and a careful investment of her means, has brought in return the success she has accomplished.

MRS. HENRY HYLAND GARNET.

Early Educator.

NEW YORK CITY has long posed as the place where so many men and women of African descent first inculcated a spirit of growing out of the conditions made noticeable by the disgrace of slavery, which destroyed the senses of refinement and carried nothing but gloom and forbodings in its train. Dr. Henry Hyland Garnett, Prof. Charles L. Reason, Bishop D. A. Payne, and a host of the leading lights of our literary and social firmament, first caught the gleam of inspiration and started their educational careers, which have so splendidly refuted the arguments that the Negro could not learn Greek and Hebrew. It was here that this talented lady answered the call to teach. History records the wonderful accomplishments of her efforts to lift up her fellow men. The wave of education she sat in motion is flowing on. That night school, the work of her heart and brain as it was forty or fifty years ago, is now possessed with that enthusiasm she injected into it, only with increasing years it has kept pace with the progress of events, conducive to grander accomplishments in an age of better educational appliances and facilities, conducted by that noble and scholarly Miss J. Imogene Howard, who for a number of years has been one of the leading educators of New York city.

Mrs. Garnett was not only a teacher, she was wife and mother—wife of a great man whom the great men of the world have delighted to honor, a minister to a foreign power, a patriot and philanthrophist—a mother of a great woman, Mary Burbosa, an educator, philanthropist and missionary, who, following in the footsteps of her father, died while engaged in the missionary work in the Dark Continent.

The triumphs and activities of this grand woman is the early fulfilment of the highest hopes of those philanthropic personages, William Lloyd Garrison, Charles Sumner, Henry Wilson, Wendell Phillips, Mr. Lovejoy, Mr. Parker, and a host of heroes who have ever watched the race with very much interest. If the history of the past, portraying the rise and fall of empires, the establishment of empires and kingdoms, republics and monasteries, can serve as an incentive to the young to be ever alert to the changes consequent of the progress made in the enlightened world during the educational centuries, surely the epochs in biography can be stepping-stones upon which the aspiring man and womanhood of a defenceless race can find sure footing.

Mrs. Garnett, exemplary in her life and character, is an example of our genius and worth as a race when placed in no indifferent position to the conditions which surrounded her young life and the facilities for encouragement which kept pace with her manifold achievements.

During the war she toiled early and late.

MRS. E. V. C. EATO.

Eminent Teacher.

THE subject of this short sketch has by her tact made for herself a name among the leading educators of New York City. The inherent principles of her art chrystalizing for years in her busy life give her the ease and readiness of imparting that which she knows to her pupils, and for a considerable time have served as a convincing argument that separate schools for the races was not a necessity, and her special fitness, as well as the fitness of other colored lady teachers, has done more to bring about the educational reform, and bridge the chasm of restriction and social life which has so long made blameful the system of education in New York, than any thing else. All credit is due these noble heroines of our race. They have not contented themselves with meagre possibilities, but have entered the higher halls of learning and taken degrees of pedagogy.

The writer has met quite a number of the young ladies who have profited by her teachings, her life and character, and he knows for a fact, that a lively recollection is cherished in their minds and hearts for this good woman whose labors show forcibly in these characters, and clearly demonstrate the quality of seed sown, principles inculcated, the inestimable value of the good work she has done for her race.   This is an instance in the life of the Negro race in a great metropolis where merited recognition equalizes the chances for their redemption from ignorance and the quagmires of prophetic chaos. Mrs Henry Highland Garnett, Miss J. Imogene Howard and others, possibly not so prominent in the public eye, have dignified the situation and enabled in every possible way the high ground of scholary attainment, which has inspired many young men and women of our land.   Mrs. Eato reflects a credit on the race that is so apparent in our literary and social life, which reminds us forcibly of our progress.

MISS FREDRICKA JONES.

Educator.

MISS JONES ranks among the leading educators of the race.   She is a grduate from the classic halls of the famous Michigan University, Ann Arbor Michigan.   And has since done very telling work for our race as teacher in the northern as well as the southern college.   She is at present lady principal of Paul Quinn college, Waco, Texas.   Her special fitness commends her to the higher educational work among our people, and the above named school has under her watchful care and tutelage, made very great advances in the right direction.

She is amiable, most agreeable in manners, and a capable counselor on topics of advanced studies.

Her prominence as well as intellectual ability, entitles her to many pages whereon might be forcibly drawn the illustrious career of one so worthy.   We, knowing, Miss Jones' love for obscurity feel somewhat reluctant in making the fore-going statement, yet by a sense of right we have thus risked our judgment.

NEALE GERTRUDE HAWKINS.

Eminent Singer.

AMONG the celebrated singers of the Negro race, Neale Gertrude Hawkins takes her place along by the side of all. It is not our purpose to give especial space to those who are actively engaged before the public, for in their realm they are seen and judged, with better satisfaction than from

NEALE GERTRUDE HAWKINS.

an open book. We therefore will not give our subject a lengthy mention.

Mrs. Clara C. Hoffman, president Women's Christian Union for the State of Missouri, says of her:

"Miss Neale Hawkins is one of the finest vocalists I have ever listened to. In compass, flexibility, sweetness, pathos and power, her voice is unexcelled.

While high culture has developed and perfected her voice, it has not detracted an atom of the mellow richness so characteristic of the Afro-American vocalist.

Miss Hawkins is a prohibitionist, has perfect articulation, and will be a drawing card in any assembly. She will sing prohibition into hearts whether they will or no."

For quite a number of years, Miss Hawkins has been singing to delighted audiences, in fact she has been the support for the famous Jinglers of California, which under the musical direction of Prof. Ed. F. Morris, has reached that point in their art that makes them one of the leading musical troups before the American foot-lights.

Indeed to write of Miss Hawkins and her capabilities as a singer, would be incomplete without the mere mention of Mr. Ed. F. Morris who has taught her step by step, to her present advanced position in the realm of song.

We append below a few testimonials:

MR. GEO. W. BAIN SAYS:

" Miss Cornelia Hawkins has a marvelous voice. It surpasses in richness of tone many prima dona's of inter-national fame.

She is as much at home in the role of a singer, as the mocking bird in his own native orange grove."

GEO. W. BAIN.

PRESS NOTICES.

" The concert given by the Jingler Concert Company in the Victoria last night was musically a great success. Probably ownig to the inclement weather there was rather a thin attendance, but what the audience lacked in numbers they amply made up for in appreciation. The programme was full of, choice selections and was supplemented by nearly as many encores. The comic part of the entertainment was inimitably rendered. The solos were uniformly good, and the impromptu rendition of " Way Down on the Swanee River," in answer to a rather unceremonious call from one of the gods was delightful. The quartette work was good and left nothing to be wished for. Several character pieces were fairly done although this is quite evidently not the company's forte. The audience was sent home in excellent humor after listening to an excellent chorus entitled ' Good Night.' "

" The Jinglers gave a concert in the M. E. church in the lecture course and had a fine audience. I have heard in my life some very fine female voices, but it seems to me Miss Hawkins has the sweetest voice I ever listened to. The Jinglers will be welome any time, especially Miss Hawkins."

"The Jingler concert company gave their first entertainment to a very fair audience in the Union church last night. The audience was very enthusiastic and the performers were recalled many times. The fine soprano voice of Miss Hawkins, the deep bass of Mr. Wallay and the magnificent tenor of Mr. Conley are such as are but seldom heard. Their selections are varied, being Negro melodies, topical selections and popular songs of the. day. For an evenings' pleasure they excel any company that has ever visited our town. They sing in Modesto to-night, giving a return engagement in the Union church to-morrow night."

"On Saturday evening last Cole's Colored Jinglers appeared at Van's Opera House before a fair sized audience. The house should have been packed full of people, and we wish it had been, for there has not been a musical combination here for years that deserves the patronage of the people more fully than does the Jinglers. The performance was complete in every respect, and all who heard them on Saturday evening were more than pleased—they were charmed. The voices blended so nicely and the songs were so well selected and sung that the audience was kept busy applauding and the applause was always cheerfully responded to. Miss C. Hawkins has a soprano voice of remarkable sweetness and Miss Chinn is a fine alto. Mr. Walley, the lion basso, is all that is claimed of him and George L. Conley is a good tenor, while Mr. B. Dozier does his part fully as a baritone. The company is, by far, the best of the kind that has appeared here since the old Tennessee Jubilee Singers. That remarkable organization contained Henry Hunley, the grand basso, and Miss Reynor, one of the best altos we ever heard. The Jinglers will appear again tomorrow evening and if you have not heard them you had better go for you will be pleased."

A FIRST-CLASS PERFORMANCE GIVEN BY THE JINGLERS LAST EVENING.

"It was an evening of music and harmony last night at Louis' opera house, and a first class peformance certainly merited a better attendance than it received, those present certainly enjoyed a treat. "The Jinglers" is the name adopted by this company of colored vocal artists, and no concert company on the road has made a greater hit. There are six voices, and each one is excellent. George L. Conley, the tenor, G. W. Wallay, the base, and B. Dozier, the baritone, are exceptionally good. Miss Hawkins has a soprano voice of singular sweetness and purity—as she demonstrated in her rendition of "The Huntsman's Horn" and "The Suwanee River"—while Miss Chinn possesses a cultivated contralto. The entire program was good and there was hardly a number but received an encore, the male quartet especially carrying off the honors of the evening. The last three numbers—"Dars a Jubilee," "Don't Feel No Way Tired" and "Good Night"— fairly enraptured the audience. E. F. Morris is an excellent pianist and was down for several piano selections, but labored under the drawback of having a miserable instrument before him. The piano used last night possibly harmonizes with a pair of cymbals and a bass drum, but is hardly up to the mark for a concert. Those who have heard Miss Hawkins sing and Mr. Morris perform, will not fail to agree that for her under her instructor a bright future awaits her."

LAISSU OF BASSA LAND.

Princess.

LAISSU was one of the most talented women of her country, and that is saying very much in favor of her sex. She is the daughter of Boyer, King of the Bassas, an African tribe. She was taken from her people when only eight years old and educated in one of the best universities in England, where she distinguished her race and elevated the sentiment concerning the capabilities of the African, from the standpoint of incapacity to her high intellectual achievement, then and there and forever.

Many of her English friends, eager to have her remain in their land of civilization, offered her special inducements; in fact, such opportunities whereby she could have further dignified her race; but on failing to charm her imaginations for future pomp and power among them, they even misrepresented her native country. Despite these entreaties, she determined to utilize her education in the training of her own people in Bassa Land.

After her residence of fourteen years in England, at the age of 22 years, she returned to her people, bearing the beacon light of Christianity into a dark and benighted land. In order that she might become favored, and later secure the coveted influence among her people, she adopted her native costume, which was next to nudity. It was through these means that she Christianized a number of her brothers and her subjects, after five years of activity, spreading the Christian religion among her people, she died in the full triumph of faith, beloved and reverenced by all her people.

AMANDA SMITH.

Missionary, Author, Minister.

WHAT is the place of Amanda Smith in American history? Has she any place there? Mrs. Smith is an historic character. The biography of great women, and especially great women of the Negro race, would be sadly deficient without her.

Of this race in the United States, since 1620, there have appeared but *four* women whose career stands out so far, so high, and so clearly above all others of their sex that they can with strict propriety and upon well established grounds be denominated *great*. These are Phillis Wheatley, Sojourner Truth, Frances Ellen Watkins Harper and Amanda Smith.

More than a score of Negro women have arisen to the heigths of fame which leaped beyond the bounds of the States in which they have resided. Nor is there a single State in our country, North or South, but that could point to Negro women, a score or so in number, who are zealous of good works, endowed with a noble spirit and a love of race, sex and self which is truly praiseworthy and distinguishing. Indeed, in every city, village, or country neighborhood, a leading Negro woman, who is a full match for its best and leading Negro man, can be found.

Were this otherwise, it would present a strong incentive for melancholy, and offer some feeble extenuation to the vague and morbid dream of redemption from race of degradation by race blending through blood mingling in unnatural and uncongenial amalgamation.

If there is a graduation from good to greater in the ordinary walks of female life among the Negroes, who does not feel his bosom heave with just and excusable pride when he reflects that among them are also those women who must be mentioned in the superlative, not only great, and greater, but greatest? Is there not substantial reason to hope that all may arise, when we behold one woman, then another, and another ascend from conditions the lowliest to a place freely ascribed as among the highest and the greatest?

This ascent from a depth was made by Phillis Wheatley, Sojourner Truth, Frances Harper, and Amanda Smith.

But if these women occupy a place superlatively great as compared to all other Negro women of modern times, we would ascertain how they stand compared to each other. For it is by this comparison that we shall be able to determine which, or whether, either is greater than the other, and wherein.

To begin with, Phillis Wheatley and Sojourner Truth were both Africans of unmixed blood. Phillis Wheatley was an African of superior tribal relations by birth. Crosses in blood are sometimes found in Africa; for many traders, if no others, have a "country wife" or so while sojourning in that country. But Phillis was a child of pure Negro parentage. Mrs. Harper and Mrs. Smith were mixed in the proportion of about one part Caucasian to three parts African; hence, whatever be their claim to greatness and goodness, their racial basis for the claim is African.

Now let us compare them.

Mrs. Wheatley was the morning star of Negro genius, being to women what Benjamin Banneker was to Negro men, the first of her line.

Her advantages were few, and her opportunities to learn limited. But such as they were she improved them, and secured fame as a poetess of rare pathos and beauty. Her claims as a poetess are attested by the few specimens of her verses which remain, and the claim is universally accorded to her.

An unfortunate marriage, with other disadvantages, may have interfered with the attainment of still greater renown but as it is, Mrs. Wheatley stands peerless among American Negro women for poetic genius.

Sojourner Truth was a revolutionist and a reformer, with great political acumen in the rough. She was in her times the peer of Frederick Douglass, being to Negro women what he was to men. Aye, in her steadfast love to God, loyalty to the interest of all, but unyielding and undeviating fidelity, preference and zeal for her own race, she was more than his peer.

She illustrates the capability of the race to rise by its own unaided efforts, and take a commanding and abiding place among those eminent for deeds worthy of commemoration. We have heard somewhere that the bust of Sojourner Truth adorns a place in the British Museum.

A slave born and reared, a fugitive among strangers, but not friendless there, Auntie Sojourner Truth has no equal in the display of natural leadership and inborn mental equipoise among the four great women with whom we class her.

Mrs. Harper, possessing superior advantages, is superior to any one of the four great women here mentioned in mental drill and versatile literary culture. She is an erudite, scholarly woman. She, too, is a reformer, an agitator, but not in the rough, or with any political tendencies.

She is polished, and may be called the greatest of school-made moral philosophers yet developed among the women of the Negro race. If Sojourner Truth was a blind giant Frances Harper was an enlightened one. What she is Sojourner, with her chances, would have been; but what Sojourner was, with no better opportunities, Mrs. Harper would never have been.

Standing outside of the Church and Churchly relations Mrs. Harper is without an equal among Negro men of her times and type of thought. To find a literary equal for her we must look either in the Negro ministry or among men who were trained for it.*

Mrs. Smith, in connection with the others, except Mrs. Harper, came up through the enthrallments of slavery and the culture of Christian faith. She is not, then, the indomitable agitator that Mrs. Harper is, nor the indomitable revolutionist that Sojourner Truth was, nor yet the brilliant genius that Phillis Wheatly was. But she matches them all in this: she is a Christian of the highest type yet produced among women of her race, and as a simple, confiding child of God has no superior among women of any race—and may we modestly say it?—nor among women of any time.

She is an evangel of the Christian powers of her race, and an evangel of that good will from God to men which is the burden of her speeches. As a demonstration of the possibilities of the Negro woman—and if the woman, then also the man—to grasp and hold a place among those who have attained the highest heights of Christian faith and perfect self-consecration to the service of God and man Amanda Smith stands without a rival.

Without the genius of Mrs. Wheatley, the daring of Sojourner Truth, the logic of Mrs. Harper, Mrs. Smith has a greatness born not of self nor of mind, but of soul culture by contact with God. Herein is she great, the equal of either, and greater than any. Among men of our race and times none equal Mrs. Smith as exemplifiers of the power of grace to save, expand and use man as an instrumentality of salvation to the human race.

She is in these particulars, then, as we have frequently said not only the greatest Negro woman, but the greatest of the race in these times.

Let Negro women study well her character and imitate it Let them read well her struggles up from sin and Satan to God, and use the same means if they, too, would rise like her in His likeness and image.

---

*Mrs. Harper is a member of the Unitarian Church in Philadelphia, and stands high in it, I learn.—AUTHOR.

What grace has wrought in her it has wrought for our example, that like her in the use of means at hand so like her we afterwards might be useful in the Master's hands.

As an enlightened, thoroughly consecrated Christian evangelist among Negro women Mrs. Amanda Smith takes the first place in American history.

MARSHALL W. TAYLOR, D.D.

MADAM WETZEL.

Ice Dealer.

MADAM WETZEL, of St Johns, New Brunswick, is an example of what a woman may achieve in the world, when energy and genius are not wanting.

Some years ago, an enterprise was started by Mr. and Mrs. Wetzel, which up to her husband's death, had not placed them in any indifferent relation to poverty, for to be sure their ice plant was not in a prosperous condition, but has been brought to its present magnitude through her energies, and business capability. Today she employs a hundred men, does her household duties, has the care and responsibility of a large family, and by virtue of her strict attention to her business, she has crushed out the competitors, who predicted her failure, and poses as a monopolist in St Johns and vicinity.

Woman has a most formidable foe to antagonize at every turn, and that foe is man. When we see such women forging their way successfully, despite the obstacles engendered by her sex, she is worth forty men in business, war, politics, bar and pulpit, she should be admitted on this portrayal of her worth, to vote, to do whatever men have a right to do. Mrs. Wetzel was left in an almost destitute condition on the death of her husband, but the power which was circumscribed in the domain of home, now had, exercise in their business, the result of which has been stated

Man will, when woman forces him to, concede to her the rights she demands. The wanting quality in woman, is yet too noticeable, to materially effect any anticipated reforms with the deep underlying principles of equality of the sexes, in the government and various forms of business.

Mrs. Wetzel is not only a success as a woman, but a Negro woman. She orders, men obey. Let others follow her example.

MISS RACHAEL L. WALKER.

Eminent Vocalist, Distinguished Teacher.

AMONG the intellectual citizens of Cleveland, Ohio, most especially those engaged in teaching music and song, Miss Walker takes a high place. Her fame has grown out of the local sphere, and become national in both her mission as teacher as well as that of a pleasing vocalist. For a number

MISS RACHAEL L. WALKER.

of years the citizens of Ohio, Indiana and Illinois have been captivated by the exquisite melody of her voice, and the great encouragements she has received (in the frequent displays of her talents) from the press, the public, and critics everywhere she has been called to play, her inspiration has quickened her energies to more vigorously pursue the art of voice culture.

She has a most excellent soprano voice, with pleasing intonations, and marvelously can she command it. She is one of the few noted singers who perform without effort. She is a talented teacher in the public schools of Cleveland, Ohio, who, in spite of obstacles on account of race, has unbidden, entered the beaten track of imparting as well as reflecting a noble character on the white, as well as the Negro children who are committed to her charge. If education is the key by which aroused intellect may enter all the repository of treasure, and take for itself available knowledge, she has the happy faculty of giving that key to the dominant race. Through no favor of friends does she enjoy the position she occupies along with the great educators of this great city, but by energy and perseverance backed by a determination to obliterate caste and race restrictions by proving the merit of her brain, and the versatile range of her brilliant faculties to serve as a convincing argument in behalf of the women of the Negro race has she become so very noble in the estimation of the leading citizens of Cleveland. She is a tireless worker, and keenly feels the necessity of setting a high example for those of her sex, and especially her race. Miss Walker is of fair complexion, elegant form, pleasing stage appearance, a lively conversationalist, and withal an aggressive race agitator. She has a most flattering hope for the race, contending that concentrated race effort to rise high in the scale to cope with other nations is the only wanting link in our condition. She is a pleasing vocalist, but a most worthy teacher.

MRS. A. J. COOPER.
Author of a Voice from the South.

MRS. COOPER'S book has been received with surprising consideration by the press throughout the country, and she is in daily receipt of clippings from quarters where least expected. As is well known, she is the widow of an Episcopal clergyman, and at present a teacher in our High School. She was graduated from Oberlin in '84, and was a class-mate of Mrs. Mary Church-Terrell. Her first attempt in literature is undoubtedly gratifying, both to her and her friends, as the following criticisms show:

New York *Independent*: "It is an open secret that the author of this volume is Mrs. A. J. Cooper. She puts a voice in her book of which she says modestly that it is only—

> "An infant crying in the night,
> And with no language but a cry,"

but it is a piercing and clinging cry which it is impossible to hear not to understand—which it is impossible to shake off. She writes with strong but controlled passion, on a basis of strong facts."

Philadelphia *Public Ledger*: "There is sound sense in this author's argument, and what is certainly rare in controversial literature, an unblemished good humor. Mrs. Cooper disdains to make use of weapons beneath the notice of a cultivated and high-minded womanhood. The book commends itself to the attention of all interested in a fair discussion of a question of the day."

Chicago *Inter-Ocean:* "It is not often that the question here raised has been discussed more candidly, more earnestly and intelligently, and in better spirit than in the volume before us. The argument is keen, seldom the least shade of vindictiveness, and yet so pointed and honest as to be convincing for its justice. She claims that the best hopes of the race rest upon the higher education of black women. That only as the woman is educated and lifted up and refined and the home made pure, will the black man advance to an honored position."

Boston *Transcript:* "Doubtless this black woman of 'Tawawa Chimney Corner,' Anna Julia Cooper, makes an intimate exposition of qualities of her people which whites are so slow to appreciate. Indeed, the very fact of her criticism in excellent English and in welcome style, and phrase, is a manifest of ability and cultivation of those she represents."

Public Opinion: "This volume posseses a fresh attraction, because it comes from the eager heart and mind of a 'Black Woman of the South,' as the author terms herself. All the order of the great race to which the writer belongs pleads for a hearing for the women of her own color. She lays down boldly, clearly and strikingly the great law that a race will finally be what it's women are. Alongside of this she puts what she claims is a fact that the new movement to lift the black race into intelligence and spiritual life, compara-

tively little place has been found for the young girls. Young
men are everywhere being pushed on and aided by societies
and friends in the struggle to get an education. But young
women are left almost wholly unaided, and very few are as
yet able to complete courses of study. The book is written
in a very judicious and elevated way. The pages are disfigured
by no extravagant ill-judged utterances, but a dignified and
womanly air pervades the whole. We commend the volume
to all who wish to keep in touch with the Negro problem. A
portiait of Anna J. Cooper, whom we take to be the author,
forms a frontispiece of the volume."

Detroit *Plaindealer :* "There has been no book on the
race question that has been more cogently and forcibly written
by either white or black authors. The book is not only a
credit to the genius of the race, but to woman whose place
and sphere in life men have so long dictated."

The Kingsley (Iowa) *Times:* "One of the most readable
books on the race question of the South bears the above title.
It is written by Mrs. A. J. Cooper, of Washington, D. C., a
colored lady with the brain of a Susan B. Anthony, a George
Eliot, or Frances Willard. The volume is attracting wide
attention, owing to its being worthy of careful perusal and
because of its originality and great literary strength. It is a
neat, cloth bound book, retailing for $1.25, but to anyone
interested in this race question it is worth many times its cost.
For sale by the author or at all book-stores. The *Times* editor
never has seen a stronger picture of the true conditions of
affairs in the South than the one coming from this colored lady."

Judge Tourgee: "The habit of a lifetime has made the
Bystander's pencil almost infallible in its indication of verbal
inaccuracy, which is, after all, the very highest test of literary
merit. The word which exactly fills the place where it is used
—neither too large nor too small for the service assigned, or to
the thought it is commissioned to convey—is to literary work-
manship what the perfect note is to music. It may be slurred
a little—often is—without constituting actual fault, as the rush
of some great movement may even hide or excuse a false note

now and then, but only precision can give the feeling of finish which attests the genuine literary artist. Rarely has the unsparing pencil passed so lightly over the pages of a book of essays as it did over the pages of this ' Voice from the South.' Its perusal would be a new sensation to many a white-souled Christian woman of the 'superior race,' who, when she had perused its bright pages from cover to cover, would be forced to admit that though she had encountered many a sharp thrust she had not received one awkward or ill-tempered blow."

Mr. Tourgee's criticism of Mrs. Cooper's book, " A Voice from the South," possesses great interest for us, because we know him to be both free from prejudice and capable of judging literary excellence. He declares that few women writers have shown a " daintier wit, and few works give promise of a purer literary art." " The deft but stinging satire, the keen but not ill-tempered wit, but the tasteful self-restraint," says Mr. Tourgee, "shows the author to be a cultured lady." According to our critic, " the white-souled Christian women of the superior race who peruse its bright pages from cover to cover will be forced to admit that, though they encountered many a sharp thrust, they received no awkward, no ill-tempered blow." While Mr. Tourgee deprecates a little parade of quotation he pronounces " the abundant use of second-hand material to be the fashion of the times," and dulls the edge of criticism by acknowledging that "the borrowed matter is always good, aptly used, in the main, shows breadth of reading, keen observation and thorough good taste in selection." Mr. Tourgee considers it neither surprising nor discreditable to the colored people of the United States that they have made so few contributions to literature. The reason is cogently and succinctly stated as follows : " The best scion grafted on the strongest stock requires some period of growth before it produces fruit, and a race by law barred from the fields of literature for two centuries need at least the lifetime of a generation in which to produce literary work. The wonder is, not that it came so late, but that it came so soon and is of such simple, genuine quality.

MISS HATTIE GREEN.

Teacher.

MISS HATTIE GREEN is one of the lady teachers of Cleveland, Ohio, who has through her own efforts unaided won for herself a name in Ohio. Her educational opportunities have been the best, as her talents show. She with others, by action has refuted the fallacy of race incompetency, in passing the rigid examinations of the school board

MISS HATTIE GREEN

of Cleveland. She is beloved by a host of persons, who admire pluck and energy, principles which if well fortified will bring success to the door of every one. These women command the attention and respect of the races whose children they instruct without favor. Their performance of duty actuated by a sense of right has won for themselves the merited recognition they deserve, and guarantees to them long tenure.

IMOGENE HOWARD.

Eminent Educator; Appointed on the World's Fair Board of Lady Managers.

A SKETCH of a remarkably clever Afro-American woman who has carved a niche for herself in the world of fame: The appointment of Miss J. Imogene Howard as a member of the Lady Managers of the World's Fair for the State of New York has met with general approval.

Miss Howard is a graduate of the Girls' High Normal School of Boston and was the first of her race to graduate from that institution. She came to New York shortly after and was appointed on the staff of teachers of Colored Grammar School No. 4. She also received the degree of Master of Arts from the College of the City of New York in 1879, and for some years taught day school, and was appointed as principal of the colored night school, only resigning her post upon the solicitations of her friends, lest the constant strain on her mental ability and physical strength impair her health. Supt. Jasper, it is said, remarked that the school gave the most flattering results under her management.

Miss Howard is the daughter of Joan L. Howard, of New York city and Edwin F. Howard of Boston.

Her brother, Dr. E C. Howard, who is an able and large practioner of Philadelphia was a graduate of Harvard College and her sister, Miss Adeline Howard is the principal of the school in the Wormly building, Washington, D. C.

Miss Howard has just received the degree of Master of Pedagogy of the University of the City of New York, and is a fit representative of the Educational Committee.

Miss Howard attended the meeting on Tuesday at the State Capitol, in the Assembly parlors, and in executive session they elected officers as follows: President, Mrs. Erastus Corning, Albany; first vice-president, Mrs. E. V. R. Waddington, New York; second vice-president, Mrs. J. S. T. Stranahan, Brooklyn; secretary, Miss Lesslie Pell Clarke, Springfield Centre; treasurer, Mrs. Frances Todd Patterson, Westfield.

An executive committee was also chosen, consisting of Mrs. Dean Sage, Mrs. Frederick P. Bellamy, Miss Annie Roosevelt, Miss Caroline E. Dennis and Mrs. Andrew G. White.

In the evening the education committee—Mrs. White, Mrs. Bellamy, Mrs. Stranahan, Miss Patterson and Miss Imogene Howard—met with the State Superintendent of Public Instruction and Professor Dewey of the State Library, in reference to the educational exhibit.

Among the associates on the board were Mrs. H. Walter Webb, wife of the vice president New York Central Railroad; Mrs. Fred P. Bellamy, sister to the author of "Looking Backward," and Mrs. Andrew G. White of Cornell College. The ladies are to meet Mrs. Potter Palmer on her return from Europe next week. They were entertained at the palatial residences of Mrs. Dean Sage and Mrs. Erastus Corning. Miss Howard is flooded with letters of congratulation from her many friends.

PRESS NOTICES.

"One of the most refreshing and sensible appointments made in this State for many a day occurred when Miss Imogene Howard was placed as a member of the Board of Lady Managers of the exhibits of the State of New York for the World's Columbian Exposition. The honor came unsolicited and was due greatly to the representation of Mr. and Mrs. James C. Matthews and Mr. and Mrs. Wm. E. Gross. Miss Howard attended the meeting of the Board in the Assembly Parlors of the State Capitol on Tuesday, and stopped with the rest of the Board at the Kenmore Hotel, Albany. The appointment is the adequate recognition of the race in the State, and is fitting in that Miss Howard ranks with the brainiest and most capable of our women; she is able to measure arms with the cleverest of the opposite race, having just been made Master of Pedagogy, and winning a scholarship from the University of the City of New York. She has a record worthy of a good teacher of many years experience, which would make her a credit to any people."

"Miss Imogene Howard is the first and only colored woman in the Empire State appointed to a managership in the World's Columbian Exposition. She is a worthy representative of her race in the great World's Fair, and colored people throughout the land may rest assured that in her hands the progress and ever increasing prosperity of the Negroes of America will be shown to all the world to the best possible advantage.

" Miss Howard is one of the most thoroughly intelligent and energetic of her people. From her earliest childhood she felt that her mission in life was to better the condition of the colored people, and in so doing she has found her life work and her pleasure. She has taught and watched and advised, and now that she has very justly been given an official opportunity to illustrate the advancement achieved she feels that she has her reward.

" She feels that her people, who have made such grand strides in intelligence, industry and importance during the past decade, are entitled to recognition in Chicago's great Fair, and it is her intention that those of New York at least shall refute the charge that has often been made, that the race is at a standstill, or is retrograding. No one knows the colored people of New York better. No one is better able to bring out their strong points, and the prospects now are that in the New York exhibit the corner devoted to the colored people will be one of the most interesting features."

SHE HAILS FROM THE HUB.

Miss Howard was born in Boston, and lived there until she was 17 years of age. She acquired her studious habits under Boston influences, and in this instance they did not lead to a life devoted only to Brown or Kendrik Isben. First she attended the Boston grammar and high schools, from which she graduated with high honors. She then became a student in the Girl's High and Normal School. She was graduated creditably in 1868, and was the first colored graduate of that high class institution. In the same year she came to New York and entered the employ of the New York Board of Education as a teacher in Grammar School No. 81, in West

17th street, where she has since remained, teaching the colored children.

Upon the resignation of Mrs. H. H. Garnett, she became principal of the high school, held in that school house, and she held that position for eight years. In spite of her arduous duties as principal and instructor, she found time to attend the Saturday sessions for teachers in the Normal College, and received the degree of A. M. This year she completed a three year's course at the University of the City of New York School of Pedagogy. She was the only colored woman of her class, but in the class of last year the Misses F. T. and H. C. Ray, and Miss Mary Eato received a like degree.

Since beginning her educational labors in School No. 81 Miss Howard has been a keen observer of her charges, and there is no one who can better testify to the increased intelligence of the colored children since the War of the Rebellion. She is a bright and interesting talker and expresses her thoughts with a forcefulness that carries conviction to the hearer.

"There is," says she, "no more interesting school in the world than ours. One must attend it day after day and year after year, as I have, to be as interested as I have become. We have much to contend with that others have not. Most of our children are of poor parentage. Many of them are the children of very ignorant parents, and home influences are not always what they should be, but in spite of all these obstacles, I think it will be impossible to find a lot of children who exhibit more actual aptitude and acuteness. Their little intellects often seem to have been sharpened by even their short contact with an unsympathetic world, and as long as we are able to direct this precocity into the proper channels they will become good and useful men and women.

SCHOLARS THIRST FOR KNOWLEDGE.

"They are all willing to learn. Many of them find their only home recreation in their study, and their advancement is often almost marvelous.

"We were formerly known as Colored Grammar School

No. 81, but by a law passed a few years ago this distinction of colored was removed. It was right that it should be, for it was unkind, and not in accord with our American institutions—we are surely all American born—that these children should be made to feel, even in their school life, that they are of a class apart. The colored schools are now all numbered in regular, consecutive order with the others. They are open to children of all colors and nationalities, and this is as it should be.

"We now have three hundred and fifty boys and girls. Of course there are more girls than boys. The percentage of girls is larger, I think, in all public schools. The boys are more often forced by necessity to go to work at an early age, and our most effective labor is, therefore, among the girls. The question as to whether the most good can be accomplished for our own people by educating the girls or the boys is one I need not discuss. The influence of one educated woman is certainly very great; but we try to educate both sexes.

"Our percentage of truancy is, I think, less than that in the average white school of equal size, and that in face of the fact that many of our pupils come from distant parts of town.

MODEL SCHOLARS THESE.

"My own class ranges in numbers from twenty-five to forty. I have one pupil who comes from 97th street, another from 44th street and the North river, and another from the Bowling Green, and these are seldom or never late or absent.

"There is more higher education now among the colored people than ever before, but in too many instances the children have to give up when they get what they can in the grammar schools and go to work.

"Their field of labor is, alas! very much restricted; but it is getting broader, and I look forward to the day when anything and everything will be open to the capable colored man or woman.

"Of my own boys many have done exceedingly well. Two are electricians, and have become quite famous. William C. Green, also one of my boys, is stenographer for Postmaster

Cornelius Van Cott. Some of them are in the public and private banking houses as messengers. One is private messenger to Archibald Rogers, and many are to be found in positions of trust in brokers' offices and big business houses. They get better employment now-a-days than ever before, and we hope for better things yet."

Miss Howard was appointed to the Exhibition management on June 3, and her selection was announced at a meeting held in Albany on June 7. She will serve on the Committee on Education, her particular branch of the exhibit being woman's part in the education of New York State. She expects to introduce educators in the work, particularly those who are engaged among the colored people.

MRS. MARY A. CAMPBELL.

Philanthropist.

TO write a sketch of the life of Mrs. Mary A. Campbell, the widow of Bishop Jabez P. Campbell, is the work that lies before me this beautiful Spring morning, April, 1893. No more delightful duty will ever devolve upon me. I only fear that I shall fail to satisfy myself or the friends of this beloved one in this attempted effort.

Mary A Campbell was born in Philadelphia, January, 1817. She was reared and trained in Christian duty and the domestic virtues by a loved mother. For many years a resident of the southern section of the Quaker City. She met and married in early life Joseph Shire. By this marriage she had four children. A widow at a later date, in good circumstances, beautiful in form and feature, with the attributes of a lovable wife, she entered a second time into the holy estate of matrimony. As the beloved wife of Bishop Jabez Pitt Campbell, her personality and its virtues won her world-wide fame. Mrs. Campbell is about the standard of her sex in height, with a soft brown skin, to which age only adds greater charms. Her hair has long been a silver crown, bound with a black velvet band, in the lovely style of our grandmothers. The one lovely charm that strikes every friend of Mrs. Campbell, both old and new, is her smile. Oh, the beauty and sweetness of it! The compelling love that lingers in it! Truly it is " a smile that is a benediction." " To know her is a liberal education." It is one of the greatest blessings I have known in life to have had the friendship of this noble woman for a quarter of a century. Her life is that of a devoted Christian; her hospitality is generosity personified; her home life teaches the young around her to love the home, make it the center of every noble effort for oneself and others; beautifully furnished, comfortable, neat, refined in all its belongings. Her husband's and her son's children have grown up in it to a pure and noble manhood and womanhood. A tender mother, a loving wife, an ever faithful friend, living close to her Savior, her good deeds and charities have been manifold.

The Colored Old Folks' Home at West Philadelphia, Wilberforce University, the Jabez Pitt Campbell College and the Women's Mite Missionary Society have been the largest recipients of her bounty; but no needy cause or worthy sufferer has ever gone empty from her door. " What have I done, my child, that I should appear among the distinguished women of the race ?" was the question asked by her in all sincere humility. My answer, from a heart overflowing in grateful remembrance of hundreds of noble deeds, was. " Not what have you done, but what have you not done, in every line of effort that would make one of the sex and race distinguished ?" And so I have tried to tell, in a few feeble words, the story of this helpful life—to set before your readers the noble, inspiring example of this lovely woman.

Intelligent, educated, aspiring beyond most of her day and generation; loved, not only by her equals but almost idolized by the young and by the humble in station. When I hear of her illness I hasten to her side, fearing it may be for the last time. The years of her life have passed the three score years and ten limit, but the prayer in many hearts is, " Lord, spare thy servant yet a little longer."

Such a character in life is valuable beyond human words to express, and in death will continue, because of noble deeds, to live on and on, by its beneficent example strengthening and guiding into higher life future generations.

MRS. N. F. MOSSELL.

AMELIA ALLEN.

Educator,

THE name of Amelia Allen is dear to the home and hearts of all Salina Kansas. She is an answer in the affirmative to the hopes of the race, and the early fulfillment of

AMELIA ALLEN.

the prophecy that the girls of the Negro race with equal chances could demonstrate their worth not only in the class room but in life as well.

Earnestness, which is indicative of strong force of character, together with her many acquirements, make possible the many accomplishments and achievements of a useful, active life. With just enough obstacles to call forth her force and ability to overcome them, these will in all probability stir other latent energies not yet awakened in her young life, and show fourth the qualifications characteristic of the many lofty expectations of those who admire her real worth.

GEORGIA M. DEBABTISTE.

Language Teacher and Writer.

AMONG the host of young ladies who are doing something in an intellectual sense for the cause of the race, we may be reasonably exultant with the triumph and activities of this talented young woman.

GEORGIA M. DEBABTISTE.

Her intellectual worth far excels her opportunities, if what a person has done is the criterion. Miss Debabtiste is quite young, but already we see signs of her labor sparkling with the brightest rays of hope. She has started right. Naturally possessing a thirst for language, she has shown her adaptability by force of her mental capacity to learn it, and as well impart it with ease. For a considerable time she has been assistant teacher in languages at Lincoln Institute under the able management of Prof. Inman E. Page at Jefferson City, Missouri.

She is a newspaper correspondent, and writes very able articles upon all the topics pertaining to the race question. Being clear in her style, forcible and pointed, she will in time cope with the leading writers of her sex.

She is the daughter of Rev. Debabtiste, of ministerial prominence, who is also a writer upon all our social as well as economic questions. She rightly inherits her talents with the pen, her logic in debate, and reflects brilliantly her capabilities to achieve much for herself, her race and prove a lasting honor to her noble parents.

ADA A. COOPER.

Lecturer, Teacher and Poetess.

I, ADA A. COOPER, was born in Brooklyn on February 6, 1861. I am the daughter of Rev. A. H. Newton, of the New Jersey Conference of the A. M. E. Church, and Olivia Hamilton, who was the daughter of Robert Hamilton, who was known through New York as a singer, and who was connected with the Anglo-African. At the age of five I was sent to school. I knew how to read at that early age; just when I learned I don't know, but it seems to me that I have always known. At the age of seven my mother died, leaving me in the care of my grandma. From childhood I was pronounced exceedingly smart; in fact, smart beyond my years. At ten years old I had read the Pilgrim's Progress, Swiss Family Robinson and Robinson Crusoe; and at fourteen I had read David Copperfield, and could repeat lots of verses from different poets. At eighteen I had read Paradise Lost and Pope's Essay on Man. I have never read either since, yet passages from both are still fresh in my mind, and I am now thirty-one. I was always peculiar as a child; I would take part in no childish sport, not even to playing with dolls that the girl so much delights in. I was always impressed with the idea that I had something to do in the world, something to live for, although I knew not what it was. At eleven years of age I met with an accident which gave me the hip-joint disease. I was thus unable to walk for nearly two years. At thirteen I again went to school, and during that year I wrote a story which I showed to my teacher. She took it and read it; after which she told me that if I persevered I would in time be able to write some. thing that would astonish the world. This opened my mind to some extent, and I determined to become a writer. At fifteen I left my northern home to go and live with my father, who was then in Little Rock, Ark. Although so young, I took the whole journey, a distance of more than 1,300 miles, by myself. Shortly after I reached Little Rock my father married a girl as young almost as myself. I was then, of course, left much to myself, and during one of my lonely hours I sat down and wrote a story which I called the " Bride of Death," and laid it away to use at some time. When I was seventeen my father removed to Raleigh, N. C., where I was sent to Shaw University. After I had been in the school a few months my teacher discovered that I was a very fine reader, hence I was given all the reading classes to teach, and thus secured my schooling free. I went to the school a part of three years, and during that time I had but three dresses. A few months after I had been in Raleigh I met W. R. Harris, who was at that time a teacher in one of the city schools. He paid marked attention to me, and I soon learned to love him. Our love was kept a secret for upwards of a year; but when it finally became known to my father he sent me to New Berne away trom Prof. Harris, because he concluded that I could not love and study too. While in New Berne mourning for my lover, I had published the story I had written at fifteen, and continued to write other stories that soon became the rage throughout the State. I was also there chosen to read the Emancipation poem on Emancipation Day. I had no dress in which to appear before the public, so I borrowed one, but composed the poem that I read. I knew that, if I could not dress, I had brain, and I was fully determined to use it. After a time I went back to school, and again I met my lover, and we determined that we would wed, let all oppose who would. He was then a professor in St. Augustine Institute, and was studying to become an Epis-

copal minister, so I promised to wait until he had completed
his course and then be his at all hazards. My father was
bitterly opposed to my union with him, on account of his creed.
I left school at twenty and went with my father north. There
an event happened which I shall never forget. My home to
me was not a pleasant place, and I was sickly, and had been
from birth. A doctor had given me laudanum to use to allay
my pains. One day, as I was about to use it as he had directed,
a thought occurred to me that, as I was sick and seemed to be
in everybody's way, I would end my life, it seemed no good to
me. Even my lover seemed to desert me, as I had not heard
from him in months. So I poured out a spoonful and started
with it to my mouth, but before I could get it there the spoon
was knocked from my hand, and the bottle fell to the floor
shivered into bits. I determined then to live and live for something. What my work in life was to be I had not yet
determined, but I knew that something lay before me
which I must accomplish e'er death came to me. After so
long a time I returned south to teach, and again met my old love
whom I found as true as steel. I had had a great many offers
of marriage, for I was a pretty girl, being a rosy brown, with
black eyes and straight, black hair; but none of them were
accepted by me, for my heart was given away. While I was
teaching in Haywood, Chatham Co., an event happened to me
which is worth chronicling. I was sick, and having to seek
for a doctor, I went to one known as Dr. Budd, who was said
to be the best in the county. On arriving at the house, which
sat back in the yard, as do the majority of southern country
homes, I met a woman coming down the path and asked her
if the Doctor was at home. Her reply was, "Yes; he is in
the back yard; go there and see him." I answered her, "I do
not go in back yards to see doctors," and went straight to the
front door and rang the bell. The woman went to the side
gate and said to me: "You may ring all day, and nobody will
come." Then she called over the fence to her servant and said:
"Kitty, oh Kitty—tell the doctor there is a nigger woman out
here who desires to see him."

Well, I have been called a plucky woman ; in fact, am said to be manish. It stood me in hand that day. I only waited to reply just long enough to see what Kitty would say. She said to the doctor, after a moment's pause : ' Doctor, there is a lady out front who desires to see you." Then I spoke and said : "The servant is a lady, hence she knows one when she sees her. The mistress never has been one and never will be one, and hence she don't know one when she sees her."

"Do you insult me in my own house," asked she.

"I care not whose house it is," said I. "You're no lady, I tell you."

"Get out of here !" said she.

"I'll not," said I, "until I get ready."

About that time the doctor came up.

"You insulted my wife," he said.

"Your wife insulted me."

"Well, get out of my yard."

"I'll not until I get ready."

"I'll hit you with this stick !" he said, grabbing a cane that lay on the porch.

"You do," I said, "and whatever law there is in Carolina for the black woman I'll get it. There is not much, but I'll get what there is."

Whereupon he threw down the stick and said :

"I'll put you out, any how."

"You may do that," said I, "for I am on your premises."

He then took me by the arm and led me out of the gate.

I had to have a parting shot, and so I said to him :

"If I were a man, I'd fight you ; but as I am a sick woman, I tell you that you are a brute, and your wife is no lady."

When this affair became generally known throughout Haywood the majority of the colored people thought that I had committed an unpardonable sin in speaking in this manner to Dr. and Mrs. Budd ; but a few of the best men of the place —Prof. S. G. Atkins and others—went to the doctor and his wife about the matter. They declared that they knew not who I was, and desired the matter hushed up. They thought that I was one of the townspeople trying to put on airs.

Shortly after this I went to R. and was married to my heart's choice, Prof. W. R. Harris, who had become an Episcopal minister. We were married in May, 1885. He was made a priest in June, and died the following January. Hence I was a bride and a widow in one year. After his death I taught in Washington graded school for three years. During that time I was the editor of the woman's column of a little paper called *The Outlook*. A Sunday school teacher, which I have been since I was fifteen, I wrote for papers and interested myself in all charitable undertakings.

At the end of three years a great sorrow came to me, which so affected me that it gave me congestion of the brain. I resigned and went to Philadelphia to the Woman's Hospital. After remaining there a while the doctors told me that I would have to undergo an operation, which was very dangerous, but which was my only hope of life. I prayed then, and I made a vow to Almighty God that if he would spare my life I would devote it to his service, doing all I could for the sick, the afflicted and the poor. He answered my prayer, and I set to work as soon as I left the hospital. I first went to Maryland to teach, and staid there eight months among the people, whom I aided in every possible way. Of my experiences there I will not stop to tell, as it would make this sketch too long. But they were many and varied.

After leaving Maryland I engaged with a Western publishing house to become a traveling agent. I entered into the work, traveling from Trenton, N. J., to Easton, Pa., where I found myself sick, unable to gain an agent, and not a dollar in the world. For a while I was nonplussed. I finally decided to go to the Methodist minister and ask his aid. This I did, and he said to me:

"I will aid you by allowing you to help yourself. Can you sing?"

"Yes," said I.

"Can you recite?"

" Yes, sir."

"And you can lecture ? "

" I have never tried to lecture," said I, "but I suppose I might ? "

" You shall try to-morrow night," said he, " in my church."

This was Saturday. True to his word, on Sunday night he gave me the stand and I lectured. Well, it was a success. Then this good brother. whose name was F. F. Smith, said to me:

" Now, to-morrow night you may sing and recite; and never be it said hereafter that you, with the brain that you possess, are left without a dollar. Start out in the lecture field, and let this book business alone."

I did as he advised, and traveled as a lecturer from then on, receiving favorable comments from the press and from such men as Bishops Turner, Lee, Dr. Coppin, and others. I lectured and visited the sick until I reached Winchester, Va., where I remained five months, working as a missionary in the Free Will Baptist Church. I accomplished much good in that community, and there decided that my life work was to be that of a missionary. I therefore hastened to New Jersey, joined the conference, and became a missionary, or evangelist, in the A. M. E. church. I felt that my work lay in visiting the prisons and places of ill repute. This I did in God's name, traveling from place to place, lecturing and preaching, until I again found myself in Raleigh, N. C. I arrived there just in time to attend the Southern Exposition, and to make a speech before the N. C. I. A. on the exposition grounds, which was said to excel any made by the men, although Gov. Pinchback and Congressman Cheatham were among the speakers. This speech was made on the 5th day of November, 1891, and on the 18th of November I met Rev. A. B. Cooper, a promising young minister of the A. M. E. church, and married him on the 13th day of January, just three days before I had ended seven years of widowhood.

So you see my life has been a romantic and an eventful one. I would tell you many things more of my life and adventures in the South were it not that it would make this too long. I am now engaged in writing a book of poems, which I purpose to finish in '93. ADA A. COOPER.

WASHINGTON, N. C.

MRS. MARTHA ANN RICKS.

Liberian Heroine.

AMONG the few Negro women of Liberia whose fame as philanthropists and race agitators is not circumscribed, but has become universal in both England and America, Mrs.

MRS. MARTHA ANN RICKS.

Ricks enjoys a prominent place. For many years her voice and pen have championed the cause of Liberia. Her prosperity has largely depended on the unabating efforts of her loyal citizens, and, regardless of sex, her leading women have figured very conspicuously in the accomplishment of every success she has attained.

Mrs. Ricks is a personal friend and correspondent of Queen Victoria, and this social attachment has been the cause of constant interchange of mementoes. Very recently Mrs. Ricks presented Queen Victoria with a "crazy-patch" quilt, which for beauty and exceptional merit, as well as the high appreciation of the gift, and her high regard for Mrs. Ricks, the Queen has placed it among the exhibits of the British Dominion in the World's Fair, at Chicago. Mrs. Ricks ranks among the leading women of her time and place, and justly merits this grand and ennobling recognition from the grandest ruler on the Eastern Continent. Her rare worth is all the more emphasized when taking into consideration the fact that her prominence asserts itself at home, and among the leading spirits of Liberia. Her power is felt. She has made herself an exponent of the progress of the people on the Dark Continent by energy and push, coupled with the other exemplary qualifications which are God-given.

MRS. DR. FRANK HAMMOND.

Race Leader.

THE remarkable signs of the times setting forth the progress of the race, based upon facts, and figures, are prophetic of what the race may accomplish in the world. With every facility to thoroughly fit and prepare the Negro to take his place along with the other great races, no one of us can grow discouraged over our possibilities.

Mrs. Hammond is a convincing unit of our progress, and demonstrates the fallacy of all doubts which have dawned upon the vision of the skeptics of her section. She is a forcible writer, a strong advocate, an active scholar in the cause of Negro progress—not easily discouraged, possessing very much physical force, strong and striking qualities capable to lead.

Her decision and discretion are very strongly marked. Her vitality bespeaks forth a long and active career in the cause of human prosperity.

MRS. DR. FRANK HAMMOND.

Alderson, West Virginia, being her home, she is so situated as to meet and explode the doctrines of incapacity, so often the ignorant conception of the Southerners regarding our intellectual progress.

MADAM SELIKA.

Singer of French and Italian Operas.

THE world has heard Madam Selika and has been delighted with her singing. The press every where has spoken in very high praise of the wonderful range of her sweet voice , the masters in music have found new beauties in their songs when sung by her, and in no compromising terms have placed her where she rightly belongs, second to none of her

MADAM SELIKA.

time. Parody nicknaming is a peculiar popularity in which many of her profession seem to have distinguished themselves, but Selika needs no gilding.

She has played as Selika and her successes demonstrate that Selika is quite as convenient a name as she could have. We may diverge from the general rule, in treating of distinguished women who have figured so very conspicuously as she, and say that there really is *something in a name*, and that name she has, by the cultivation of her voice, dignified and made quite as prominent as the many adopted by persons not near her equal. She has, by study and unceasing practice in the foreign languages, prepared herself so artistically in the realm of song as to acquit herself far beyond the expectations of the many thousands who have flocked to hear her.

Indeed she is so well known, and the sentiment is so general as to her excellency in her art, that she requires no additional comments.

She continues to raise the scale of our intellectual possibilities, and demonstrate before the world that the Negro can not only sing jubilee songs, and ballads, but they can enter all the repository of music and song, and discriminate between the lettered and unlettered operas, yea, can sing the French and Italian as well as the English operas.

Madam Selika has been on the stage seventeen years, during which time she has traveled five years in Europe, has sung before the Czar of Russia, and her many triumphs abroad have won for her such fame as no other Negro woman of our time can boast. By special invitation she has sung for President Hayes, and on more than a dozen occasions where thronged thousands of the lovers of her sweet intonation, she has been universally pronounced " the greatest colored singer of the globe."

We append below a brief extract from *The Colored American,* on the event of her expected appearance before a Washington audience :

"SELIKA CONCERT POSTPONED.

" Despite the awful inclemency of the weather, hundreds came to hear the greatest colored singer of the globe last Wednesday night. Postponed until Monday night, May 8th. Everybody will be there. Tickets for Wednesday night good on Monday night.

" The concert to be given Wednesday night would, without doubt, have drawn the largest gathering ever assembled in the Metropolitan Church on M street northwest. The talent and programme were the finest, combining in one the magnificent soprano, Madame Selika; the peerless little Lotta, the renowned tenor and instrumentalist, Prof. Laurence, and the famous baritone, Prof. Velosko. But Æolus and Jupiter Pluvius took a hand in the matter with disastrous results. These old and antiquated gentlemen, who never wore white shirts and laundried collars and had no such musical artist to please their tympani with musical strains, concluded and did give us a combination of wind and water that made all shiver in their boots.

"The many people who bravely faced the rainstorm on last Wednesday night showed the appreciation in which Madam Selika, Profs. Laurence and Velosko and Little Lotta are held by the Washington people. The concert was postponed until Monday night, May 8, 1893, to accommodate the many who did not come out Wednesday night. Everybody will be there at 8 p. m. sharp. The managers of the concert have decided that all tickets issued for Wednesday night will be good on Monday night. The managers have also arranged 'A Parlor Match' with Mr. Æolus and Mr. Jupiter Pluvius, and they will take 'A Night Off' 'Down On the Bowery,' and will not be here to interfere with 'The Crust of Society.'"

Her rightful position as an accomplished singer is by the side of Jenny Lind, Parodi, Nilsson, Patti and Elizabeth Taylor Greenfield. When other aspirants for such honors from the public pulpit and press startle the world with their matchless voices, as Selika has, shall shine upon our musical horizon and have dignified as well their names, they, as she, will be doing much to compensate for the evil practices of some who feel honored in passing a mimetic name. "There all the honor lies."

MRS. SARAH LEE.

A Noble Mother and Race Benefactor.

MRS. SARAH LEE, the mother of Bishop B. F. Lee, was one of a family of nine children—seven girls and two boys, and was born in the year 1818, in Cumberland county, N. J. She was the daughter of Benjamin and Phebe Gould, and comes of an old family, tracing from one generation to another, in regular succession, to the first settlers of New Jersey, ranking with Sir George Carteret and John Fenwick, and other English Quakers who secured that part of the State from William Penn. Sarah is fifth in generation. Her father possessed a small farm and large tract of woodland, and did an extensive business in the hoop-pole trade. There being so many more girls than boys, Sarah was often called into service out of doors as well as in the house ; and in such rural pursuits and activities her early life was spent.

The educational facilities of the country were those of the earlier ages, and the three R's were taught in the winter months, and by this Sarah acquired a common school education. She was always fond of books and study, and was considered both handsome and accomplished. At the age of twenty-one she was married to Abel Lee, who was also one of a large family and native of the same State. They settled in life and purchased a small farm, and had six children, three girls and three boys, born to them. But, alas! when the eldest had only attained the age of thirteen years the hand of death took away the fond husband and loving father, and left the children orphans and Sarah a widow. She has never fully aroused from that stolid grief ; but with a set purpose and firm will she turned her face to the world to defend and take care of her children and sustain the honor of her husband. His promises of debts on the place she would pay, and though the law of New Jersey would not claim such she did pay to the last dollar; and she had a home secure for her children and herself in her declining years.

As she began to have a little leisure in life her love of reading increased ; she sought the strongest minds and information from the best authors in literature.

Of her children she has lived to see them all grow up to honorable man and womanhood : the girls and one son, the bishop, to marry ; two sons still remain at home with her; one of them, who had become a smart farmer worth several thousand dollars, is afflicted with blindness, upon whom she waits now with tenderest care.

A great lesson of life is taught by this woman having lived —that in working out the every day affairs we are laying foundations deep and strong; that at home, and unobserved, we are sending minds to search for the beautiful, the great and good, and verifying the saying that thoughts spoken in the bedchamber are repeated on the housetops, and that honor, strength and perseverance will bring forth a never-failing harvest; so surely as it is said, what a man sows shall he also reap.

Mrs. Alice S. Felts,
6 Emerson st., New Bedford, Mass.

MRS. MARY E. LEE.

Educator.

MARY E. LEE, wife of Bishop B. F. Lee, was born in Mobile, Ala. In this sunny clime she spent the earliest days of her childhood.

In about 1858 her parents moved to Wilberforce, Ohio, and there on a farm, near the college, the days of her youth were spent. She attended Wilberforce University and graduated in 1873, receiving the degree of Bachelor of Science, and composed the "Class Ode." Previous to the completion of her course, she had two years' experience as a teacher in Mobile, Ala., and was quite a successful teacher.

At an early age she showed great talent for writing. Poetry seemed to be her specialty, for there was something in the natural surroundings of Wilberforce which harmonized with her nature, and inspired her thoughts.

On Dec. 30, 1873, she was married to Rev., now Bishop, B. F. Lee, then a professor at Wilberforce, and during his presidency of eight years her influence was greatly felt by the pupils.

For many years she has from time to time contributed poetry and prose to *The Christian Recorder*, and also to the *A. M. E. Review* and other journals, and is at present editor of "The King's Daughters" department of *Ringwood's Journal*.

She has written many short poems, and several lengthy ones, such as "Tawawa," and "Afmerica." Although still young, she has seen much sorrow, having lost by death both father and mother, with two brothers and five sisters since her marriage, and having been the mother of nine children, three of them have been carried to the better land, so that now, but for a number of nieces and nephews, she would be quite alone in the world; yet she is of a cheerful and pleasant temperament, treating every one she meets with affability, and all who come to her home are met with a generous welcome and made to feel at ease during their stay. As a wife and mother, she is very devoted and careful, overseeing the management of her house, and, to some extent, the education of her children and controlling every department with a skill that brings success.

As has been said, during the eight years that her husband was president at Wilberforce University, she was a great help to him in caring for the students and helping them with their studies; there are many young women, and men as well, who owe to her, and they do not fail to recognize it, a debt of gratitude for the instruction and sympathy they have received while students, at that university.

Her reading has been extensive and varied, her book stands abounding only in the classics of both prose and poems, but also of the latest and most wide-awake authors, so that she continually revels in a wealth of literature equaled by few of her race.

APPENDIX.

"Out of my lean and low ability
I'll lend you something."

W. H. S.

INTRODUCTORY.

These are a set of random facts, gathered from the great central lights of the subject, and flung, as it were, on the skies, to be viewed as our telescopic visions, early fulfillment of our highest hopes, a forcible index to our progress, a conclusive pledge to redeem ourselves from the thraldom of inferiority and incapacity. Twenty-seven years of freedom and education has not only made us men and women worthy of honor and trust, but we have become features of *help* and *maintenance* in every avenue of the world's progress. Not far removed from our former condition, it is not difficult to prove the great loss of a nation that for more than 250 years in holding one-fourth of its population in abject slavery, when facts and figures speak so very eloquently for us to-day. But, "we are coming."

Mrs. Josie D. Heard's prophecy (in "Morning Glories") is already here, and more than fulfilled in Mrs. Frances E. W. Harper's "Iola; or, Shadows Uplifted," as well as in Miss Anna J. Cooper's "A Voice From the South;" Mrs. Octavia V. R. Albert's "House of Bondage," all of which forcibly show their capability as *authors*.

The poems from the pens of Phillis Wheatley, Mrs. Josie D. Heard, Mrs. Harper, Mrs. Charlotte Forten Grimke, Miss Mamie E. Fox, herein, are strong as proofs of Holy Writ, and remove Mrs. Heard's prophecy far from vain imaginings.

THE AUTHOR.

WOMAN AS EDUCATOR.

BY MATTIE E. DOVER.

IN the beauty, the fullness and inspiration of his soul the poet Milton has said that woman is God's latest and best gift to man. And if it is incumbent upon the lesser gift to teach humanity, it must be a two-fold duty of woman that splendid gift of divinity. It is an acknowledged fact that a moral, intellectual and a religious foundation is necessary for our success in life. That is, truth should be the basis of human action. It is said that the first impression the human mind receives is the most lasting. Who teaches the first principles? Who gives the mind the first turn, a start and a thought? Woman. Education, means to lead out, draw out, set forth, and in those countries where woman's influence as an educator is recognized there you find civilization most advanced, piety most sincere, morality most progressive and knowledge most extensive.

England, for instance, one of the grandest, noblest, and most influential nations on the globe, is only great because she recognized the powerful influence of the intellectual force of woman as an educator. There, too, our own country keeps pace to the music of mental improvement by conferring upon woman the rare privilege of instructing the youth. Go to the public schools—the celestial arch upon which our government rests—who constitute the majority of our teachers? Women, for the people know that woman by her neatness, her accuracy, her patience, her faithfulness and her zeal, can most deeply impress the aspiring student, than man by his vigorous enforce-ments. Napoleon once asked Madam DeStael what was the best thing he could do to elevate France. She replied " instruct the mothers." That very expression was the essence of true greatness, the very archstone upon which the greatest prosperity of the greatest nations rest.

People have often wondered why the Indian does not become civilized, though the government does more for him than any other nation does for its wards, and yet he still " sees God in the wind " and seeks the happy hunting ground as his final resting-place. I say that people still wonder; the solution of that question is easy, because in the dark ages and savage nations woman is not recognized as a partner, as an equal, as a consoler, as an instructor, but as a servant, as a slave. They haven't learned that " where woman is most respected, man is most elevated," and it is a fact that no nation kindred or tongue, can become powerful or great until their women are .nstructed in the high principles of morality and truth. For, when once her heart is lighted up with those high principles it shines forth with the intensity of a meridian brilliancy. In no department in which woman has been placed has she disgraced the position. Which is forcibly illustrated by Miss Sweet, the agent who handles millions of dollars of pension money and is always found correct in her accounts. The energetic Lockwood's pleas are commended by the bar. Elizabeth Fry and Mrs. Vancolt's words sink as deep into the heart of the erring and fallen as their stern brothers. Ellen Foster, Susan B. Anthony and Sojourner Truth are as eloquent on the platform as most of the bearded sex, and I know that Frances Nightingale and Clara Barton, those " angels of mercy " Whittier calls them, have done as much to lessen the sorrow, to cheer the faint and lift up the fallen, as their more elevated brethren. Woman's influence as an educator may be likened unto the rays of the sun, which come quietly, silently upon the realms of nature. The clearer woman is of her knowledge of her duty, of her relation, of her reponsibility so more powerful will her influence be as an educator and as an elevator of suffering humanity, Then I would say that the " chiefest " duty of the age, of the pulpit, of the school, of the statesman and of the press is to bend all their energies in assisting woman as an educator.

Miss Lucy E. Moten, of Washington, D. C., is an able woman. She has a broad knowledge of men of letters, she has traveled abroad and took in store the great and wonderful experiences of a diplomat; she took the classic or gentlemen's course in Oberlin college and graduated with high honors.

At the annual session of the American Association of Educators of Colored Youths, she elicited the following comment:

" The program of the Association embraced many valuable papers by the most experienced teachers of colored youth. One of the most interesting occasions of the entire session was when the beautiful and talented Miss Lucy E. Moten, of Washington, D. C., delivered an address on the Theory and Practice of Teaching.—*Christian Recorder.*

Miss Lucy E. Moten, principal of the Miner normal school of the 7th and 8th divisions, is one of the most popular and highly educated teachers in the United States. She has recently been made one of the vice-presidents of the educational conference which meets in Chicago during the time of the World's Fair. It is conceded by those best posted on educational affairs that the explanation of the art of teaching by Miss Moten is equal to any of either race in this country. Her appointment is a tribute in her deserving ability.—*The Colored American.*

Miss Moten occupies a very high place among the great educators of the age. Her work in the school room portrays the success to which our race has attained, and marks the highest nitch in the art of teaching. She is mentally the peer of her sex, and is working for the race an enviable name by the side of the leaders of her art.

MISSES RACHEL AND LOUISA ALEXANDER are worthy scholars and teachers of renown.

MISS CHANIE PATTERSON, of Washington, D. C., is a graduate from the classic halls of Oberlin, and takes front rank among our leading educators. Her experience as a teacher is long, varied and full of rare experiences. As a cultivated woman her usefulness has added much to the culture and refinement of the race.

Mrs. Mary Withers, also emerged from the classic halls of Oberlin, and stands very high in the art of teaching.

Mrs. Dr. Vanella, of Topeka, Kansas, is one of the prominent female educators of the West.

MRS. PROF. GARNETT,
Louisville, Ky.

Mrs. Sadie Newton, of St. Louis, Mo., is another classic graduate from Oberlin, who has done much in the educational cause for the race.

Misses Hurlburts, teachers and elocutionists of Trenton, New Jersey, are entitled to our notice because of their literary labors and real worth in the cause of education.

Miss Mattie A. Henderson graduate of Lemoyne Institute, more recently of Cincinnati Business College, now editor of the *Future State* of Kansas City, Mo., ranks very high as a teacher having completed her course at Lemoyne Inst. graduating at the head of her class, she was offered a position in her *alma mater* which she accepted, giving in every way entire satisfaction to all concerned.

Miss Ramsey, of Philadelphia, ranks among the grand educators of the race in the Quaker City.

MISS M. E. MATLOCK,
Mathematician.

First and foremost among the leading scholars of the Negro race from the South, stands Mrs. Mollie Church Terrell. She entered Oberlin at quite an early age, and prosecuted the studies in the gentlemen's course, graduated with honors, and was tendered a position in the Oberlin faculty. She has traveled abroad, studied the dead languages in their native haunts, in fact became a disciple under the instruction of the very best foreign instructors. Her field for usefulness is very extensive. To say the least Mrs. Terrell is a very grand young woman, destined to do some mighty act, that will place higher value upon the integrity and character of the race, and cause a general change of opinion concerning our fidelity, and loyalty. The School Board of Washington, D. C., immediately after her European travels tendered her a very high position in the High School.

Miss Addie Jackson, of Baltimore, claims space for her name wherever the subject of Negro education is given consideration.

The Misses Wilsons, teachers of distinction of Indianapolis, Indiana, are mentioned here because of their worthiness as educators.

The Misses Howards, of Philadelphia, are classed very high in literature and the arts and sciences.

KATIE B. CHAPMAN,
Yankton, S. D.

Rev. Kershaw of the A. M. E. Church in a letter to the *Christian Recorder* concerning Edward Waters College noted the following:

At the class room No. 1, we found Miss P. B. Weston controling and leading on the primary division; in class room No. 2, Miss M. E. Brown, one of Edward Waters' first graduates is teacher. The trustees made no mistake in electing her to take charge of the intermediate department. We found her drilling her class in that part of hygiene that relates to strong drink. Masterly and convincing was her instruction to her class " wine is a mocker, strong drink is raging ; whosoever is deceived thereby is not wise."

Miss L. M. Johnson presides over the musical department, and there is where 'get along' is the order of the day. After hearing her I said, " Lord it is good to be here."

In room No. 3, Miss E. N. Phelps is holding the crayon in front of the Normal department, at the time of our visit to a class in United States History. The particular subject was the treason of Arnold. Miss E. N. Phelps is surely mistress of the position which she occupies.

MISS BEULA V. GARNER,
Winchester, Tenn.

DR. GEORGIA E. L. PATTON bade farewell to her many friends, Saturday, Feb. 11th, and started for New York, where she expects to meet Miss E. Millard, who will assist her in making the last arrangements for her long journey. The ship in which she is to embark for Liberia, her future field of labor quick and ready, and this trait she injects into her pupils. She possesses more than usual power, and propels her children seemingly along. Her fitness as an instructor has also won for her the position of assistant supervisor of the colored schools.

AMONG the noted people of Kansas, Mrs. Prof. Wadkins, of Topeka, takes high rank as an educator, scholar and race agitator.

DR. CARRIE V. STILL ANDERSON, of Philadelphia, daughter of the great Still, of underground railroad fame, is able as a scholar, teacher, lecturer and champion race advocate.

DR. CARRIE V. STILL ANDERSON.
Philadelphia, Pa.

MISS MATTIE E. ANDERSON, principal female seminary, Frankfort, Ky., ranks very high as a teacher and disciplinarian. Mrs. Sarah G. Jones of Cincinnati says of her: "Miss Anderson has labored faithfully for years in Kentucky and has assisted much in elevating the educational interests of our people in the locality where she resides. Such influence as she exerts cannot, however, be confined to a narrow limit, but asserts itself positively in every direction for good."

Our Female Teachers who have distinguished themselves are many, almost innumerable in fact, a tiresome count, but among them we shall simply name a few.

Miss Lucy Laney of Georgia, stands pre-eminently ahead of those of our southern ladies. The *Christian Recorder,* says of her:

One of the most remarkable and successful women, is Miss Lucy Laney principal of the Haynes Normal and Industrial School, Augusta, Ga. This school is now under the auspices of the Presbyterian church, but like most of their schools in the South, is open to everyone who comes and complies with the rules. Miss Laney manages this large school which has an enrollment of 320 scholars with such an ability and business tact as would do credit to any institution in the land. She is a model for her numerous pupils in everything that the word implies.

MISS LUCILLA WASHINGTON,
Memphis, Tenn.

Mrs. Minnie L. Phillips *nee* Brinkley, of Houston, Texas, ranks among the greatest modern molders of clay, and teachers of the paper folding art. She enjoys a lucrative salary in the Austin public schools, and it's a very easy task to single out the little fellows who are under her immediate care. She is as medical missionary, will sail about the 10th of April. We ask for her a prosperous journey and that her work may be a blessing to many.

Mrs. Lucy Thurman's work for the cause of Temperance among the race is so very well known that we shall not necessarily emphasize for her. The American people know her as Miss Lucy Simpson. Mrs. Christine Shoecraft Smith says of her, "She has lectured extensively in Illinois, Indiana, Kentucky and Michigan as a woman of note, distinguished for her tireless advocacy for the Temperance cause, she is worthy a place in your book."

CARRIE L. GRIFFIN
Dayton, Ohio.

Mrs. B. W. Arnet, Mrs. Susie I. Shorter, Mrs. Tanner, Mrs. Bishop Campbell, Mrs. Bishop Hood and indeed a host of female giants are worthy of extensive mention in this chapter, but let the above serve as a hint to those so careless as to be doubtful. Through these, God is working out the plan of redemption for mankind. Others will catch a gleam of the bright spark they hold aloft and succeed these womanly patriots until wine is proven to be a mocker, and strong drink forbidden in our christian land.

MISS ANNIE FAIRCHILD is another primary teacher of note. She is worthy the mead of praise when we consider that prompt attention is given to her grades to the extent that column after column ascends each year and in no instance has she let her little lambs diverge from the path of duty, that of learning or losing a grade.

MRS. LAURA ALLEN *nee* WATSON of Nashville, Mrs. Bessie Carter *nee* Gibson, Mrs. C. C. Goudy, Mrs. Bessie Brady Ballad, and a host of Nashvillians rank very high as teachers especially in the primary art of teaching.

Nashville, Tenn., being the Athens of the South the habit of striving to excel has grown in the teachers until now par excellence is the rule.

A Georgia paper says: Miss Selena M. Sloan, proprietress of Edward Waters Seminary, in Tallahassee, Fla., is a living example of the excellence of Georgia teachers. She is a charming young woman, and is an inspiration to any girl with whom she comes in contact. Georgia cherishes a remarkable pride in her, and she deserves the esteem of everyone.

MISS IDA GIBBS is an able teacher, a graduate from Oberlin College and a classic student. She is principal of the Preparatory Department of the University at Tallahassee, Florida.

MISS IDA BELLE EVANS a graduate of the academic, scientific and collegiate departments of the Central Tennessee College is a teacher with an excellent record. She has taught three years in the Prairie View State Normal institute of Texas, having resigned she returned to Nashville, Tenn., and entered her Alma Mater, and resumed the position as pupil and teacher in the college, taking in 1891 the degree of A. B. from the classic department. Miss Evans is destined to be heard from, not only as a scholar but a singer, a poetess and a mathematician. She has traveled through the North with the Tennessee singers and has been richly endowed with press comments.

MRS. AMANDA S. MULLEN, *nee* PERRY, is among our talented teachers of the South.

Miss VARA LEE MOORE is a classic graduate of Central Tennessee College who has taught unceasingly in Texas, Waco and Ft. Worth for six years. Recently she has been appointed Lady Principal of the Central Alabama Academy at Huntsville, Ala., under the auspices of the Freedman's Aid Society.

Miss HALLIE Q. BROWN ranks among the leading teachers of the race, at present acting as lady Principal of Tuskegee University. Her sketch is given elsewhere.

MRS. FRANKIE E. HARRIS WASSOM is making her name not only as an instructor of the future man and woman, but that of a poetess, she ranks high among the alumni of Oberlin.

Miss CLARISSA M. THOMPSON is a disciplinarian whose sketch is given in another part of our book.

Miss A. L. EVANS, we may justly say is entitled to be styled a teacher. Having for some years taught in the capital city of Texas, and feeling her inability to give value for value. she went to Oberlin College in 1888, remaining until 1890, finishing in one of its departments.

Miss ELNORA BOWERS, a classic graduate of Fisk University, located at Galveston, Texas, is a very efficient scholar and able teacher. All Texas is proud of her.

MRS. ELLA AYLER, *nee* JONES, of Macon, Ga. is a graduate of Fisk University and is gifted for generosity and sincerity among not only her pupils, but all others who come in her way. She has for many years taught in the Lone Star State; Dallas, Waco and Huntsville being the fortunate cities that can boast of her sojourn as teacher.

MRS. MARY SINCLAR, *nee* LE McLEMARE, is classed among the finest musicians of Tennessee. Not only was she a most pleasing musical performer, but a composer of songs and music. She is the author of many notable pieces of music that have found their way into the recognition of the great writers. She is widely known as a musician of a very high order, and many surprises has she given when bringing into full view of her audience her dark skin.

Mrs. Haydee Campbell, *nee* Benchley, is a native Texan. For some years past she has resided in St. Louis, Mo. Three or more years ago she distinguished herself by actually going before the school board of St. Louis, as an applicant for the position as principal or instructress for the kindergarten department. Here she was confronted with the task of making the highest average, and leaping the obstacle of white applicants, who for so many years have stood in the way. She, with

MRS. HAYDEE CAMPBELL.

courage undaunted, went into the examination .. , the surprise of the board of examiners, the white applicants and the city of St. Louis, she captured the department with the highest average percentage ever made in St. Louis, for that work. Mrs. Campbell is a tireless worker, and it is never too cold, too wet, for her to do a charitable act. The people of St. Louis love her. She is an ex-student of Oberlin, a scholar but not a graduate.

Among the host of teachers in the public school service of Cleveland, Ohio, we delight to mention several ladies of our beloved race, who are making for themselves a comfortable living, teaching not only colored children, but white as well. Since this is a demonstrable fact, we must lay down the excuse so often made, and say, the way is open, enter while you may. *Merit* before examining boards is the watch-word.

Misses Sarah L. Mitchell, Rachel Walker, Hattie Green, Ida Deaver, Cora Bean and Mary Trappe, have met boldly the requirements and pursue their pleasing tasks to the satisfaction of all.

MRS. FLORENCE A. T. FLEMMING, *nee* HAYES, is a graduate from the normal department of Central Tennessee College, who has achieved some distinction in the Quincy (Ill.) public schools as a teacher and efficient disciplinarian. Prior to her going North Dr. William Wells Brown, in his book "The Rising Sun," gave almost a chapter to Mrs. Fleming, *nee* Hayes, who was brutally beaten by a white coward, who, if a man, was not manly. This was in the seventies, when colored teachers were an experiment in the South, and many there were who entered upon this pioneer mission. Among these was the subject of this short sketch.

MRS. I. GARLAND PENN is a gifted teacher, whose sketch appears in another part of this book.

MISS GRACE G. SAMPSON is among the brainiest young women of the race. As a scholar she is without a peer. She is the first and only woman who has secured a first-grade certificate from the Dallas City public school board. Having been reared in Chicago she has enjoyed exceptional advantages for education. After graduating from the high school of her native city she came to Texas and accepted a position as teacher in the Paul Quinn College. Thence she took the first-grade examination and got the highest average per cent. ever made in Corsicana, Texas, where she taught one year. Prof. Kealing, now president of Paul Quinn College, Waco, Texas, hearing of the rigidness of the Dallas board of examiners, took the examination in 1888 and passed it with a very high mark, as the boast had been made by the whites that "a nigger could not get sufficient average." Thus Prof. Kealing exploded the doctrine of incapacity, being the first Negro to pass the board. The remark was made afterward that "no Negro woman could get a first-grade certificate in Dallas." This remark was grating on Miss Sampson's ear, hence in 1889 she went to Dallas and applied for a first-grade certificate, to the utter surprise of the board. She was examined and awarded the coveted certificate, and thus put an end to the doubts and dogmas of Negro inferiority. She is at present teaching in the city schools of the great and future metropolis, Chicago.

We have thus sketched a few of the great, grand and good teachers of the race. This subject could be carried to infinity, as they are legion. The work is telling on the present generation, and who can doubt the harvest, if they reap as they have sown?

Among the musicians of the race we mention MRS. E. C. NESBIT, nee Clark, as peerless, while MISS GIBBS, of conservatory fame, now at the head of the first and only Afro-American Conservatory of Music in the United States, founded by the late and lamented Dr. William J. Simmons, at Cane Springs, Ky., is an accomplished musician, mistress of both key and stringed instruments, and none her equal. She is the daughter of Judge Gibbs, of Little Rock.

MISS MYRTLE HART is among the noted female musicians of the race, and the pride and boast of Indianapolis, Ind.

MRS. CORA L. BURGEN, nee MOORE, of Detroit, Mich., now of Oakland, Cal., sister to Prof. A. J. Moore, like him is a pianist, a graduate in the musical art and a most pleasing performer, an ex-musical teacher in the Texas Blind, Deaf and Dumb Asylum.

MISS ANNA AUGUSTA RIDLEY is a musician, and at present is teacher of music in the Tennessee State Deaf, Dumb and Blind Asylum. Miss Ridley is yet quite young. She is destined to become excellent in the pianoforte art.

Miss WILLY BENCHLEY, of Oberlin, is one of the best known organists perhaps in the world. For many years she has played for the original Fisk Jubilee Singers, who have sung themselves into the hearts of many nations and traveled around the world. She has played before the crowned heads of the Eastern world, besides delighted the audiences of their many

MISS WILLY BENCHLEY.

thousands of concerts in the United States by her harmony and cadence. She being a good organist is, almost of necessity, a pianist; yes, a pianist most difficult to surpass, not to be criticised, never to be frowned upon. Miss Benchley, now residing in St. Louis, a cousin to Mrs. Haydee Campbell, of kindergarten fame, is a Texan lady, and has for years been proving that locality is nothing when the mind is made up and the opportunities are not wanting.

Mrs. J. E. Edwards, of Washington, D. C., now of Galveston, has enjoyed superior advantages for learning music, being the adopted daughter of Right Rev. Richard Cain, D.D., whose heart and mind were fixed on the bringing out of the talents of the Negro. She is a scholar in piano music, both a composer and a pleasing performer.

Of the many great literary women of the race Mrs. Harper, being the oldest, ripe with theory, practice and experience shines alone. Mrs. Coppin, with her rich opportunities for showing her stored-up knowledge, most especially in the field of pedagogy, takes rank by the side of the former; while Mrs. J. Silone Yates, being the youngest of the three, in her special field of science, takes the front rank and seems to distance all of her sex, when age is considered. Where then shall we place Mrs. Anna J. Cooper? For readiness of speech, for disciplinarian qualities, for her analytical foundation upon which her principles of instruction are built, forces us to say that she is equal to all. For depth and solidity, firmness and conservatism, Mrs. Zelia R. Page takes her place among the galaxy of bright intellectual stars; so also does Mrs. Blanch V. H. Brooks. While Mrs. Mollie Church Terrill, being the youngest of all, stands in no indifferent relation to the eldest.

As martyrs for the cause of education, the untimely death of Mrs. Olivia Davidson Washington, Miss Arimenta Martin Mrs. Octavia V. R. Alberts, Miss Louise Mortie and Miss Julia Hayden, all thrill our minds with sorrow and regret. As Mr. Lincoln beautifully said of his comrades who had fallen on the battle field, so may we say :

> " Their swords are rust,
> Their bodies dust,
> Their souls are with the saints
> I trust."

How young, yet how noble in heart and mind, with purpose fixed and bent upon doing what others had done for them; but sometimes we overshoot the mark and bring unwelcome grief and sorrow upon ourselves. They, in the morning of their lives,

had just begun the earthly, heavenly, task, and scarcely had
they learned their duty well ere the summons came to pay the
debt which all must pay.

We have this comfort, that their deeds still live. The
asylums founded, orphans homes builded, the enlargement of
our universities, are works of their hands and hearts.

Our Temperance Union women are many; and, indeed, that
subject alone would fill a volume doubly the size of our book,
hence we restrict ourselves to the mention of a few who rank
with any and all in every land of civilization.

Mrs. Abbie Wright Lyon is not only a singer but a Christian temperance woman. Mrs. Naomi Anderson is among the
noted females who took the lecture platform in the palmy days
when Mrs. Mary A. Livermore and Sojourner Truth stood, in
their gigantic independence, battling for woman's rights. In
1869 she spoke from the platform in Chicago with the leader of
the movement, Mrs. Livermore, and traveled through the States
of Illinois, Indiana and Ohio advocating that cause; but in
recent years Mrs. Anderson has become famous as a temperance
advocate, and is also engaged in the founding of orphan homes for
the poor of the race. We may justly style Mrs. L. A. Westbrooks
a tireless, energetic advocate of the temperance cause. Many
years of her life have been spent in organizing temperance
bands among the race in the Southern States. Perhaps no lady
is more widely known for work in this cause, most especially in
Texas, than Mrs. L. A. Westbrooks, A. M. She is president of
the Woman's Home Mission work for the M. E. Church in
Texas. While the Caucassian race is proud of Miss Frances E.
Willard, who is in every way a pure genuine type of tireless
Christian devotion, we, seemingly the unfortunates of earth,
delight to honor the name of Mrs. S. J. W. Early, the peer of
any human advocate for the Christian temperance cause.
While Mrs. Early has not met with the encouragement that
Miss Willard has, yet, with no meager idea of Christian temperance devotion characterizing the race with which she is
identified—she labors among the illiterate—has accomplished
a two-fold result—that of educating and christianizing. She

has been in the lecture field for more than two decades, we believe, and in the educational work more than forty years. Her opportunities for education have been the best. After receiving the honors from the classic halls of Oberlin, she became the first colored teacher in Wilberforce University. Here she sowed the seeds of the temperance cause, which have brought forth fruit a hundred fold. She is beloved by many thousands of her race. The presidents of Fisk University, Central Tennessee College, and Roger Williams University delight to be honored by a yearly visit of this talented female lecturer. As an intellectual woman, Mrs. Early ranks fairly with our very best educators; but being more than an educator we place her in her respective two-fold sphere. Living up to her teaching, she has all her life enjoyed the very best of health. We remember when a school boy, at Central Tennessee College, hearing her say that she had not suffered an unwell day in all her active life.

MRS. M. E. LAMBERT, of Detroit, Michigan, is one of the leading spirits of her city in all the higher social and intellectual activities among the race. She was born in Toronto, Canada, where she enjoyed the very best educational facilities, preparatory to the place she occupies among the grand people of our time. She is a poetess, as well as a contributor to the leading magazines. For a number of years she has been a special correspondent to the *Monitor*, *Plaindealer*, and takes a leading part in all the life and prosperity of St. Matthew's Episcopal church. Her poems teem with that beauty, reinforced by her high rhetorical faculties, convincing by her logic, and betraying very deep imaginative powers.

MISS FRANKIE BUCKNER, an accomplished organist and pianist, received her training at Detroit. She has been praised by the papers of Madison, Wis.; was at one time pianist to a large singing society; and is a contralto vocalist.

MISS IDA PLATT ranks among the finest female pianists of the Negro race. In fact, to say that she is brilliant in performing is putting it mildly.

Miss May Withers emerged from the classic halls of Oberlin, and stands very high in the art of pedagogy.

Mrs. Dr. Vanella, of Topeka, Kansas, is one of our prominent female educators.

Miss Eva Lewis, of 19 Grant street, Cambridge, is employed by the Mass. Inland Fish Commission under the Civil Service.

Chicago has an Afro-American woman physician, Mrs. Dr. Carrie Golden.

Mrs. Addison Foster, of Philadelphia, Pa., will manage the undertaking business, formerly owned and managed by her husband, recently deceased.

Mrs. Dove of Keokuk, Iowa, wife of Rev. Dove is a lec. turer, author, and tireless agitator. Sne has compiled her deceased husband's sermons into book form, and is now traveling through the South lecturing and selling the work of her hands. This is indeed noble, a splendid lesson full with rare instruction to our girls.

Mrs. Georgia Green Majors has done something in the educational cause for her race. Having attended Oberlin College and Fisk University, thereby preparing herself for life's duties, she returned to Texas and for seven years has labored earnestly in her public schools. She has been favorably endorsed by such educational men as State Supt. Carlisle, Professors Hand, Gambrell, George Hunter Smith, Esq., and Hon. George Clark. She ranks with the best primary teachers of the State in which she lives.

Miss Ida R. Griffin, Mabel Moffard, Birdie Williams, Adel and Alice Baines and S. A. Owens are energetic teachers, and are doing much in the cause of Negro education in the South.

Mrs. Smothers is one very good and noble woman who for many years has taught school and lectured throughout Texas and other Southern States. She is a W. C. T. U. woman, and one of the brightest stars in the Baptist cause.

GIRLHOOD AND ITS OPPORTUNITIES.

BY KATIE D. TILMAN.

" The hours are flying.
Each one some treasure takes,
Each one some blossom breaks
And leaves it dying."

IT is the May-time of the whole world, dear girls, and it is also the May-time of your lives.

Do you realize as you go carelessly on through life that yo are now at the most critical period of your lives?"

It is, alas, too true. You who have been watched and guarded from harm from babyhood will now be brought into contact with vice, sailing under the garb of virtue; sin robed in the most alluring forms; passion under the guise of love. All of these influences will be brought to bear upon your impassionable natures, and unless you are on your guard you will not cross the boundary line and gain the crown of bright womanhood without having stained your dainty robes.

While there are hundreds of girls belonging to the Afro-American race who are models of virtue, industry and intelligence, there are thousands who are living aimless, unhappy lives, never heeding the truth of the following sentiments :

" Life is a leaf of paper white,
Whereon each one of us may write,
And then comes night."

Among the evils that tend to destroy your lives are novel reading, bad associates and love of finery.

I maintain that the reading of an impure book is more injurious to one's moral health than an hour's conversation upon an immoral subject, for in such a book, as nowhere else, you will find wrong painted so as to resemble right. I do not condemn the reading of a good story, far from it ; indeed, much good hath often been wrought by the pen of the novelist. A book written in vindication of truth, such as " Uncle Tom's Cabin," " Bricks Without Straw " and " Ben Hur," or to inculcate a good moral, as " A Golden Gossip," " The

Home at Greylock," together with the bright, helpful stories
found in such magazines as the *Century, Scribner, Ladies'
Home Journal*, and the *A. M. E. Review*, furnish reading of
the best sort and contain nothing hurtful, but too much cannot be said against promiscuous novel reading.

The mind that revels constantly in the pages of Bertha
Clay and Laura Jean Libby's sensational romances will, in
time, become a weak, flabby affair unfitted to contend with
the stern realities of life.

Some one has said, " A man is no better than his thoughts;"
so, dear girls, you must be careful of your reading, for low
reading will surely introduce low thoughts into your minds, and
low thoughts will lead to deeds of a similar nature.

You have the opportunity of storing your mind with the
best literature of the age. Books, at American prices, are in
the reach of all.

Dickens pleading in his inimitable style for the poor of
England; Reade, on his tour through the British prisons;
Goldsmith, Byron, Lowell, all look down at you from their
lonely shelves and sigh as you hasten past them to procure the
latest edition of the *New York Weekly* or the *Saturday Night.*

If you had only yourselves to consider,—but think of it, if
God spares your lives, in a few years the majority of you will
become mothers, and upon you rest the destiny of your children.

Is there a single line in all the trashy novels that you have
read that will help you to train a soul for all eternity?

But some of you say, you do not make a practice of reading novels, you only read occasionally, and that is all right
you think. Well, it would be if all were like you, but remember that there are many girls around you, who, like the drunk-
ard, are always crying for more, and I would cite you to that
passage of the Bible which reads, " If meat maketh my brother
to offend," etc. If you are strong enough to take only an
occasional draught, then you are strong enough to give it up
altogether for the sake of those around you. Here is an
opportunity to influence say a dozen girls to renounce the

reading of impure books. Will you do it? You can if you will.

I myself owe much to the influence of other girls in the halcyon days of girlhood. You cannot begin too soon to muster your forces and find out how many advocates you have for pure, healthy literature.

"Let us, then, be up and doing."

We have all heard the old adages, "Evil communications corrupt good manners," and "Tell me the company you keep and I will tell you what you are."

Evil associates will bring you nothing but heartaches and woe.

Now by evil associates, I am not speaking especially of those who are outcasts of society, pariahs who have chosen to live in sin. I take it for granted that none of you have such girls for your associates. But of all those with whom you are brought in contact at home, school, church or anywhere, whom you know in your soul are not suitable persons for you to be with, let not lively conversation, wealthy appearance, beauty or any other attraction cause you to make intimate of unworthy persons. There is a pretty safe test of such persons; feeling their own inferiority, they will invariably flatter you. Beware! Many an innocent girlhood has been blighted by flattery.

As one has said, "If we watch our friends our enemies will have no power to harm us."

Another person to avoid is the person who tries to create strife between you and your best earthly friend, your mother. Out of all the women in the world God in His infinite wisdom has chosen your mother as the guardian of your young life. Be sure that you give her all the love and respect that are due her.

It seems to me that the saddest sight in the world is the estrangement of mother and daughter. Remember that in the majority of cases it is the daughter's place to submit, not the mother's.

To you who have associates who are not what they profess to be comes the opportunity to do them good, by refusing to associate with them any longer unless they act as they should. Convert them if possible to your own plan of thought and then enlist their friendship and services in behalf of others.

Let this thought inspire you. If the majority of our girls are pure, earnest-hearted women, what a grand race we shall become ! Our children shall sing our praises to their little ones.

You have also the opportunity of helping the young men to lead noble lives. You stand in your dainty fresh girlhood before their eyes, and your smile is more potent with them than all the counsel of their fathers. In your slim brown hand lies " the balance of power." How will you use it? If you will refuse to associate with all young men of immoral character, there would be a decided reformation among them and you will infinitely better your own future happiness.

There are girls who do not read anything, and who do not associate with evil companions, but are almost insane on the subject of dress. Dear girls, the sooner you give up the unequal struggle in the race for dress and display supremacy, the happier you will be.

It is said "that the love of money is the root of all evil," but with many girls it is the love of dress. Not to be desired in the height of fashion is the greatest curse in their category.

Poverty is no disgrace, if you are not able to afford a dress for Easter, for every new picnic or excursion, don't try to do it any way. Be sensible, girls, dress according to your means and you will win more real friends than by any other means.

A COLORED BUSINESS WOMAN.

Mrs. Lizzie Young, a colored woman of Jacksonville, Fla., has established quite a draying business in that city. She owns three drays, and employs from twenty to thirty more when occasion requires. She pays each drayman $1.50 a day, calling fourteen loads a day's work. At present she is employed in hauling away the sand from the excavation on the government lot, and so far has sold every particle of the sand dug out. Mrs.

Young knows by face and name every drayman in her employ. But draying is not her only business. For six months every year this enterprising young woman runs an extensive wood yard at North Springfield, and four or five teams are kept busy delivering wood. She sells, besides, many hundreds of dollars worth of pork every year, and does a good trade in poultry and eggs.— *Tonguelet.*

The first ballot ever cast by a woman in the State of Mississippi was that of Mrs. Lucy Tapley, a colored woman.

The silk quilt presented to Queen Victoria by Mrs. Ricks, of Liberia, will be exhibited at the World's Fair.

Miss Carrie L. Dickerson, of San Francisco, has been appointed to a Federal position after a rigid examination.

Mrs. D. A. Evans, of Columbus, Ohio, is an exceptional lady, exceptional in her ambition and in the successful prosecution of a profitable business. She is a successful builder and fire insurance agent. Her success offers encouragement to other Afro-American ladies to enter other useful employments besides those of the home and school-room. Society and the apparent fixtures of position have made them the only places suitable for the employment of ladies. But in this aggressive age of competition the environment disqualifies a large number of women for domestic and educational service. Yet they are dependent upon themselves for a livelihood and have to bestir themselves in acquiring a living. We who are mothers should try to direct the attention of our daughters to the avenues in which an honorable livelihood may be gained. As the scope of their knowledge of the industrial world is enlarged they are made more self-reliant and capable of caring for themselves and assuming the responsibilities of matured years. The success of this Afro-American woman suggests that others may' be successful in similar pursuits.—*Mrs. Julia Ringwood Coston.*

Nancy Garrison, an Afro-American living at Holly Springs, Miss., has the longest hair, probably, of any woman in the world. She is about sixty years old. Her hair she wears in

three plaits. The side plaits just touch the floor, while the
third plait drags two feet nine inches on the floor and measures
eight feet in length. It is a silver sable in color, and she wears it
coiled up on her head.

Miss E. O. Miles, who sailed to Europe lately, writes that
she has the pleasure of ranking in the best London society,
where no American caste and prejudice dare to exist. She has
been invited to the best public places, most popular churches,
sang in a hall, was a guest and ate at the tables with members
of the royal family, and there was no hint of discrimination.
She adds, that on a visit with a company of Grecian and
London ladies to the Women's Christian Association she was
escorted to one of the large branch associations on Regent
street, one of the most popular thoroughfares. There, to her
surprise, she was introduced to one of the principal secretaries
of the department, a Miss Gardner, who is an educated African young lady, doing business with much grace and aptitude,
speaking the English and many other languages with great
fluency and ease.

COLORED WOMAN'S NOBLE WORK.

The most notable colored woman in Georgia to-day is Miss
Carrie Steele. She is now about fifty years of age, and is a
bright mulatto. For many years she was stewardess of the
Central Railroad at Macon and later held the same position in
Atlanta, receiving therefor $100 a month. It was while there
that she became impressed with the necessity of doing something to take care of colored orphans. She daily saw them
rushed off to the penitentiary for trivial offenses. She took
several orphans under the shelter of her house, and from this
developed the idea of having an orphan asylum entirely for
colored children. She undertook the collection of funds herself,
and was so successful that the whites insisted that she should
finish up the work, and thus have the entire credit of the under-
taking. The result is a building worth $20,000 on a site worth
$10,000, all paid for and under Negro management. She has,
in the prosecution of this work, had to address the City Council,

to juggle with legislative committees and to appear before large white congregations, calling for aid. Every request she made was favorably answered, and she was freely trusted in the handling of the money and completion of the work.—*Chicago Inter Ocean.*

Mrs. Amanda Merchant, the amiable wife of Rev. E. W. Merchant, of Lawrence, one of the gifted daughters of Missouri, is president of the Woman's Baptist Home and Foreign Mission Convention of Kansas. She is a lady of excellent qualities and high aspirations. In the district convention Mrs. R. M. Goins, of Fort Scott, Kansas, presides over a grand, intelligent body of ladies, second to none in the West. Her able, dignified, impartial caste is unimpeachable and without a peer in the category of feminine parliamentarians. She is president of the Woman's Home and Foreign Mission Convention under Central Baptist Association. Mrs. M. C., the president of the Woman's Home and Foreign Mission Convention, an auxiliary to the Northwestern Baptist Association, is a woman of broad ideas, intensely Christian in motive, full of zeal and oratorical ability. She is the Queen Esther of her tribe, and is doing great service as organizer. Mrs. M. E. Merchant is noted for her eloquence and push, and is said to be the Laura M. Sohnson of Kansas in the mission field. Miss Ophelia Moran, of Frankfort, heads the list as an elocutionist. During the past two years the women of Kansas have raised more than $1,300 for mission work.

INDEPENDENT AFRO-AMERICANS.

IN New Richmond, Ohio, a town about twenty miles above Cincinnati, there was, a few years ago, much opposition shown by the whites to the mixing of the schools. Finally a settlement was made in court in favor of mixed schools. Since that time a number of young Afro-Americans have attended the high school, but for some reason none have ever graduated. Now, however, a young lady, Miss Alice Paxton, has shown a determination to do so that must indeed be trying to the patience of the school management. For some time she had been put off with promises, although having passed her examinations. At the end of this school year Miss Paxton would be put off no longer. So the school decided to have no commencement exercises this year. Miss Paxton was given her diploma and the other members decided to take another year in school and come out when there would be no "nigger" graduates.

The Afro-American citizens, not to be outdone, secured the largest hall in the town, sent to Cincinnati and secured one of Cincinnati's best vocal quartettes, and on Friday evening, April 22d, Miss Paxton read her graduating essay before one of the largest mixed audiences ever assembled in New Richmond. She received an ovation, and was the recipient of many beautiful flowers. The musical programme, which was well rendered, met with hearty applause. Many white citizens, who have outgrown the prejudice that still clings to their more ignorant townsmen, helped to meet the expenses of the affair and attended the exercises with their families.

By the way, Miss Paxton is not only a very bright young lady intellectually, and quite a musician, but is not afraid to use her hands. I have among my souvenirs a horseshoe made by the young lady. Her father is a blacksmith, and she likes to spend an occasional hour or two in the shop with him.—A. E. W. in *Ringwood's Journal.*

Miss Fannie Hicks, artist and teacher of drawing in the University, at Louisville, has applied for space at the World's Fair, in which to exhibit work of the pupils of the University.

Iola Leroy, or Shadows Uplifted.—By Frances E. W. Harper (Philadelphia: Garrigus Bros., No. 608 Arch street). Perhaps no woman, white or colored, has during the last decade labored more earnestly and effectively for the upbuilding of the colored race than Mrs. Harper. She has written half a dozen volumes, either one of which would be creditable if it had emanated from the brain of the most cultured white woman. But her books do not measure her influence for good.

Since the close of the war she has been a constant laborer among the colored people of the South. Her favored work has been among the colored women of the South, discussing temperance, education, home purity, industry, morality; and helping them to break away from the thoughts and customs and methods instilled into them during the ages of slavery. No field has a riper harvest of good to be gathered than in the upbuilding of the colored man's home in the South. She knows every intricacy of the condition of the race freed from bondage. The volume before us, " Iola Leroy," as effectually discusses caste prejudices on account of color as " Uncle Tom's Cabin " portrayed the iniquities of the inhuman institution. The plot, though simple, is clear, clean, and delightfully interwoven with facts and incidents of the war of thrilling interest. The story is beautiful in its symmetry, its pictures and characters never overdrawn, and its lessons so pathetic and impressive as to move the coldest reader into sympathy. No story of the war is more profoundly interesting as a story, and certainly no writing will be more likely to exert a helpful influence in cultivating public opinion to a more humane and Christian standard. The black race has its faults, and a multitude of them grow directly out of its training during all the generations of the past. But it is well to stop and remember that as a race the black man now has a score of merit. Had he been white, Indian or Asiatic when his case was pending in the South, thousands of homes and villages of the South would have been the scene of bloodshed and crime. He knew the situation, and yet the wives and daughters of his enslavers were safe under his protection. It is a wonder that Negro chivalry, as displayed during that period, has not oftener been acknowledged by the people of the South. But read " Iola Leroy." It is a remarkable book.—*Chicago Inter Ocean.*

Mme. Flora Batson has taken permanent residence in Chicago.

Mme. Lizzie Pugh Dugan scored a success in Cincinnati, as she does everywhere.—*Indianapolis Freeman.*

A number of ladies of the two Kansas cities met last week at the Lincoln High School, Kansas City, Mo., and formed an auxiliary league, which has for its object the bettering of the condition of young women.—*Freeman.*

Miss Rachel L. Walker, of Cleveland, appeared with great success at the Indianapolis Musical Festival.—*Indianapolis Freeman.*

Lulu Vere Childers, who is studying in the Oberlin Conservatory of Music, is considered its best contralto.—*Indianapolis Freeman.*

THE KING'S DAUGHTERS.

The King's Daughters gave a delightful entertainment at Grace Presbyterian Church Wednesday night. The program, which was varied and interesting, was enjoyed by a large audience.

The "Workers for the King" was organized in 1871 by Mesdames John Jones, J. Bryant, Jessie Young, C. E. Jones. There are now fifty members. The officers are as follows:

Mrs. Sarah Curd, president.

Mrs. Robert Young, vice-president.

Miss C. E. Jones, second vice-president.

Miss Theodora Lee, secretary.

Miss Eliza Johnson, treasurer.

The object of the organization is to do good, and many are the wants of the poor and needy which have been relieved during the past year.—*Chicago Appeal.*

Mrs. Minnie Watson, a lady of Louisville, Ky., is a graduate of the Clark school for embalming. She is the youngest female graduate in the world. She graduated in February, '92, in a class of forty-five, three colored and forty-two male students. Mrs. Watson took the first honor. She is a great assistance to her husband, Wm. Watson, who is running an under-taking establishment at 312 Ninth street. This little lady made her husband, who is a graduate himself, open his eyes with amazement when she embalmed a man who died with the dropsy, a case that all undertakers dread to handle.—*Freeman.*

Sarah J. Earley, of Tennessee, addressed the congress on the organized efforts of Afro-American women in the South to improve their condition. She could not present all of her ideas on account of the lateness of the hour. Briefly, she said :

"In this age of development and advancement, of multiplied methods and opportunities, all the forces which have been accumulating for centuries past seem to be centered into one grand effort to raise mankind to that degree of intellectual and moral excellence which a wise and beneficent Creator designed that we should enjoy. No class of persons are exempt from this great impulse. The most remote, as well as the most obscure, the most refined as well as the most unlettered, seem to have felt the touch of an unseen power which caused them to arouse, and to have heard a mysterious voice calling them to ascend higher in the scale of being and bask in the light of the eternal. It is not a strange coincidence, then, that in this period of restlessness and activity the women of all lands should simultaneously and at once see the necessity of taking a more exalted position and seeking a more effective way of ascending to the same plane and of assuming the more responsible duties of life with that of her favored brother.

Step by step, as the dark cloud of ignorance and superstition is dispelled by the penetrating light of eternal truth, men begin to think, and thought brings resolution, and resolution changes the condition of men and leads them into a happier and brighter existence, so have the great revolutions of the age affected the condition of the Afro-Americans of the State and brought them into a more prominent and more hopeful relation to the world. Afro-American hearts are inspired with all the ambitions which swell the breast, and have pushed forward in the line of progress their equal advantages ; they will take an equally prominent part in every movement which has for its purpose the advancement of a higher and better civilization.

Mrs. Earley was followed by Hallie Q. Brown, who entertained the audience with Afro-American dialect songs and an interesting discussion of the position of the Afro-American in modern civilization.

Mrs. Coppin was called upon for some remarks, but she declined on account of the lateness of the hour, except that she regretted ·the fact that more attention had not been given to the papers upon the kindergartens. Then she requested the privilege of introducing her friend, Mrs. Ellen Watkins Harper, as it would be the only opportunity of securing her attention. Mrs. Harper entertained her admirers in a few well-selected words on the way the Afro-American girl has improved her opportunities of education, and how she devoted herself to the spreading of God's word.

The Washington *Pilot* is an able exponent of the progress of the colored race, and includes in its sheets many items indicative of the aspirations and achievements of its women. This representative of the woman's side of life is perhaps due to the fact that the editor is Mrs. R. Douglass Sprague, a daugter of the Hon. Frederick Douglass. In the last issue are these items of interest :

Mohango Corpassa, the African girl who has been one of the students at the Howard Asylum, Brooklyn, N. Y., has been sent to Northfield Seminary to prepare for missionary work in Africa.

Miss Estella I. Sprague, grand-daughter of the Hon. Frederick Douglass, has volunteered her services gratis for one year to the Agricultural and Industrial High School at Gloucester, Va. She is a graduate of one of the best cooking schools in Washington.

Miss Emma Reynolds, sister of the Rev. G. Reynolds, formerly of Chicago, graduated from the Provident Hospital as a trained nurse, and will enter the medical college of the Northwestern University in Detroit. She is the first colored that has entered the institution.

Miss Celestine O. Browne, of Jamestown, New York possesses fine ability as a pianist. She is thus mentioned by the *Folio,* of Boston, in the number for December, 1876 :

> She is a fine pianist, very brilliant and showy as soloist and accompanist.

Again, the same journal in the number for February, 1877, said of Miss Browne :

> A pianist of great merit. Her natural abilities have been well trained. She has a clear touch, and plays with a great deal of expression.

For more than two seasons she was an honored member of the Hyers Sisters Concert Troupe.

In his able contribution to the Negro literature of this 19th century, Mr. J. M. Trotter pays some very high compliments to our race in music, some of which I take the liberty of appending. He says :

> Madame Browne was long regarded as the finest vocalist of her race in this country, while only a few of the other race could equal her. Although now no longer young, she still sings artistically and beautifully. Her repertoire comprises the gems of the standard operas ; and these she has sung and does now sing, in a style that would reflect honor on those far more pretentious than herself.

Out of compliment to her singing, Miss Sarrah Sedgwick Bowers, "The Colored Nightingale," is rather conservative as well as natural.

The *Daily Pennsylvanian,* in speaking of her vocal triumphs of May 3, 1856, says :

> We have never been called upon to record a more brilliant and instantaneous success than has thus far attended this talented young aspirant to musical honors. From obscurity she has risen to popularity. She has not been through the regular routine of advancement, but, as it were, in a moment, endowed by nature with the wonderful power of song, she delighted the circle in which she moved, and is now enchanting the public. Last evening the hall was thronged at an early hour. In every song she was unanimously encored.

"Miss Bowers now lives quietly at her home in Philadelphia," writes Mr. Trotter, "singing in public only on special occasions."

Miss Mary F. Morris performs upon the piano-forte with fine skill and taste, and is a vocalist of excellent powers. She has pursued her musical studies in the Cleveland Convent, the teachers of which enjoy a high reputation; and also under Professor Alfred Arthur, one of the finest instructors of Cleveland; and under these very auspices, opportunities and musical advantages we also add the name of Miss Annie Henderson, who is a very pleasing vocalist.

MISS CLARA MONTIETH HOLLAND, the daughter of the celebrated guitar virtuoso, Justin Holland, gives evidence of a fulfilled prophecy by Mr. Trotter of her musical powers, and especially on the piano-forte.

MRS. ANN S. BALTIMORE is an accomplished pianist, and possesses, besides, a melodious voice. She has been favorably noted by the press, and enjoys the happy faculty of pleasing all who hear her. Her life before the public is long and varied. She stands along with the great women of this age.

MISS MARY AND FANNIE COLE, members of the Mozart Circle, are distinguished for the beauty of their voices.

MISS SARAH WERLES has a voice which is much appreciated, and under her fingers the cabinet organ itself seems to sing.

For public musical occasions we shall not fail to mention Miss Ella Smith and Ella Buckner, who have delighted thousands of Cincinnati's music-loving citizens at various times.

In this connection, and under the head of music, we call your attention to the fact that, owing to the World's Fair being held at Chicago, many of our leading and, in fact, most celebrated singers are taking up a permanent residence there; hence, to give a long list of Chicago's musical talent, I trust, will not be expected here—as elsewhere in this book is a sketch of Mrs. Flora Botson Bergen, the Hyer Sisters, et al

MISS BESSIE WARWICK, soprano and brilliant pianist, was formerly a pupil of Prof. Baumback, of Chicago.

MRS. HETTIE REED possesses a contralto voice of remarkable beauty, purity and sweetness. She was one of the principal singers of the Chicago Colored Musical Society, and has been highly complimented by the critics of Illinois and Wisconsin.

Miss Eliza J. Cowan, educated in Chicago, a member of the Olivet Church choir, is a very sweet singer.

Miss Flora Cooper has a voice of such great depth that it really may be styled baritone. She was educated in Chicago, and is a teacher in one of the public schools of that city.

Mrs. Esther Washington (*nee* Miss E. Fry) is a finished performer on the organ and piano-forte. She is a graduate in thorough-bass and harmony from Warren's Conservatory of Chicago.

Mrs. Frances A. Powell is the leading soprano of the Olivet Baptist Church choir. She was educated at Buffalo, New York, and her superior powers as a vocalist have been made the occasion of very flattering testimonials by the press of Chicago, and of the States of Illinois and Wisconsin.

Mrs. Harriett E. Freeman, an excellent mezzo-soprano, leading the singing of Quinn Chapel choir, has been showered with press notes and compliments. She was educated at New Bedford, Mass.

Mrs. P. A. Glover (*nee* Whitehouse) and Mrs. Hester Jeffreys (*nee* Whitehouse) inherited their rich vocal talent from their mother, who in her earliest youth and even to middle life delighted and pleased, with music and song, her host of friends and admirers. The daughters are not at all lacking in this sublime feature. When and wherever they have appeared before the public they are received and applauded after the fashion of all great singers. Mr. Trotter says of them: "They possess voices of rare natural beauty, considerably cultivated. These sisters, had they so chosen, could have long since become public singers of much prominence; since their rich vocal gifts are supplemented by a fine knowledge of music, to which are added, also, very graceful, winning manners."

Miss Fannie A. Washington has for some time afforded much pleasure to public audiences as a contralto singer.

Mrs. Ellen Sawyer sings soprano most beautifully. Her voice, says a noted author, "is quite elastic, of great range, and strong and clear in the upper register." She has become a favorite of music lovers, and encore after encore is the rule on occasions that bring her before the public.

Miss Rachel Thompson is an erudite scholar in music and sings soprano with the clearness of the nightingale.

Mrs. Phebe Reddick possesses a ringing soprano voice and has done much toward choir-directing and soul-stirring with her vocal accomplishments.

THE NEGRO'S TRIUMPH

Over Obstacles Under which Nations go Down—Unequal in the Start, He Outdistances Other Enslaved Nations—His Chart for Guidance.

GOD hath made of one blood all nations of men, and the human family finds a common origin in the one man, the original creation of Almighty God, but the flight of centuries has so diversified the original man that there stands to-day five distinct and separate races, peculiar in color, different in physical features, to represent the one creation. One phase of this great family, dark in complexion, unsymmetrical in form, made so by manner of life and climatic influence, is called the Negro.

This race for centuries slumbered in ignorance and superstition amid the burning sands and tangled wilds of their African home, until designing men led many captive from their sunny clime and doomed them to a life of hopeless servitude. In the so-called "land of the free and home of the brave" for more than two centuries they toiled without the hope of recompense, until the just wrath of an angry God is kindled against their masters, and amid the fatricidal strife that deluged this country with blood, the voice of God speaks through the sainted Lincoln and four million bondsmen are freed from the withering curse of slavery.

The newly enfranchised African, grateful for the tardy justice done him, amid the smoke of battle and rattle of musketry fought so valiently for the flag that had wronged him that the song of the poet and the page of the historian eloquently proclaim his deeds of heroism. During all the subsequent years of freedom no other race since the beginning of time has had so much to overcome as the Negro. He measures arms with a race having centuries of civilization behind it, while he has centuries of barbarism.

He starts this unequal contest without learning, without money; he encounters the formidable opposition of deeply routed prejudice; every avenue of advancement is closed against him; the gates leading to every lucrative employment are shut, and against the merciless oppression of an inimical South no law protects him. Against these weighty impediments and formidable barriers, what race could move onward? What race could exhibit such patient endurance amid persecution and wrong except that race, that prophetic race, of which it is promised in the Book of Truth that she shall stretch forth her black hand unto God.

In order to fulfill the glowing words of this prophecy, the Negro must be possessed of two essential elements of success, namely: Belief in God and confidence in himself. That race that trusts in the Almighty will be exhalted, for though he must overturn the foundation of every government, God will make his own to triumph.

> " And this sin-cursed guilty Union
> Shall be shaken to its base,
> Till it learns that simple justice
> Is the right of any race."

To succeed, the Negro must believe in his own possibilities and take pride in his own capabilities. He who believes he cannot do will not do. The Negro has not yet done much to make him renowned in the world's history, but his capabilities of greatness, which the near future must develop, will cause his name to be written in the unperishable records of time. Every nation must love its own. How the Irish look with pleasure to that Emerald Isle, lying like an oasis upon the trackless deep; how the Italian strikes his harp and sings of his historic land, the home of art and song; how the Englishman points with pride to the long line of illustrious ancestors that have graced his country's history in peace and war. The Negro has no such history, but let him believe in and boast of a future, bright with promise. Oh Ethiopia! may thy future be bright and hopeful, as thy past has been dark and hopeless, for already we see coming up from the schools and colleges of the land the young of this race girding on their armor and preparing for the conflict with odds and opposition, and we believe that they shall succeed in planting the banner of Ethiopia on the dizzy heights of distinction.

The future African shall fit himself to move with this progressive age; he shall chisel from the rugged stone the angelic forms of beauty; he shall charm the listening world with the fervor of his song and the eloquence of his speech; he shall man the ships of commerce and bring them back laden with the wares of many climes, and in the fields of literature he shall move on to take his place among the foremost of the world. Should he fail in this, he shall disappoint our fondest expectations, and varying the speech of the eloquent Lyman Beecher, "May God hide from me the day when the failure of my people shall begin." Oh, thou beloved race, bound together by the ties of common interests and brotherhood, live forever, one and undivided! ⸙ STELLA HAWKINS.

CINCINNATI, OHIO.

RETROSPECTION.

BY DR. H. T. DILLON.

THE word "socialism" was coined in England in 1835, and the definition of this often misunderstood word, as given by all of its sturdy defenders, tends the recognition on the part of the strong the rights of the weak.

Glancing along the pages of history, the world has ever been slow to realize that the weak had any rights which demanded recognition on their part.

In the early forms of government slavery, according to the views of Dunoyer, flourished as the industrial and agricultural interests of a nation increased. While their services were considered indispensable to the commercial wealth of the country, the influence of slavery was, and always will be, degrading and demoralizing in its effects upon master and slave alike. Hume very justly observes "that the severe, I may say barbarous, manners of the ancients were due in large degree to the practice of domestic slavery, by which every man of rank was rendered a petty tyrant, and educated amidst the flattery, submission and low debasement of his slaves."

As Christianity advanced, civilization took higher forms and society became organized, we find serfdom taking the place of slavery.

The datum of the transition from the position of a serf to a free individual, with all the rights of citizenship, is one of the obscure points of modern history.

The change was evidently gradual and due, according to Adam Smith, to political and economic reasons. As serfdom became more and more an institution of the past among advanced countries we find history repeating itself in the slave trade of the colonies, and with less just cause than in the slavery of the middle ages. But the same baneful influence of this pernicious system is exercised and the same triumph of right is felt and seen.

To Denmark belongs the honor of being the first European nation to abolish slavery; next England, and gradually the other European powers followed suit.

In reading the history of these nations we find that as freedom from the bonds of slavery and serfdom, freedom of religious thought and individual liberty was allowed and encouraged in the same proportion did that nation flourish and prosper. The old tower of public good, upon the walls of which were engraved the laws of subordination to the society in which one lived and one common property, began to totter and fall. The family became to be recognized as the social unit upon which the safety of the government rested. Private property with private enjoyment was the last of those three periods which marked the ownership of lands and found expression in the eighteenth century. The end of the eighteenth century marked also an important epoch in the history of England as regards the share which the poor working classes had in the industrial era which had just begun to dawn. At that time the English worker "had no fixed interest in the soil; he had no voice in either local or national government. The right even of combination was denied him till 1824." It was at this period, under the influence of Robert Owen, that the term "socialism," which has since been so misinterpreted and abused, originated.

The philanthropy of this man cannot but be appreciated by those who have read of the sufferings of the lower classes in that country, and while his doctrine flamed and lighted the dark places of misery and degradation and then suddenly seemed to go out, good, which was lasting in its effects, was the result of his efforts, in spite of them having been regarded by some as Quixotic. The truths which he attempted to unfold to the world are just and true—recognition on the part of the strong the rights of the weak.

But what does all this hasty review of the past signify to us as a people? Much. We have been in slavery as were some of the nations mentioned; and in some sections of this fair land of America, the historic home of the brave, the land of the free, are in a condition which, in its tyranny and misery, resembles the serfdom of the middle ages.

Again, our present condition resembles the condition of the working classes of Great Britain before that wave of socialism passed over her. True, we are not exactly denied voice in "local or national government," but our voice is often silent because of the fraud and chicanery of a supposed superior race. But all these things should not discourage us. If, after centuries of civilization, a nation like the English could so trample upon the rights of her own flesh and blood as late as 1824, what may we not hope for the Afro-American? Let us not grieve too much over our present trials, but look back and see what other races have come through, work steadily onward, living in bright anticipation of a glorious future, which, if we do not live to realize, our children may.

Weak and poor races of other ages have pleaded for recognition on the part of stronger ones, for individual liberty, for rights withheld; and to-day the same cry is heard from the Negro.

Not as a black man or woman do we plead that our rights shall be recognized, but as man to man, woman to woman, irrespective of color or previous condition. We do not clamor for any special privileges because of our color, but simply for those which are given to those of fairer skin. Treat us as citizens, with all the rights and privileges embodied in this word, and let us work out our own destiny. That the rights which are now denied will eventually be ours, because they are right, cannot be doubted.

It matters not how firmly evil may be intrenched behind the massive walls of wealth and prejudice, the great sea of right and time will surely sap the foundation and conquer in the end.

The truth is, many of our white enemies and friends do not realize what we are doing, mentally, physically and morally as a race. And while we have much to do in the future, we can congratulate ourselves upon the past. The mixed schools in the North are doing much toward opening the eyes of our white friends as to the Negro's intellectual capacity, while the opposition in the South is teaching him how to depend upon himself.

If one will but refer to past history, there is no need for discouragement about the Negro's future.

The weaker races of every age have had to suffer indignities at the hands of the stronger; but eventually, through industry and perseverance, they rose above the obstacles and conquered; and we will do likewise.

We shall not, however, do as the Nihilist in Russia, or the Irish in Ireland; rather let our pens be our swords, our brains our dynamite, and with firm confidence in the Hand which guides the affairs of nations abide our time.—*Christian Recorder, June 30, 1892.*

THE VOODOO PROPHECY is undoubtedly the product of a fertile brain, yet Mr. Maurice Thompson, poetically speaking, puts the wrong lens to his telescope and sees the scattered effusions of his own gifted soul, and as many random thoughts, the delusion of an alarmist. His poem for vindictiveness and promised retribution may be ever so fitting, yet for boldness and uncouth coloring the Negro is not so much of a strike-back, get-even-with-you race, as he pictures him to be. In fact, it is out of tune and makes a terrible discord in our harmonious feeling, so much so that we have placed ourselves under the burden of such a responsibility as to procure from the pen of one of our most talented verse writers an answer; in the accomplishment of which we place the race in their proper modes and tenses. "The Voodoo Prophecy" will have been very badly used up when two such women as Mrs. A. J. Cooper and Mrs. Frances E. W. Harper have pounced upon it with their peerless pens. The former in her philosophical prose; the latter in her rhythmical poetry. It is an oft' asserted remark that "God holds the destinies of nations in his hands," and it is not always the uppermost thought in the Negro's mind to do some "awful thing." He does not think that way. He neither prays for "God to speed the day of retribution on." He means to "tote fair" with the world.

We take special pleasure in the placing of the Voodoo Prophecy on our pages that it may meet its fate in Mrs. Harper's answer. The prophecy the emanation from the encephalon of an alarmist, the answer simply a mild vindication of a quiet, peaceable people of humble habitation.

THE VOODOO PRO PHECY.

I am the prophet of the dusky race,
The poet of wild Africa. Behold .
The midnight vision brooding in my face !
Come near me,
And hear me,
While from my lips the words of Fate are told.

A black and terrible memory masters me ;
The shadow and the substance of deep wrong.
You know the past, hear now what is to be,
   From the midnight land,
   Over sea and sand,
From the green jungle hear my Voodoo song:

A tropic heat is in my bubbling veins,
Quintessence of all savagery is mine,
The lust of ages ripens in my veins,
   And burns
   And yearns
Like venom-sap within a noxious vine.

Was I a heathen ? Ay, I was—am still
A fetich worshipper ; but I was free
To loiter or to wander at my will ;
   To leap and dance,
   To hurl my lance,
And breathe the air of savage liberty.

You drew me to a higher life, you say ;
Ah, drove me with the lash of slavery !
And I unmindful? Every cursed day
   Of pain
   And chain
Roars like a torrent in my memory.

You make my manhood whole with equal rights ?
Poor, empty words ! Dream you I honor them—
I who have stood of Freedom's wildest heights ?
   My Africa,
   I see the day
When none dare touch thy garment's lowest hem.

You cannot make me love you with your whine
Of fine repentance. Veil your pallid face
In presence of the shame that mantles mine.
   Stand
   At command
Of the black prophet of the Negro race !

I hate you, and I live to nurse my hate,
Remembering when you plied the slaver's trade
In my dear land. . . . How patiently I wait
   The day,
   Not far away,
When all your pride shall shrivel up and fade.

Yea, all your whiteness darkens under me !
Darkened and bejaundiced, and your blood
Take in dread humors from my savagery,
   Until
   You will
Lapse into mine and seal my masterhood.

Your seed of Abel, proud of your descent,
And arrogant, because your cheeks are fair,
Within my loins an inky curse is pent,
   To flood
   Your blood,
And stain your skin and crisp your golden hair.

As you have done by me so will I do
By all the generations of your race ;
Your snowy limbs, your blood's patrician blue,
   Shall be
   Tainted by me ;
And I will set my seal upon your face !

Yea, I will dash my blackness down your veins,
And through your nerves my sensuousness I'll fling ;
Your lips, your eyes, shall bear the rusty stains
   Of Congo kisses,
   While shrieks and hisses
Shall blend into the savage songs I sing !

Your temples will I break, your fountains fill,
Your cities raze, your fields to deserts turn ;
My heathen fires shall shine on every hill,
   And wild beasts roam
   Where stands your home ;
Even the wind your hated dust shall spurn.

I will absorb your very life in me,
And mold you to the shape of my desire ;
Back through the cycles of all cruelty,
   I will swing you,
   And wring you,
And roast you in my passion's hottest fire.

You, North and South ; you, East and West,
Shall drink the cup your fathers gave to me ;
My back still burns, I bare my bleeding breast,
   I set my face,
   My limbs I brace,
To make the long, strong fight for mastery.

My serpent fetich lolls its withered lip,
And bears its shining fangs at thought of this;
I scarce can hold the monster in my grip,
So strong is he,
So eagerly
He leaps to meet my precious prophecies.

Hark for the coming of my countless host ;
Watch for my banner over land and sea ;
The ancient power of vengeance is not lost!
Lo, on the sky
The fire clouds fly,
And strangely moans the windy, weltering sea.

A FAIRER HOPE, A BRIGHTER MORN.

BY MRS. FRANCES E. W. HARPER.

From the peaceful heights of a higher life
I heard your maddening cry of strife ;
It quivered with anguish, wrath and pain,
Like a demon struggling with his chain.

A chain of evil, heavy and strong,
Rusted with ages of fearful wrong,
Encrusted with blood and burning tears,
The chain I had worn and dragged for years.

It clasped my limbs, but it bound your heart,
And formed of your life a fearful part ;
You sowed the wind, but could not control
The tempest wild of a guilty soul.

You saw me stand with my broken chain
Forged in the furnace of fiery pain.
You saw my children around me stand
Lovingly clasping my unbound hand.

But you remembered my blood and tears
'Mid the weary wasting flight of years.
You thought of the rice swamps, lone and dank,
When my heart in hopless anguish sank.

You thought of your fields with harvest white,
Where I toiled in pain from morn till night ;
You thought of the days you bought and sold
The children I loved, for paltry gold.

You thought of our shrieks that rent the air—
Our moans of anguish and deep despair;
With chattering teeth and paling face,
You thought of your nation's deep disgrace,

You wove from your fears a fearful fate
To spring from your seeds of scorn and hate
You imagined the saddest, wildest thing,
That time, with revenges fierce, could bring

The cry you thought from a Voodoo breast
Was the echo of your soul's unrest ;
When thoughts too sad for fruitless tears
Loomed like the ghosts of avenging years.

Oh, prophet of evil, could not your voice
In our new hopes and freedom rejoice?
'Mid the light which streams around our way
Was there naught to see but an evil day?

Nothing but vengeance, wrath and hate,
And the serpent coils of an evil fate—
A fate that shall crush and drag you down;
A doom that shall press like an iron crown?

A fate that shall crisp and curl your hair
And darken your faces now so fair,
And send through your veins like a poisoned flood
The hated stream of the Negro's blood?

A fate to madden the heart and brain
You've peopled with phantoms of dread and pain,
And fancies wild of your daughter's shriek
With Congo kisses upon her cheek?

Beyond the mist of your gloomy fears,
I see the promise of brighter years.
Through the dark I see their golden hem
And my heart gives out its glad amen.

The banner of Christ was your sacred trust,
But you trailed that banner in the dust,
And mockingly told us amid our pain
The hand of your God had forged our chain.

We stumbled and groped through the dreary night
Till our fingers touched God's robe of light;
And we knew He heard, from his lofty throne,
Our saddest cries and faintest moan.

The cross you have covered with sin and shame.
We'll bear aloft in Christ's holy name.
Oh, never again may its folds be furled
While sorrow and sin enshroud our world !

God, to whose fingers thrills each heart beat,
Has not sent us to walk with aimless feet,
To cower and crouch, with bated breath
From margins of life to shores of death.

Higher and better than hate for hate,
Like the scorpion fangs that desolate,
Is the hope of a brighter, fairer morn
And a peace and a love that shall yet be born;

When the Negro shall hold an honored place,
The friend and helper of every race;
His mission to build and not destroy,
And gladden the world with love and joy.

IN FLORIDA.

In Florida, to-day, the roses blow,
  And breath of orange blossoms fills the air
In blooming thickets, by a brook I know,
  The mocking-bird is pouring forth his rare
    Rich song, thrilling the charmed listener's heart.
In deeper woods the fair, pink lily grows ;
    Pale as the wind-flower she droops apart,
Or, glowing with the blushes of the rose,
    From the dark pool she lifts her lovely head,
A radiant presence 'mid the woodland gloom,
    While, smiling on her from their mossy bed,
Sweet purple violets in beauty bloom.
    'Mid their dark, shining leaves magnolias gleam,
White as the snows that o'er our fields extend,
    And oleander trees above a stream,
O'erladen with their rosy blossoms bend.
    O'er hedge, and bank, and bush, the jasmine flings
Its graceful, golden leaves, with lavish hand
    To boughs of ancient oaks the gray moss clings,
Its long, weird tresses by the soft breeze fanned.

* * * * * * * * * *

How sweet to linger in the shaded bowers !
　　How sweet to catch gleams of the blue blue, sky !
To dream away the softly-gliding hours,
　　As on the fragrant, flower-sown earth we lie !
Alas, it may not be !　Our lot is cast
　　In bleaker climes.　'Neath sadder skies we stray—
Still haunted by bright visions of the Past.
　　Sweet, sweet to be in Florida to-day !

　　　　　　　　　　　　　　　CHARLOTTE F. GRIMKE.

MARCH, 1893.

———

On the death of the Rev. Geo. Whitfield, Phillis **Wheatley**
wrote:

Thou, moon hast seen and all the stars of light,
How he hast wrestled with his God by night.
He prayed that grace in every heart might dwell ;
He longed to see America excel ;
He charged its youth that every grace divine
Should with full lustre in their conduct shine.
That Savior which his soul at first receive
The greatest gift that even a God can give
He freely offered to the numerous throng
That on his lips with listening pleasure hung.
"Take him, ye wretched, for your only good,
Take him, ye starving sinners, for your food ;
Ye thirsty come to this life-giving stream.
Ye preachers take him for your joyful theme ;
Take him, my dear Americans," he said ;
" Be your complaints on his kind bosom laid ;
Take him, ye Africans, he longs for you ;
Impartial Savior is this title due ;
Washed in the fountains of redeeming blood,
You shall be sons and priests to God."
But though, arrested by the hand of death,
Whitfield no more exerts his laboring breath,
Yet let us view him in the eternal skies,
Let every heart to his bright vision rise ;
While the tomb safe retains its sacred trust,
Till life divine reanimates his dust.—

TIME'S PAGES.

The fast-flying years are as leaves of a book,
On which all mankind is permitted to look ;
Some pages are written with judicious care,
While others are blotted that but here and there
Can we discern words ; other pages are blank,
Left so by those men whose superior rank
Could boast of no deeds done to benefit men,
And surely no record had they to leave, then !
Some leaves have been torn from this ponderous book,
By persons ashamed for their brethren to look
On records of lives that were useless to earth,
And only to sorrow and trouble gave birth.
But how are our pages ?   Well-written and clean ?
Or so filled with blots scarce a word can be seen ?
Have we left blank pages, and are all our deeds ?
Unworthy the sight of creation who reads ?
Do traces of pages completely torn out
Betray lives enveloped in shame and in doubt ?
If such be our records, make haste to amend,
Lest we to Plutonian darkness descend ;
But rather let all of our pages be clean,
And worthy by God and mankind to be seen.

MAMIE E. FOX.

CHILLICOTHE, O., Jan. 5, 1892.

THE END.